LONDON
FICTIONS

LONDON FICTIONS

Edited by
Andrew Whitehead
and Jerry White

Five Leaves Publications

www.fiveleaves.co.uk

London Fictions
edited by
Andrew Whitehead and Jerry White

Published in 2013
by Five Leaves Publications,
PO Box 8786, Nottingham NG1 9AW
www.fiveleaves.co.uk

ISBN: 978-1907869662

Cover illustration:
Belinda Davies, 'Guardian Angels' (1976),
courtesy of Tower Hamlets
Local History, Library and Archives

Typeset and design by
Four Sheets Design and Print

Printed and bound by CPI Group (UK) Ltd, Croydon, CR0 4YY

CONTENTS

Introduction

No city has been written about more than London. The centre of printing in English for more than half a millennium, London has found itself the muse of poets and playwrights, journalists, essayists and historians and — most important of all — fiction writers, the men and women who have imagined the city and its people since the time of Daniel Defoe, if not before. London is truly unknowable, but we get closest to it through the novels and short-stories whose characters work out their destinies in this most complex and multilayered of cities.

Fiction has peopled London in the mind, and indelibly so. However hard historians try to unearth the lived reality of, say, Victorian London, we still get our sharpest insights in the fiction, both great and small, of the time. The fiction writers have the benefit of immediacy, of material that is fresh and real to them as they write, of what it feels *now* — at the time of writing — to be a Londoner and to deal with the city's challenges and changing imperatives. 'Dickensian London' has retained an indelible resonance almost a century-and-a-half after the novelist's death. Although the years that followed provided no such transcendant figure, similar revelations might be sought for the London of the 1930s, to choose just one fruitful decade among many, in the novels of Patrick Hamilton, J.B. Priestley, George Orwell, Pamela Hansford Johnson, Ethel Mannin, Rosemary Lehmann and a host of others.

In these fictions we find the great themes of London life as they have been etched out generation by generation. The mesmeric draw of London, for instance, for the talented youth of provincial England and the nations of the British Isles, and indeed for Londoners from the whole world over. A small library of fictions has been constructed around the desires and temptations that have brought people to London, and the joys, tribulations and disappointments of metropolitan life once they arrive there. Of the difficulties in their way, none has been weightier than finding somewhere decent to live, so that housing has itself become the main subject of scores of London novels (from Richard Whiteing's *No. 5 John Street*, 1899, through Lynne Reid

Banks's *The L-Shaped Room* of 1960 to J.G. Ballard's dystopic London futurama of 1975, *High-Rise*, and many more). Of the dangers of London life none has been more potent than sexual desire, enlivened by uncountable encounters in street and workplace and pub, an enduring theme that stretches from the very beginnings of London fictions to today (we might instance stellar examples in Samuel Richardson's *Pamela* of 1741 and Martin Amis's *London Fields* of 1986). Most of all, perhaps, the novelists remind us that it is love and money — not necessarily in that order — that keep this city ticking.

One of the great themes of London life is change, especially the restless transformation of the city's intricate social geography. In London fictions, more often than not, this theme for the modern reader is implicit. Some novels have indeed made a changing London district their own theme, like Monica Dickens's 1960 novel of Notting Hill, *The Heart of London*, or Mervyn Jones's East End family saga *Holding On* (1975). More often, readers will be struck — often intrigued and moved — by just how the London they know now has altered since the novel was written. The Hoxton carefully and tenderly represented in Walter Besant's *Children of Gibeon* (1886) was recognisable even into the 1960s: there's nothing left of it now. For those newcomers who have made a life there in the twenty-first century it must come as a considerable shock to see just how far this tiny and difficult area of inner north-east London has rewritten itself; and how the Hoxtonites have altered in the process.

It is this single theme on which we've focused in *London Fictions*. We asked a selection of contemporary Londonists — the term is coming once more into fashion but is originally Marcus Fall's from 1880 — to write about a novel they love or admire or maybe hate, to tell us something of plot and character and just what makes it special in the London canon, and to dwell briefly on how the city described there differs from the London of 2013. From a long tradition, and given the prominence understandably accorded to Charles Dickens in his bicentenary year, we decided to restrict our contributors' choice of novels to writers active after his death in 1870. We believe their selection will contain surprises, while refreshing delight in some old favourites. We think the variety of books surveyed will appeal to all who are interested in London's literary heritage. And we hope that there will be scope for subsequent collections that explore a tradition that has been built by literally hundreds of writers. For London, while ever unknowable, is inexhaustible too.

Jerry White

George Gissing
The Nether World (1889)

ANDREW WHITEHEAD

G eorge Gissing, a northerner, came to London as a social outcast. He was a stranger in an immense city which he explored ceaselessly, which absorbed his intellectual energy and fed his creativity, and about which he had little good to say. The London of *The Nether World* is grim, sulphurous and suffocates the human spirit. Gissing's great novel of working-class Clerkenwell has little of the picaresque humour of Dickens's jaunts into London slums. It is not a work of social reform, for while the author's anger sears through his story, it is burdened by a despairing resignation rather than a prescription to achieve change. All the most obvious remedies — political radicalism, philanthropy, self-help, slum clearance — are tried during the course of the novel and found wanting. Even in Gissing's bleak underworld there are good people with noble motives, yet the finest of his characters still find their lives crimped and their aesthetic senses blunted in the brutal snare of poverty and exploitation.

The novel's title has two meanings. It is the out of view, out of mind universe of the urban poor — for almost every character in *The Nether World* has his or her roots in the working-class. It is also the hellish world of the dead. Gissing invests his London with a stygian gloom. An incidental character, Mad Jack, a crazed itinerant preacher, gives voice to this metaphor while reciting a message received in a vision: '...There is no escape for you. From poor you shall become poorer; the older you grow the lower shall you sink in want and misery; at the end there is waiting for you, one and all, a death in abandonment and despair. This is Hell — Hell — Hell!' The location of his prophecy is the most infernal of Gissing's slums, Shooter's Gardens, a 'winding alley', a 'black horror', possessed by 'filth, rottenness, evil odours', where each room houses a separate family, and where wife beating, drunkenness and petty crime are the order of things.

The story of *The Nether World* concerns Michael Snowdon's increasingly obsessive determination to use the wealth with which he returned from the colonies to help London's poor. His kind-hearted granddaughter, Jane, is raised modestly, and with the intention that she will execute her grandfather's philanthropic ambitions. Sidney Kirkwood, a working man of integrity, is enlisted in the venture. A series of contrivances which owe much to Victorian melodrama — the plot includes an unsigned will, disguised identities, chance encounters, veiled faces and a scheming lawyer — deprive Jane of her inheritance. She cannot achieve her purpose, though she succeeds in touching people's lives simply by the quality of her character. Sidney Kirkwood and Jane Snowdon come across as honourable but insipid characters. In true Gissing style (there is something of the author in this) they are confined by a sense of duty and responsibility. They are soul mates, but cannot live their lives together.

The great rivals Clem Peckover and Pennyloaf Candy are more memorable characters; two women who would not be out of place in *Eastenders*. There is a touch of Dickens about them, not least in their names. Pennyloaf, a seamstress, is a brutalised, feckless but good-natured inmate of Shooter's Gardens. Clem, from a slightly less squalid slum in Clerkenwell Close, is earthy, coarse and cunning. They compete for the affections of the ne'er-do-well Bob Hewett. Surprisingly, he chooses Pennyloaf, and the couple spend their wedding day, a bank holiday, on an outing to Crystal Palace — where Clem and her friends are also enjoying a day out. The grounds are packed. There's a band, coconut shies, high tea, fireworks, and (for Bob, and many others) plenty of drink. Gissing had taken trouble to spy out his landscape. 'What a day I had yesterday at the Crystal Palace!' he commented to his sister. 'I brought back a little book full of scribbled notes. You will read it all some day.' And there it is in *The Nether World*, a 'great review of the People':

> See how worn-out the poor girls are becoming, how they gape, what listless eyes most of them have! The stoop in the shoulders so universal among them merely means over-toil in the workroom. Not one in a thousand shows the elements of taste in dress; vulgarity and worse glares in all but every costume. ... Mark the men in their turn: four in every six have visages so deformed by ill-health that they excite disgust; their hair is cut down to within half an inch of the scalp; their legs are twisted out of shape by evil conditions of life from birth upwards. Whenever a youth and a girl come along arm-in-arm, how flagrantly shows the man's coarseness!

10

For Clem and Pennyloaf, the bank holiday outing to Crystal Palace ends in the spectacle of a brawl on Clerkenwell Green. 'Pennyloaf flew with erected nails at Clem Peckover. It was just what the latter desired. In an instant she had rent half Pennyloaf's garments off her back, and was tearing her face till the blood streamed. Inconsolable was the grief of the crowd when a couple of stalwart policemen came hustling forward, thrusting to left and right, irresistibly clearing the corner.' For Gissing, as for his imaginary onlookers, the brutalism of the urban poor was a spectacle, though one that he found profoundly sad rather than exciting.

An early review of *The Nether World* described George Gissing as 'a modern Dante' — a particularly prescient comment. Gissing, a classicist at heart, had read Dante attentively as a means of learning Italian. 'Ye Gods, what glorious matter!' he declared. It's probably where the novel's title came from. The phrase 'the nether world' appears in Henry Cary's hugely influential translation of Dante, with which Gissing was familiar. He was not the first to make the association between Dante's realm of the tormented and the streets and courts of Clerkenwell. A local clergyman had, in the mid-1880s, likened the noises emanating from the deep trench built for the underground railway to 'the shrieks and groans of the lost souls in the lowest circle of Dante's *Inferno*'.

Hellish imagery and references to death set the tone from the opening pages. The story starts as the ageing Michael Snowdon, in search of his family, walks past the graveyard of St. James's, Clerkenwell, to the walls of the Middlesex House of Detention. He stops to glance at a nightmarish effigy above the prison gateway. 'It was the sculptured counterfeit of a human face, that of a man distraught with agony. The eyes stared wildly from their sockets, the hair struggled in maniac disorder, the forehead was rung with torture, the cheeks sunken, the throat fearsomely wasted, and from the wide lips there seemed to be issuing a horrible cry.' (The jail was much as Gissing describes, though he can have had only indirect knowledge of the tormented face above the gateway which appears to have been removed in the 1840s). The Peckover household nearby, introduced in the first chapter, is 'dark and cavernous' and home to a corpse awaiting burial. Clem has been reared in the 'putrid soil of that nether world'. The book ends in another cemetery, at Michael Snowdon's grave at Abney Park in Stoke Newington. The recurring refrain is of a populace trapped, entombed, in a cycle of suffering.

There's an inescapable sense that Gissing alighted on his setting and theme and then populated the story, rather than the other way round. As a result, *The Nether World*'s depiction of the urban environment is more convincing than its account of those who dwell in it. The underworld Gissing describes is very circumscribed. Much of the action takes place within a quarter of a mile of the opening scene on Clerkenwell Green, and almost all within a mile or two. He is precise in his topography, as if this exactness demonstrates the authenticity of his urban landscape. The word 'Clerkenwell' appears seventy-four times. The routes taken by his ever perambulating characters are set down in detail. They are always on the move, though — until the closing sections of the story — they rarely move far. Dozens of street names are mentioned, and Shooter's Gardens is the only important setting that can't be found in a gazetteer.

Most of Gissing's fiction is imbued with a powerful sense of London. His novels stretch north and south of the river, from inner city tenements to the newer middle-class suburbs. London is not simply the setting, but a wellspring of his imagination, and while the urban panorama he offers is unsettling, he provides a more compelling sense of the late-Victorian city than any other contemporary novelist. That is in part because Gissing lived among the people he wrote about. He had married into the underworld, and knew the poorer parts of the city more intimately than most of its chroniclers.

George Gissing moved to London as a nineteen-year-old in the autumn of 1877. He was a Yorkshireman, born in Wakefield and northern educated, a product of the provincial middle-class. By the time he came south, his life was in a groove from which he could not, or would not, escape. He had been expelled from Owen's College in Manchester, where he had proved an exceptional student, for stealing money and had served five weeks in jail. He remained haunted by that disgrace. The theft was to help support a young Manchester prostitute, Nell Harrison, who became Gissing's wife, and with whom he endured a miserable few years in London garrets — not themselves slums of the Shooter's Gardens kind, but uncomfortably close vantage points. That tragic relationship tainted him, and provided much of the fire and fury in his early work. Gissing's five novels of the London poor, of which *The Nether World* was the bleakest and the most accomplished, were all the product of his first decade or so in the city — written while living with Nell, during their uneasy separation, or amid the catharsis of her drink-ridden decline.

'I have a book in my head which no one else could write', George Gissing confided to his sister in 1886, 'a book which will contain the very spirit of London working-class life.' Nell Harrison's death two years later provided the impulse behind the novel that most lived up to his goal. She succumbed to what may well have been syphilis at the

12

age of thirty. Gissing went to her room in a dingy lodging house in Lambeth to see the body, and recorded the scene in his diary:

> Linen she had none; the very covering of the bed had gone save one sheet and one blanket. I found a number of pawn tickets, showing that she had pledged these things during last summer, — when it was warm, poor creature! All the money she received went in drink...
>
> She lay on the bed covered with a sheet. I looked long, long at her face, but could not recognize it. It is more than three years, I think, since I saw her, and she had changed horribly...
>
> Came home to a bad, wretched night. In nothing am I to blame; I did my utmost; again and again I had her back to me. Fate was too strong. But as I stood beside that bed, I felt that my life henceforth had a firmer purpose. Henceforth I never cease to bear testimony against the accursed social order that brings about things of this kind. I feel that she will help me more in her death than she balked me during her life. Poor, poor thing!

Gissing had been toying with a novel set in Clerkenwell. 'I have something in hand which I hope to turn to some vigorous purpose', he wrote to Thomas Hardy in the summer of 1887, 'a story that has grown up in recent ramblings about Clerkenwell, — dark, but with evening sunlight to close.' Prior to Nell's death, repeated attempts to embark on a fresh book had proved stillborn. Within three weeks, Gissing has begun to write *The Nether World* and it took just four months to complete.

'It is far from finished yet, but I am satisfied on the whole with the completed parts', Gissing told his sister-in-law in April 1888. 'It deals exclusively with the lower-classes'. This unrelenting focus on the impoverished sets *The Nether World* apart from his other novels. Many of his books, before and after, concern the chains of social convention, and feature men and women who straddle social classes or are caught awkwardly between them. But here, he makes a working man the central character — albeit one who bears some traits in common with his creator. As he set to work, Gissing returned again and again to the streets he had chosen for his story. 'Evening spent in Clerkenwell, wandering' he jotted in his diary. In the following weeks, there are similar entries: 'Morning spent in Clerkenwell'; 'Good Friday. Morning in Clerkenwell'; 'In evening to Clerkenwell Green'.

Gissing never lived in Clerkenwell, but some of his London homes were strolling distance away. George and Nell took refuge in a succession of drab rented rooms in unfashionable districts of inner London. One of these was at 5 Hanover Street in Islington, just north of and backing on to the Regent's Canal. The house is now 60 Noel Road. They moved there in November 1879 — about the moment that the story told in *The Nether World* opens — and stayed for over a year.

13

The street is described in the novel as 'a quiet byway... Squalor is here kept at arm's length'. Michael Snowdon and his granddaughter take lodgings there, and it becomes one of the novel's principal venues — a level or two above the grim depths of Gissing's underworld just to the south in Clerkenwell.

The area that he alighted upon as his setting was a densely populated locality squeezed between Islington, Holborn and the City. 'For some years many of the well-to-do residents of the parish have been gradually leaving their houses, which become occupied by a poorer class of people, many of the houses which were formerly held by one family, being now let to several', reported the local Medical Officer of Health in 1883. Clerkenwell had for a century or more been associated with highly skilled artisan trades, watchmaking in particular, but also jewellery and precious metal work, and specialist printing, bookbinding and furniture trades. 'Here every alley is thronged with small industries', records the novelist, 'all but every door and window exhibits the advertisement of a craft that is carried on within.' By the 1880s, standardisation and mechanisation were making craft skills redundant, forcing many who had once enjoyed high wages and status to take on any work they could find.

Gissing reflects the pain and dislocation of the declining years of artisan inner London, and performs a task few of his contemporary novelists were sufficiently confident to attempt — taking the reader inside the workplace. Bob Hewett works in a die-sinking workshop making moulds. For Bob's father, Gissing explains, 'it was no slight gratification that he had been able to apprentice his son to a craft which permitted him always to wear a collar' — though Gissing observes that die-sinking 'is not the craft it once was; cheap methods, vulgarising here as everywhere, have diminished the opportunities of capable men.' Hewett junior uses his skills to make counterfeit coins. Hewett senior, once a self-employed cabinet-maker, is reduced to responding to a newspaper advert for an odd-job man paying a paltry fifteen shillings a week, and even then finds himself in a melee of five-hundred desperate jobseekers.

The transition from a proud, craft-based economy to attic workshops for those with skills still in demand, and casualised labour for the rest, is captured in one of the novel's most celebrated and vivid passages.

> It was the hour of the unyoking of men. In the highways and byways of Clerkenwell there was a thronging of released toilers, of young and old, of male and female. Forth they streamed from factories and workrooms, anxious to make the most of the few hours during which they might live for themselves...

14

... In Clerkenwell the demand is not so much for rude strength as for the cunning fingers and the contriving brain. The inscriptions on the house-fronts would make you believe that you were in a region of gold and silver and precious stones. In the recesses of dim byways, where sunshine and free air are forgotten things, where families herd together in dear-rented garrets and cellars, craftsmen are for ever handling jewellery, shaping bright ornaments for the necks and arms of such as are born to the joy of life. Wealth inestimable is ever flowing through these workshops, and the hands that have been stained with gold-dust may, as likely as not, some day extend themselves in petition for a crust.

There is a compassion and social concern in Gissing's account of his underworld which alleviates a pessimism that otherwise threatens to overwhelm the reader.

At times, Gissing veers towards polemic and exaggeration, as in his description of slum housing. Shooter's Gardens stands in a long tradition of the classic literary slum. Yet he takes the trouble to look beyond the veneer of dilapidation and overcrowding to explain how money was to be made out of bad housing. 'This winter was the last that Shooter's Gardens were destined to know', he writes. 'The leases had all but run out; the middle-men were garnering their latest profits; in the spring there would come a wholesale demolition, and model-lodgings would thereafter occupy the site.' The role of middle-men, house farmers as they were called, in pushing up rents while allowing the buildings' fabric to decay, and in using local political influence to obstruct the enforcement of public health regulations, was one of the main findings of the landmark Royal Commission on the Housing of the Working Classes of the mid-1880s. Clerkenwell was one of the districts to which the Commission paid particular attention, and local clergy, landlords and school board officials — though not the slum dwellers themselves — were called to give evidence.

The Royal Commission was part of a wave of social concern about outcast London which developed from the early 1880s, reflected in the writings of concerned clerics, sensationalist journalists and social investigators. Gissing's novels of London poverty, all products of the 1880s, were not born from the same reflex, but they fed into the same process of developing public awareness and unease about what was sometimes called (though not by Gissing) 'darkest London'. The vogue for slum novels gathered pace in the following decade, complemented by Charles Booth's monumental and revelatory *Life and Labour of the People in London*, which sought to map the city's poverty and criminality. Gissing helped set the tone for the slum fictions of the closing

15

years of the century, though he privately dismissed Arthur Morrison's *A Child of the Jago* as 'poor stuff'.

The clearing of the worst slums and the building of model dwellings, multi-storey blocks of workers' flats, was one of the most conspicuous responses to concern about poor housing. Many vermin-ridden rookeries met the same fate as Gissing's Shooter's Gardens. In the novel, Sidney Kirkwood and the Hewett family move into newly-built industrial dwellings on one of Clerkenwell's main roads — a building which Gissing finds repulsive:

> What terrible barracks, those Farringdon Road Buildings! Vast, sheer walls, unbroken by even an attempt at ornament; row above row of windows in the mud-coloured surface, upwards, upwards, lifeless eyes, murky openings that tell of bareness, disorder, comfortlessness within. One is tempted to say that Shooter's Gardens are a preferable abode... Barracks, in truth; housing for the army of industrialism...

The dousing down of the human spirit horrifies Gissing even more than the contagion of the old courts and alleys.

If *The Nether World* is testimony against the 'accursed social order', it is also contemptuous of those who seek to overthrow it. All five of Gissing's novels of working-class London are concerned in some degree with popular politics and unbelief. When writing his first published novel, *Workers in the Dawn*, he described himself as 'a mouthpiece of the advanced Radical party.' In the early 1880s, Gissing dallied with positivism, a bookish strand within progressive radicalism. It was a brief interlude. When in 1886 he wrote *Demos*, subtitled 'a story of English socialism', he was disdainful of organised radicalism and scathing of the shallowness of socialist leaders.

If Clerkenwell's name was known in late nineteenth-century London, it was as a hotbed of working-class radicalism. The district's craftsmen had fostered a culture of artisan radicalism which still found powerful expression in the 1880s. The Patriotic Club on Clerkenwell Green (the eighteenth-century building is now, appropriately, the Marx Memorial Library) was one of the most active of London's many working men's radical clubs. Clerkenwell Green itself was a forum for radical oratory and a venue of notoriously turbulent popular protests. Gissing spent a Sunday evening there in 1887, and reported back to his family in Wakefield that it was 'a great assembly-place for radical meetings, & the like. A more disheartening scene it is difficult to imagine, — the vulgar, blatant scoundrels!'

In *The Nether World*, the most Gissing-like character, Sidney Kirkwood, briefly embraces working-class politics. His friend John

Hewett is portrayed as a more determined radical, an embittered orator, soured by the hardships endured by himself and his family. Eventually, Hewett's radical passion is spent, disillusioned in part by the collapse of the savings scheme run by his workmen's club, for radicals — Gissing suggests — are no more honest than those they disparage.

For all the sense of hopelessness, Gissing was able to find the 'evening sunlight to close' that he had spoken of to Thomas Hardy. At the end of the novel, Sidney Kirkwood and Jane Snowdon meet at the grave of her grandfather.

> In each life little for congratulation... Yet to both their work was given. Unmarked, unencouraged save by their love of uprightness and mercy, they stood by the side of those more hapless, brought some comfort to hearts less courageous than their own. Where they abode it was not all dark. Sorrow certainly awaited them, perchance defeat in even the humble aims that they had set themselves; but at least their lives would remain a protest against those brute forces of society which fill with wreck the abysses of the nether world.

Simply surviving uncorrupted amid the brutalism and misery constituted a challenge to the social order that tolerated such injustice. And telling the story of the nether world helped Gissing gain some closure on years of personal misery. His biographer, Paul Delany, argues that in the process of writing the novel, 'Gissing paid off his debt to Nell's memory, and decided that he need no longer walk the streets of outcast London'. He went on to write many successful London novels, among them *New Grub Street* and *The Odd Women*, but never again chose to focus on the London poor.

References and Further Reading

George Gissing, *Workers in the Dawn*, 1880

George Gissing, *The Unclassed*, 1884

George Gissing, *Demos*, 1886

George Gissing, *Thyrza*, 1887

Pierre Coustillas (ed.), *London and the Life of Literature in late-Victorian England: the diary of George Gissing, novelist*, Harvester Press, 1978

Pierre Coustillas, *The Heroic Life of George Gissing, Part 1: 1857-1888*, Pickering & Chatto, 2011

Rev. William Dawson, *A mid-London Parish: a short history of the parish of S. John, Clerkenwell*, 1885

Paul Delany, *George Gissing: a life*, Weidenfeld & Nicolson, 2008

The Collected Letters of George Gissing, Ohio University Press, multi-volume, 1990 onwards

John Goode's introduction to the Harvester Press edition of *The Nether World*, 1974

John Halperin, *Gissing: a life in books*, Oxford University Press, 1987

P.J. Keating, *The Working Classes in Victorian Fiction*, Routledge & Kegan Paul, 1971

Royal Commission on the Housing of the Working Classes, 1884-85

Survey of London, vol. XLVI: South and East Clerkenwell, Yale University Press for English Heritage, 2008

Andrew Whitehead, 'Clerkenwell as Hell — Gissing's "nether world"', *Gissing Journal*, October 2010

Today's 'Nether World'

Clerkenwell was on the cusp of profound change as Gissing wrote about the area. The road buildings and slum clearances are captured in his pages, as are the new commuter services. Sidney Kirkwood ends the book travelling to work in Clerkenwell from an industrial cottage in Crouch End 'on the northern limit' of London, where the streets 'have a smell of newness, of dampness'. Fronting the main thoroughfares, old and new, warehouses and light industrial buildings sprang up. The wars brought down more of the old buildings (a plaque on Farringdon Road marks premises 'totally destroyed' by a zeppelin raid in September 1915), and much of the housing that remained was swept away to make space for huge new municipal estates.

So much has gone, yet fragments of Gissing's Clerkenwell remain. Hidden away on Albemarle Way, a two minute stroll from Sidney Kirkwood's workshop on St. John's Square, is a last vestige of what was once the area's defining trade. Gleave & Co. 'watch and clock materials', situated next to a gemstone merchant, now does much of its business online, but can still supply the moving parts to almost any old fashioned timepiece. Nearby Clerkenwell Green remains something of a backwater, its character preserved by four defining buildings: the commanding Sessions House, once a court and now a conference centre, the refurbished Marx Memorial Library, the Crown Tavern, and looming over all, the bleached, rounded, elegant spire of St. James's. The Green's old centrepiece, a pump, has gone, but it remains a public space — and now much more fashionable than in Gissing's day.

Off the Green, Clerkenwell Close follows its old serpentine path, graced by buildings with which Gissing would have been familiar. Pear Tree Court is the site of the Peabody Clerkenwell Estate, a step up perhaps from the 'terrible barracks' which so appalled Gissing, but of the same period and

Barnabas House, Central Street EC1

purpose. Pockets of stylish Victorian terraced housing survive in and around Sekforde Street. As recently as the 1980s, much of the area was down-at-heel, and the passer-by was occasionally assailed by fumes from metal plating workshops. South Clerkenwell is now fashionable, 'a synonym for urban rejuvenation and energy' in the rose-tinted judgement of the *Survey of London*, and reputed to have more architects and design studios to the acre than anywhere in Europe.

A little further towards Islington, the streets have more vitality, a more rooted community, than gentrified south Clerkenwell. On a sunny weekend afternoon, Spafields — once an even more insurrection-minded meeting place than Clerkenwell Green — still has a touch of the cockney about it. Clarks on Exmouth Market — about as a traditional an eatery as you can find, 'jellied eels £2.70, hot eels £2.75, eels and mash £4.10' — still sits its customers on pew-like benches, and serves its mash in scooped out spherical globules. 'Hi Nan, you alright?!' shouts a young man called Tel as he cycles past the open door — his nan is one of a triptych of elderly white women behind the serving counter.

But here too, the last emblems of industrious Clerkenwell are fading. Doors away is the much-in-demand Moro, 'known for its award-winning Moorish cuisine'. The street is a foodie's delight — tapas bars, open air food stalls, 'artisan' bakeries in place of artisans' workshops.

Round the corner on Farringdon Road, the Quality Chop House 'progressive working-class caterer' is the same style and vintage as Clarks, with similar high-backed wooden seats. Within my memory, you could read the communist *Morning Star* over a breakfast of bloaters. Then it went up-market, with oysters topping the menu. It didn't work. The place has, in keeping with the area, found a mid-market niche, selling homemade meatballs. Happily, the choir stall seating remains.

Further down towards the City, Farringdon Road gets a little louche. Not all that far from Gissing's 'terrible barracks' — in a building he would have seen being constructed as he researched and wrote *The Nether World* — is the Chatterbox Topless Bar, 'drinks £10, no other charges: hostesses wanted'. That would have given Gissing something to write about.

Andrew Whitehead

Arthur Conan Doyle
The Sign of Four (1890)

ANDREW LANE

I had neither kith nor kin in England, and was therefore as free as air — or as free as an income of eleven shillings and sixpence a day will permit a man to be. Under such circumstances, I naturally gravitated to London, that great cesspool into which all the loungers and idlers of the Empire are irresistibly drained. There I stayed for some time at a private hotel in the Strand, leading a comfortless, meaningless existence, and spending such money as I had, considerably more freely than I ought.

These are the words that Arthur Conan Doyle uses at the start of his novel *A Study in Scarlet* to introduce us to narrator Dr John Watson, and to set the scene for Watson's later meeting with the eccentric consulting detective Sherlock Holmes. *A Study in Scarlet* was published in 1887, and is set somewhere between 1881 and 1885 (more on the author's offhand approach to dates in a moment). Conan Doyle went on to write three more novels and fifty-six short stories using Sherlock Holmes as the central character. The last-written story ('The Adventure of Shoscombe Old Place') was published in 1927 but set much earlier. The last chronological story ('His Last Bow') was published in 1917, but set in 1914.

In Sherlock Holmes, Arthur Conan Doyle created one of the best known and longest-lasting characters in English fiction. The Sherlock Holmes stories have justifiably never been out of print, and rather than languishing on the shelves designated for 'classic literature' they sit proudly in the 'Crime' section of bookshops and libraries, alongside the latest (usually Scandinavian) authors. As well as having been adapted into too many films, TV programmes, comics and computer games in too many countries to count, they have also given rise to a whole industry of literary pastiches and parodies. Conan Doyle did this by accident — he never set out to make a lasting impact with Sherlock Holmes (in later life he thought that his historical novels would be his legacy to the literary world). His secrets were firstly a writing style that, paradoxically, had no style — it spoke directly to the reader, without artifice — and secondly an extraordinary central character who was superficially unlovable except through the filtering eyes of his friend and biographer, John Watson.

To counterbalance his extraordinary literary achievements, Conan Doyle has come in for a great deal of criticism over the years for, amongst other things, his slapdash approach to continuity. Dr Watson's wound, for instance, received during military service in Afghanistan, moves mysteriously from leg to shoulder and back, and his first name varies between John and James, while the faithful housekeeper and landlady Mrs Hudson becomes Mrs Turner on one occasion. He has also been criticised for his cavalier approach to time — *The Sign of Four* itself takes place in both July and September, according to the text, and the only way to rationalise the various appearances and mentions of Holmes's nemesis Professor James Moriarty on the dates that the stories are supposedly set is to assume that the evil Professor has two brothers, and that all three siblings are named James.

What has not been criticised to any great extent is his description of London, which is where the majority of the stories are at least partially set. Quite the opposite — it's probably fair to say that Conan Doyle's Sherlock Holmes stories have heavily coloured people's image of Victorian London, but is this fair? His initial characterisation of that city as a 'great cesspool' full of 'idlers and scroungers', for instance, indicates to the casual reader that Conan Doyle will be placing the stories against a richly detailed Dickensian background of slums, sordid taverns and grotesque inhabitants, but this promise is never satisfied. Anybody looking to Conan Doyle for a contemporaneous critique of social conditions in the great metropolis will have to look elsewhere.

A quick look at Conan Doyle's biography will indicate why this is the case. He was born in Edinburgh and educated first in Lancashire and then, briefly, in Austria. He returned to Edinburgh to study medicine and, having qualified, was initially employed as a ship's surgeon on a voyage to West Africa. On arrival back in England he set up in practice first in Plymouth and then in Portsmouth, which is where he wrote *A Study in Scarlet*. The location absent in all of that peripatetic existence is London. Admittedly he visited the city before finally moving there in 1891 (he had a notable dinner at the Langham Hotel in London in 1889) but these would have been fleeting visits, not enough to soak up the rich atmosphere and to explore the subtle (and sometimes not so subtle) differences in social class that could (and still can) exist between streets only a few minutes' walk from one another.

The irony is that Conan Doyle's writings have produced a vivid picture in people's minds of what Victorian London was like. The vision is of thick fog, clattering hansom cabs, gas-lit streets, taverns resounding with Cockney sing-songs, pavements cluttered with beggars and ragged urchins, and telegrams arriving at all hours of the day and night containing vital facts. This picture is, however, largely an invention. It is based firstly on an extrapolation of just a handful of comments in the stories and secondly on the imaginations of several generations of film and TV producers who have interpreted the stories and converged on a convenient shorthand representation. Consider the fact that Holmes's recorded career covers some thirty-four years between the earliest and latest chronological stories. In that time gas lamps were replaced with electric lighting, hansom cabs were replaced with cars and telegrams were replaced with telephones. Mention the name 'Sherlock Holmes', however, and it can be guaranteed that people will not be thinking about electric lights, cars and telephones. Fog, hansoms and gaslights are, and forever will be, the first things that come to mind.

Of the four Sherlock Holmes novels written by Conan Doyle, both *A Study in Scarlet* and *The Valley of Fear* use Holmes as a 'wrap-around' for a flashback story set in America, and *The Hound of the Baskervilles* takes place largely (and famously) on Dartmoor. Only his second Holmes novel *The Sign of Four* (or *The Sign of* the *Four*, as it was originally titled), takes place in numerous London locations — but the book was first published in 1890, the year before Conan Doyle relocated to London from Portsmouth, and it shows.

The plot of *The Sign of Four* is relatively direct for a book that is supposed to be a mystery. Holmes and Watson are whiling away the time at their residence in Baker Street when a visitor arrives. It is a Miss Mary Morstan, and she tells them a story about the disappearance of her father and the mysterious arrival once a year of a parcel addressed to her containing a pearl. Now a letter has arrived from the same source asking her for a meeting, and she wants Holmes and Watson to accompany her. The three of them travel to a house in Brixton, south London, where they meet Thaddeus Sholto. He tells them that his father, Major John Sholto, had been sending her the pearls. The reason was that John Sholto and Mary Morstan's father were stationed together in India and came into possession of a treasure chest of jewels. The two men had argued, back in England, and Mary Morstan's father had suffered a heart attack, which Sholto then covered up by hiding the body. Since that date he had been sending Mary the pearls as a kind of apology, but Sholto himself has now died. For months Thaddeus and his brother, Bartholomew, have been searching their father's house for the treasure, and now Bartholomew has sent word that he has found it.

The four of them travel the short distance to Upper Norwood, where brother Bartholomew is still living in their father's house. Bartholomew is dead, however — pricked by a poisoned thorn — and the jewels are missing. Holmes and Watson follow the killers, but eventually lose the trail at the edge of the Thames.

Holmes sets out by himself to investigate, and determines that the killers are using a steam launch to travel on the Thames. He alerts Watson and the police, and together they try to catch the steam launch with their own steam-powered police boat. A chase ensues down the Thames during which one of the killers (a midget Andaman islander) drowns and the other (a one-legged sailor named Jonathan Small) is rescued.

In a descriptive account that echoes those in *A Study in Scarlet* and *The Valley of Fear*, Small tells his questioners the story of how he and three confederates came into possession of the treasure, how Sholto and Morstan took it from them, and how he has spent years searching the world for it.

Setting aside the plot, the detective work, the characterisation and the historical backdrop, it's instructive to examine how *The Sign of Four* treats the city in which most of its action takes place. Promisingly, early in the book we find an atmospheric and yet rather generic description of London as seen through the filter of the kind of unpleasant autumn day with which most people will be familiar:

> It was a September evening and not yet seven o'clock, but the day had been a dreary one, and a dense drizzly fog lay low upon the great city. Mud-coloured clouds drooped sadly over the muddy streets. Down the Strand the lamps were but misty splotches of diffused light which threw a feeble circular glimmer upon the slimy pavement. The yellow glare from the shop-windows streamed out into the steamy, vaporous air and threw a murky, shifting radiance across the crowded thoroughfare. There was, to my mind, something eerie and ghostlike in the endless procession of faces which flitted across these narrow bars of light—sad faces and glad, haggard and merry. Like all humankind, they flitted from the gloom into the light and so back into the gloom once more.

This is Watson describing London, but it might just as easily have been Liverpool, Manchester, Glasgow or Edinburgh.

During the course of the book, Holmes and Watson seem to be perpetually rushing from one London location to another; sometimes together, sometimes apart, and occasionally accompanied by Miss Mary Morstan, Inspector Athelney Jones and a dog named Toby. They start in Baker Street, at number 221b. This has become a world-famous address since publication of *A Study in Scarlet*, but it doesn't take the casual investigator long to discover that the address itself was and is completely fictitious. Baker Street at the time that *The Sign of Four* is set was considerably shorter than it is today, running only from Portman Square in the south to the junction with Crawford Street and Paddington Street. From there up to Marylebone Road it was called York Place. North of Marylebone Road it was Baker Street again, but this time *Upper* Baker Street (a distinction never mentioned by Conan Doyle). The numbering is as problematic as the street name: the Baker Street numbers only ran from 1 to 84 at the time, so there never was a 221 Baker Street, let alone a 221*b*. And while we are on the subject, what exactly did that *b* mean? The basement flat? A flat above a shop or an office? Neither possibility was ever mentioned by Watson in the entire Conan Doyle canon.

Watson does tell us, at various points in the stories, that 221b Baker Street had a bow window in their first floor sitting room, and that the house backed on to a mews. This hardly helps us track it down: no upstairs room in Baker Street ever had a bow window, and there were no mews at the back. Don't look to Conan Doyle for accuracy.

From Baker Street our intrepid heroes travel by cab to the Lyceum Theatre. In the hands of another writer we might get a detailed description of the theatre and the theatre-going public, but Conan Doyle is more concerned with the actions of his characters and the dialogue between them. At the time the book was set the Savoy Theatre, not too far away, was lit by electricity, which in the hands of an author nowadays writing about the 1880s would form an interesting diversion, but no, not here.

From the Lyceum our characters are taken on a cab ride to parts unknown. It is foggy outside, and Holmes narrates the journey for us:

> 'Rochester Row,' said he. 'Now Vincent Square. Now we come out on the Vauxhall Bridge Road. We are making for the Surrey side apparently. Yes, I thought so. Now we are on the bridge. You can catch glimpses of the river.'
> We did indeed get a fleeting view of a stretch of the Thames, with the lamps shining upon the broad, silent water; but our cab dashed on and was soon involved in a labyrinth of streets upon the other side.

'Wordsworth Road,' said my companion. 'Priory Road. Lark Hall Lane. Stockwell Place. Robert Street. Cold Harbour Lane. Our quest does not appear to take us to very fashionable regions.'

This is nothing more than a list of street names. One can imagine Conan Doyle sitting at his desk in Southsea, Portsmouth, consulting a gazetteer of London as he wrote.

The journey ends shortly afterwards in Brixton (assuming, of course, that Conan Doyle meant Coldharbour Lane rather than Cold Harbour Lane). Conan Doyle describes the area with economy and precision:

> We had indeed reached a questionable and forbidding neighbourhood. Long lines of dull brick houses were only relieved by the coarse glare and tawdry brilliancy of public-houses at the corner. Then came rows of two-storied villas, each with a fronting of miniature garden, and then again interminable lines of new, staring brick buildings — the monster tentacles which the giant city was throwing out into the country.

It is interesting to note that in those days Brixton counted as the edges of the countryside. One would have to travel many more miles these days before seeing a green field.

Following a brief interlude in a 'third-rate suburban dwelling house', our heroes head for nearby Upper Norwood. There they arrive at a very different place of habitation — the opulent Pondicherry Lodge, which stands by itself in an expanse of garden (which has itself been heavily dug up by the Sholto brothers in search of the treasure). The suggestion — and it is no more than that — is that Upper Norwood is, in this year, a very countrified area, and the houses are all isolated from one another. That is certainly not the case now.

Watson takes Miss Morstan back to her lodgings in Camberwell, also conveniently located that side of the river, and then heads to Lambeth to fetch a tracker dog for Holmes to use. With Toby the dog leading, the two men follow the scent trail of the killers of Major John Sholto:

> We had during this time been following the guidance of Toby down the half-rural villa-lined roads which lead to the metropolis. Now, however, we were beginning to come among continuous streets, where labourers and dockmen were already astir, and slatternly women were taking down shutters and brushing door-steps. At the square-topped corner public-houses business was just beginning, and rough-looking men were emerging, rubbing their sleeves across their beards after their morning wet...
>
> We had traversed Streatham, Brixton, Camberwell, and now found ourselves in Kennington Lane, having borne away through the side streets to the east of the Oval. The men whom we pursued seemed to have taken a curiously zigzag road, with the idea probably of escaping observation. They had never kept to the main road if a parallel side

> street would serve their turn. At the foot of Kennington Lane they had
> edged away to the left through Bond Street and Miles Street. Where
> the latter street turns into Knight's Place, Toby ceased to advance...

Again, we find ourselves a victim of Conan Doyle's London gazetteer
and his wandering finger. A contemporary author writing of a foot-
slog through South London would indulge in a great deal more
description of the houses, the shops, the people and the various sights
that were experienced on the way. Not here, alas.

> Our course now ran down Nine Elms until we came to Broderick and
> Nelson's large timber-yard just past the White Eagle tavern...   It
> tended down towards the riverside, running through Belmont Place
> and Prince's Street. At the end of Broad Street it ran right down to the
> water's edge, where there was a small wooden wharf.

Holmes and Watson end up on the south side of the Thames, opposite
Millbank. They then head back to the mythical 221b Baker Street,
with mentions of Greenwich and Gravesend being made. Watson
makes two trips to Camberwell (he is now courting Mary Morstan),
and Holmes goes wandering off by himself in disguise. When he
returns, he tells Watson that he has tracked their quarry to a boat
yard near the Tower of London. The two of them join a Scotland Yard
detective (not, alas, Inspector Lestrade) at Westminster Pier and
pursue the killers of Bartholomew east along the Thames from the
Tower all the way down to Plumstead, where the final confrontation
is played out and the treasure is dumped into the murky waters.

That final section, with the police steam boat desperately trying
to overtake the villains' steam boat, and with the murderous
Andaman islander shooting poison darts at our heroes, is amongst the
most thrilling in the entire canon of English literature. It is, alas, far
too short, and it still tells us nothing of the historical Thames, which
has been the backbone of London since before there was a London.
Like everything else geographical in the book, it is a convenient and
thinly sketched out backdrop. If the book had been set in Liverpool
and the final chase had occurred on the River Mersey, (or the book
had been set in Newcastle and the final chase had occurred on the
River Tyne), then virtually no words would need to be changed. And
221b Baker Street would be equally as realistic as an address.

It has been said that you can read all of Jane Austen's books without
realising that the Napoleonic wars were going on in the background. In
the same way, you can read all fifty-six short stories and four novels that
Arthur Conan Doyle wrote about Sherlock Holmes without finding out
much about the London of the time. For instance, Conan Doyle does
mention various types of transport used by Holmes and Watson —

hansoms, four wheelers, jarveys, and even the horse-drawn buses that plied set routes — but he never describes the piles of manure that must have been left by those horses, or the sheer stench that must have been the result. And he almost never tells us about the Underground trains. The first underground line — the Metropolitan — opened in 1863, about twenty years before Holmes and Watson met, but there are very few mentions in the stories, and no descriptions at all. Similarly, the first telephone exchange opened in London in Lombard Street in 1879, and a contemporary account from 1882 mentioned an employee giving notice by telephone which means that they must have had quite a degree of "market penetration" as it is known, but there is no mention of a telephone in 221b Baker St. until sixteen years later (although Conan Doyle does have Holmes crossing the road to use the telephone in the Post Office in 1888). Conan Doyle tells us that when Watson first arrived in London he was living on eleven shillings and six pence a day, but he never puts this in context. In those days a man could live in a hotel in Central London for less than two pounds a week — including breakfast and dinner. A bottle of Bass beer cost three pence; less for a bottle of Guinness. A First Class return to Paris cost £2/12s and 6d. And in a wider social context, Scotland Yard detectives such as Lestrade, Gregson, MacDonald and so on get regular mentions in the canon but there is no hint of police corruption, ignoring the fact that in 1878 fully three out of the four Chief Inspectors of London's Detective Branch were found guilty of corruption. This led directly to the formation of the Criminal Investigation Department (CID), which the humorous magazine Punch subsequently referred to as the Defective Department.

Much of the above could be taken to be a critique of Conan Doyle as a writer. It is not meant that way — his achievements far outweigh any shortcomings in his prodigious output. It is rather a reminder that while Conan Doyle was trying to accomplish many things with his Sherlock Holmes stories, writing about London was not one of them.

References and Further Reading

Michael Harrison, *The London of Sherlock Holmes*, David & Charles, 1972

H.R.F. Keating, *Sherlock Holmes — The Man and His World*, Thames and Hudson, 1979

Pondicherry Lodge

Pondicherry Lodge is the most memorable of the many London locations in *The Sign of Four* — a suitable name for the retirement home of an old India hand such as Major Sholto. Conan Doyle locates the house in Upper Norwood — a building which 'stood in its own grounds, and was girt round with a very high stone wall topped with broken glass. A single narrow iron-clamped door formed the only means of entrance'. Once through that door, 'a gravel path wound through desolate grounds to a huge clump of a house, square and prosaic, all plunged in shadow save where a moonbeam struck one corner and glimmered in a garret window. The vast size of the building, with its gloom and its deathly silence, struck a chill to the heart.'

Conan Doyle knew Norwood well. He lived there for three years and was keenly involved in the local cricket club and even more so in the Upper Norwood Literary and Scientific Society (as I discover from Alistair Duncan's *The Norwood Author: Arthur Conan Doyle and the Norwood years*). But he moved there in the year after *The Sign of Four* was published, and there's nothing to indicate that he was familiar with the locality at the time he devised the Sholtos' forbidding family home.

That hasn't prevented two very different schools of research prising into the meaning of Pondicherry Lodge. Students of colonial and post-colonial literature have explored the novel's engagement with India and Indians — indeed one writer has commented on the Lodge's 'orientalist character both inside and out' and mused about the meaning of its transnational name (Pondicherry was a French enclave in southern India), so choosing to overlook the possibility that Conan Doyle was attracted simply by the resonance and rhythm of the word.

The remarkably assiduous body of Sherlockians have taken on the more daunting task of locating an (please forgive the heresy) imagined Lodge. Not so much the building that Conan Doyle had in mind as the model for Pondicherry Lodge, but the one that he should have had in mind — the house that most approximates to the fictional version. Holmes enthusiasts are now generally agreed that Kilravock House on Ross Road in Upper Norwood, built as the retirement home of one Major Thomas Ross, is the best fit. It stands close to the brow of quite a steep hill — a huge, squat ('clump' was Conan Doyle's word) mid-nineteenth-century mansion, now divided into thirteen flats, with a commanding southerly outlook over the Crystal Palace football stadium and far beyond.

The spot has a slightly out-of-the-way feel. Across the road is the cosy but somewhat neglected Grangewood Park — its bandstand, museum and café all long since swept away. On a spring afternoon, squawking ring-necked parakeets flit around the park, flashing their bright green plumage — not as menacing as an Andaman islander with a blow dart but an enduring touch of the sub-continent nonetheless.

Andrew Whitehead

Israel Zangwill
Children of the Ghetto (1892)

NADIA VALMAN

*C*hildren of the Ghetto: A Study of a Peculiar People, Israel
Zangwill's sprawling fictional ethnography of Jewish immigrant life in late nineteenth-century Whitechapel, was first
published in 1892 to great critical and commercial success. Blasting
into an increasingly politicised public debate about immigration, it
gave voice for the first time to Jewish perceptions of living in London's
East End. Zangwill's authority as a university-educated journalist
who had also lived and worked in Whitechapel for most of his life provided readers with a privileged perspective on the much-discussed but
little-known world of Russian and East European Jews and their
English-born children. The book's exotic 'panopticon of Ghetto scenes
and characters' was widely considered to outweigh a straggly plot; the
Athenaeum, for example, enthused about its 'vividness and force', and
the *Manchester Guardian* deemed it 'the best Jewish novel ever
written'. Zangwill himself claimed that his aim was 'less to tell a story
than to paint a community', and the novel gave him an opportunity to
reflect at length on the bonds that knit individuals into collectives, a
question that was to preoccupy him for many years to come.

When *Children of the Ghetto* was published, Zangwill was at the
beginning of a literary and activist career that was later to flourish
around women's suffrage, pacifism and territorialism (the movement
seeking an autonomous Jewish homeland anywhere in the world).
Born in Spitalfields in 1864 to immigrant parents, he spent most of his
childhood in the East End, attending and later teaching at the Jews'
Free School there. He went on to graduate from the University of
London and began work editing and writing humour and social criticism for a range of satirical publications in London. His journalism on

the changing character of Anglo-Jewish religious life led to a commission from the Jewish Publication Society of America, which hoped to foster a Jewish version of *Robert Elsmere* (1888), Mrs Humphry Ward's bestselling novel of Christian doubt and redemption. These themes are indeed pursued in the second part of Zangwill's book, 'Grandchildren of the Ghetto', which stages possible futures for Judaism — orthodox, rational and universalistic — through the divergent destinies of a group of young Jewish intellectuals. In the first part, 'Children of the Ghetto', however, Zangwill produced something more unexpected: a series of overlapping vignettes that created a detailed panorama of the Jewish East End, shifting seamlessly between moments of comedy, pathos, cruelty and idealism.

The elements of realism he deployed made the novel often uncompromising, with Yiddish vocabulary and arcane religious debates woven into the fabric of the text so that as a reader you always feel as if you are eavesdropping on a subculture you'll never quite fully comprehend (a glossary was added for the third edition). Taking the everyday dramas of immigrant life as his subject — the conflicts generated by poverty, aspiration, the impact of modernity, the influence of Victorian values — Zangwill depicted a community riven with deep divisions, caught at a moment of critical generational change.

Children of the Ghetto was published at the end of a century that was transformative for Anglo-Jewry both demographically and politically. Expelled from England in 1290, Jews had been officially readmitted in 1656 and remained a tiny religious minority. By the mid-nineteenth century the Jewish population was slowly growing: from 27,000 in 1828 to 40,000 in 1860, but it did not exceed 0.2 per cent of the population. Apart from a small, more assimilated number of wealthy Sephardi (Iberian and eastern Mediterranean) Jews, they were mostly Ashkenazi immigrants from Holland, the German states and Poland and made their living as street traders and itinerant peddlers. In the course of the nineteenth century, Jews became economically mobile; by the 1870s the majority were bourgeois and there was also a high-profile elite whose wealth derived from financial activities, and a small professional middle-class.

However the character of Anglo-Jewry was dramatically altered by immigration from Russia and Poland in the second half of the century, accelerating between 1881 and 1914. Between 120,000 and 150,000 East European Jews settled permanently in the United Kingdom, expanding the Jewish population to 300,000. Escaping religious persecution and chronic economic hardship, these new immigrants were poor, often religious-minded, and some were politically radical — socialists, anarchists and Zionists. Their presence was most concentrated in the East End of

London, where low-wage employment was readily available (though highly insecure) in small garment, shoe or furniture workshops and where an earlier generation of Jews had established synagogues close to the City. In *Children of the Ghetto*, Zangwill faithfully documents the idiosyncratic immigrant subculture that was developing in Whitechapel, with rivalrous institutions: synagogues, religious schools and a secular cultural life centred around Yiddish-language newspapers, political organising and social clubs.

The stark economic, cultural and religious differences between immigrant and native Jews by the end of the century provided Zangwill with a rich source for satire in the mode of Charles Dickens. Highly conscious of their public image, middle-class Victorian Anglo-Jews were uncomfortable with the visibility of large numbers of poor foreign Jews in London. By the time Zangwill was writing, moreover, an initial wave of public sympathy towards Jews suffering persecution had begun to ebb and the area's social and economic problems were being ascribed, both in Parliament and on the street, to the immigrant influx. In this context, the Jewish upper classes redoubled their efforts at anglicizing the poor through welfare schemes, schools and youth clubs — efforts regarded with a healthy disrespect by their clients, as Zangwill makes clear. One reason for the broad general appeal of *Children of the Ghetto* for its original readers is the way that Anglo-Jewish London could be seen as a microcosm of the *fin-de-siècle* city. For Victorians, the East End lay across a gulf that was symbolic as much as it was geographic — dividing respectability and poverty, order and unruliness, progress and stasis. And yet Zangwill offered readers a literary East End quite different from that of his contemporaries Arthur Morrison and George Gissing — a place not of degenerate brutality but social warmth and political and religious faith.

Jewish Whitechapel was not, as Zangwill notes in his first paragraph, literally a ghetto. That term referred to the walled enclave into which Jews were forcibly confined in European cities centuries earlier. But the neighbourhood was frequently referred to as a ghetto or a Jewish colony by contemporary observers, who were astonished at how it barely felt like London at all. 'My first impression on going among them,' remarked the journalist Mrs Brewer in the *Sunday Magazine* in 1892, 'was that I must be in some far-off country whose people and language I knew not. The names over the shops were foreign, the wares were advertised in an unknown tongue, of which I did not even know the letters, the people in the streets were not of our type, and when I addressed them in English the majority of them shook their heads'. When Zangwill uses the term 'ghetto', however, it's a metaphor, indicating not a physical place but a mentality — a worldview shaped by inherited memory. As he writes in the novel's prologue:

> The folk who compose our pictures are children of the Ghetto; their faults are bred of its hovering miasma of persecution, their virtues straitened and intensified by the narrowness of its horizon...
>
> The particular Ghetto that is the dark background upon which our pictures will be cast, is of voluntary formation.
>
> People who have been living in a Ghetto for a couple of centuries, are not able to step outside merely because the gates are thrown down, nor to efface the brands on their souls by putting off the yellow badges. The isolation imposed from without will have come to seem the law of their being.

Underpinning Zangwill's stories of the Whitechapel immigrants and their children, then, is a consideration of the existential impact of a heritage of isolation. But although Zangwill wants the reader to grasp this history, he is also critical of its power to determine modern lives. For Reb Shemuel, the rabbi who rarely ventures beyond the Ghetto boundaries, for example, 'the radius of his life was proportionately narrow' and 'the restless life of the great twinkling streets was almost a novelty'. Reb Shemuel cannot comprehend his children's instinctive desire to participate in the wider city's 'restless life'. And his daughter Hannah, who contemplates flight with an enterprising lover, ultimately finds it impossible to abandon the Ghetto. While part of Zangwill's purpose is to explain the fearful insularity he observes in Jewish Whitechapel, his tales of broken or unhappy families indicate a deep frustration with the immigrant community's resistance to modernity.

Yet it is not only this more abstract question of modern Jewish identity that interests Zangwill. In *Children of the Ghetto* more than any of his other fiction on Anglo-Jewry, he roots the immigrant experience in the environment of the East End itself. The novel's story is told as much through its locations as its plots — the East End settings of buildings and streets where the particularities of immigrant collective life come into especially sharp focus.

First of all, there are domestic spaces. In the opening chapter of *Children of the Ghetto* Esther Ansell, the novel's child protagonist, climbs the 'dark flight of stairs to the attic in Royal Street' where her grandmother and younger siblings wait in the cold and gloom for her to return from the charity soup kitchen in a nearby street. One of the formerly grand mansions of Spitalfields, passing in the early nineteenth century to wealthy City Jews, the house where Esther lives is now close by 'some of the vilest quarters and filthiest rookeries in the capital of the civilized world' and occupied by several immigrant working-class families as well as a synagogue on the ground floor. The building shows signs of long-term physical neglect: 'It was stoutly built and its balusters were of carved oak. But now the threshold of the great street door, which was never closed, was encrusted with black mud, and a musty odour permanently clung to the wide staircase'.

Zangwill was not the only Anglo-Jewish writer to find a meaningful irony in the dilapidated Huguenot houses of Spitalfields now inhabited by another generation of immigrants. A few years earlier, Emily Marion Harris had opened her novel *Benedictus* (1887) in the very same location, a garret in 'a street which was, years ago, fashionable enough... but time has changed all that, and altered the destiny of the roomy houses... And time and progress have turned the lofty chambers to separate tenements, transformed some to workrooms, others to manufactories, institutions, shabby lodgings'. Harris's elegiac description does more than create a material setting for her novel however; it is also used symbolically to suggest that a similarly tragic fate has befallen the Jews who now live and work there. 'Behind narrow counters, or bending above heavy garments,' she writes, 'are assembled many a specimen of a kingdom whose descendants bear the trace of its royalty, and greatness yet, in the flash of the dark eye, in the gestures of the grand figure, strikingly apparent at times'. These highly romanticized images of East End immigrants, whose 'height and bearing are of a kind familiar in scriptural illustrations' were designed to counter more prevalent contemporary representations of Jews as uncivilised and culturally alien. For Emily Harris, the ruined chambers provide a picturesque backdrop for viewing both the residents and the neighbourhood itself as innocent, noble and enduring victims of historical change.

Children of the Ghetto, by contrast, is much less concerned to persuade readers that Jews are quiet, respectable citizens (or tragic victims). Despite its dirt and decay, the house in Royal Street is 'close packed with the stuff of human life' and for Zangwill it is precisely the vitality and vulgarity of the Whitechapel Jews, rather than their refinement or pathos, that should be celebrated. Nowhere is this clearer than in the novel's exuberant descriptions of the commercial and social hub of the Jewish East End, Petticoat Lane market. In the late nineteenth century the market was in its heyday, with over a thousand stalls selling groceries, household goods, second-hand clothes and above all food. Zangwill remembers it as a place of uninhibited excess, its narrow streets teeming with crowds, smells and noise:

The Lane was always the great market-place, and every insalubrious street and alley abutting on it was covered with the overflowings of its commerce and its mud. Wentworth Street and Goulston Street were the chief branches, and in festival times the latter was a pandemonium of caged poultry, clucking and quacking and cackling and screaming... The confectioners' shops, crammed with 'stuffed monkeys' and 'bolas,' [sweet pastries] were besieged by hilarious crowds of handsome girls and their young men, fat women and their children, all washing down the luscious spicy compounds with cups of chocolate...The famous Sunday Fair was an event of metropolitan importance, and thither came buyers of every sect... A babel of sound, audible for several streets around, denoted Market Day in Petticoat Lane, and the pavements were blocked by serried crowds going both ways at once.

As the century wore on, Zangwill laments, 'the community was Anglicized... respectability crept on to freeze the blood of the Orient with its frigid finger, and to blur the vivid tints of the East into the uniform grey of English middle-class life'. But even in the late nineteenth century, when *Children of the Ghetto* is set, Petticoat Lane retains something of its unruly foreignness. It is the one place where Jews of all classes come together: where social distinctions that are otherwise so carefully policed collapse with joyous abandon. On the eve of the festival of Passover, Zangwill writes,

> great ladies of the West... came down again to the beloved Lane to throw off the veneer of refinement, and plunge gloveless hands in barrels where pickled cucumbers weltered in their own 'russell' [brine], and to pick fat juicy olives from the rich-heaped tubs

In the crowded market, wealthy, assimilated Jewish women revel in the coarse sensualities of Whitechapel, embracing the Eastern European origins they share with the new immigrants. Equally, as other writers of the time noted, the Sunday market brought Jewish and gentile traders together, breaking down the Ghetto's isolation. *Living London* (1902–03), a series of essays edited by the journalist G.R. Sims, characterises Petticoat Lane as 'a howling pandemonium of cosmopolitan costerism, a curious tangle of humanity'. Descriptions like this show that alongside sustained attempts to foment anti-alien hostility in the East End at the turn of the century, there was also considerable public fascination with this early example of a shared, multiethnic London space, the meeting place for jellied eels and bagels, Cockney stalwarts and recent arrivals.

But for Zangwill the streets are not just a colourful spectacle; they are a place of cruelty too, where the poor compete for survival at the inevitable expense of those who are weaker. Here, Esther Ansell is pickpocketed of the meagre shilling she has brought to buy fish for the festival. For Esther, the chaos of the market has a harsher aspect; it gives her 'a sense of the hollowness and uncertainty of existence'. This apprehension of the powerlessness of an East End child to shape her own destiny and of the miserable 'martyrdom of her race' to poverty and piety will lead to Esther's bitter rejection of the Ghetto and her longing to escape.

Esther's story is picked up again in the second part of the novel, 'Grandchildren of the Ghetto', which switches style from the episodic series of portraits to a more sustained narrative focus. In the meanwhile, Esther, a promising school pupil, has been plucked from obscurity and adopted by a wealthy Kensington Jewish family. She has abandoned her religious beliefs, put the Ghetto behind her, graduated from London University and is about to launch her career as a writer when she experiences a crisis of faith in the world of her anglicised patrons. Disillusioned by their social ambition, hypocrisy and fear of gentile disapproval, she feels a longing to go 'back to her true home... where hearts were open and life was simple... back to her father's primitive faith like a tired lost child that spies its home at last'. The final chapters of the novel thus return with Esther to Whitechapel, where she struggles to make sense of the formative environment of her childhood.

But the East End is not as she remembers it. Geographical and social distance from Royal Street has filled Esther with yearning, but once she finds herself there again her sentimental feelings dissipate. The appearance of the locale has radically altered. The slum clearances of the late nineteenth century have begun to reshape the urban landscape: 'Instead of the dirty picturesque houses rose an appalling series of artisans' dwellings, monotonous brick barracks, whose dead, dull prose weighed upon the spirits'. Here, Zangwill borrows from George Gissing, who in *The Nether World* (1889) famously described Clerkenwell's new model dwellings as 'terrible barracks... for the army of industrialism'. Similarly, Zangwill is dismayed by the crushing uniformity imposed by the architecture of social reform on the inhabitants of the East End. Regeneration, he suggests, is yet another way to 'freeze the blood of the Orient'.

There is also a more unsettling disjunction between the East End of Esther's memory and that of her present experience. The streets appear 'so unspeakably sordid and squalid. Could she ever really have walked them with light heart, unconscious of the ugliness?' Other roadways, she observes, 'seemed incredibly narrow. Was it possible it could have taken even her childish feet six strides to cross them, as she plainly remembered?' Of course, it is hardly surprising that the adult Esther — older, taller, more accustomed to comfort but also wearier of life — finds the physical encounter with the streets utterly different. Nonetheless, her disappointment at failing to find a ready connection — her lonely alienation from the landscape of her memory — is one of the novel's most despondent moments; it is also what prevents *Children of the Ghetto* from becoming a work of easy nostalgia. As the scholar of Zangwill's life and writing Meri-Jane Rochelson puts it, the novel 'is meant to eulogize a culture perceived both as the source of Jewish spiritual identity and as dying'.

Only in the final chapter is there some resolution of Esther's ambivalence. This scene is staged in another of the East End's distinctive spaces — a small synagogue [*chevrah*], often located within a residential building, which on this occasion, the Day of Atonement, is especially crowded with worshippers. Ostensibly, the cramped space of the *chevrah* epitomises the religious and intellectual confinement that Esther has emphatically rejected. Yet in a sudden moment of identification with the congregation united in prayer, she feels her horizons expand:

> She was overwhelmed by the thought of its sons in every corner of the earth proclaiming to the sombre twilight sky the belief for which its generations had lived and died — the Jews of Russia sobbing it forth in their pale of enclosure, the Jews of Morocco in their *mellah*, and of South Africa in their tents by the diamond mines; the Jews of the New World in great free cities, in Canadian backwoods, in South American savannahs; the Australian Jews on the sheep-farms and the gold-fields and in the mushroom cities.

The novel ends by drawing the reader's attention to another aspect of Whitechapel life that Zangwill regards as remarkable, mysterious and moving. For the Jews at prayer in the *chevrah*, the East End is a place of diaspora consciousness. Their synagogue may be small and inward-looking but in the religious imagination of its congregants it is a space that figuratively stretches across the globe.

In many ways, then, Zangwill's Whitechapel is far from parochial. The commercial, culinary and affective life of its residents connects them to a host of other places and people: countries of birth, wealthier co-religionists in the West End, gentile neighbours, Jews overseas. But the novel itself is also less insular than its first few chapters may suggest. Although set within the boundaries of the Ghetto and densely packed with the minutiae of immigrant politics and family feuds, its central narrative, focussed on the struggles of a young female writer, has a wider contemporary resonance. The literary ambition and vacillating confidence of Zangwill's heroine closely resemble the protagonists of many New Woman novels of the 1890s, written as professional opportunities, economic independence and mobility in the city began to open up for women for the first time. Esther Ansell inhabits the same London that we see in Ella Hepworth Dixon's *Story of a Modern Woman* (1894), for example, where the protagonist Mary Erle, like Esther, researches in the British Museum, traverses the city by foot or omnibus, and experiences the metropolis as a place full of new possibilities and uncertainties. The dilemmas of Anglo-Jewry, seen in this context, are part of the wider current of social and political upheaval sweeping London in the late nineteenth century.

As a novel that captured the fine detail of East End Jewish life at the same time as pointing to the more universal questions with which contemporary Jews were grappling, *Children of the Ghetto* hit a winning combination. By 1900, the book had been reprinted eight times and successfully produced as a stage drama; Zangwill had become a celebrity — the press's favourite commentator on matters concerning Anglo-Jewry. The Jewish East End, too, was a subject of enduring public interest throughout the 1890s, as the novel joined a cacophony of competing voices — journalists, social scientists, political activists — seeking to interpret the phenomenon of the Ghetto. And although the Aliens Act of 1905 — the first legislation restricting immigration for nearly a century — was to put an end to much of this discussion, Zangwill's novel, especially its evocation of '[s]uch a jolly, rampant, screaming, fighting, maddening, jostling, polyglot, quarrelling, laughing broth of a Vanity Fair', continued to shape the memory of the Jewish East End for decades to come.

References and Further Reading

Israel Zangwill, *The King of Schnorrers: Grotesques and Fantasies*, 1894

Israel Zangwill, *They That Walk in Darkness: Ghetto Tragedies*, 1899

Israel Zangwill, *Ghetto Comedies*, 1907

Eitan Bar-Yosef and Nadia Valman, eds, *'The Jew' in Late-Victorian and Edwardian Culture: Between the East End and East Africa*, Palgrave, 2009

Eugene C Black, *The Social Politics of Anglo-Jewry, 1880–1920*, Basil Blackwell, 1988

David Englander, (ed.), *A Documentary History of Jewish Immigrants in Britain, 1840–1920*, Leicester University Press, 1994

David Feldman, *Englishmen and Jews: Social Relations and Political Culture 1840–1914*, Yale University Press, 1994

William Fishman, *East End 1888*, Duckworth, 1988

David Glover, *Literature, Immigration and Diaspora in Fin-de-siècle England: A Cultural History of the 1905 Aliens Act*, Cambridge University Press, 2012

Meri-Jane Rochelson, *A Jew in the Public Arena: The Career of Israel*

Zangwill, Wayne State University Press, 2008

Jerry White, *Rothschild Buildings: Life in an East End Tenement Building*, new edition, Pimlico, 2003

Zangwill's Whitechapel Today

Jewish life in the East End of London flourished between the late nineteenth century and the Second World War, declining rapidly in the following decades as assimilation and upward social mobility increased. After decades of indifference, it is only recently that the built environment of immigrant life has come to be regarded as 'heritage' by Anglo-Jewry. It has, meanwhile, played a significant role in the redevelopment of Spitalfields since the 1980s as a richly historic site of immigrant settlement. For this reason, fragments of the Jewish East End as semi-fictionalised in *Children of the Ghetto* remain with us today.

Spitalfields' more austere Victorian remnants, like the artisans' dwellings that appal Esther in the novel (known locally as the Rothschild Buildings and located in Flower and Dean Street) have disappeared. Those with more aesthetic appeal, notably the ornate Soup Kitchen for the Jewish Poor in Brune Street (formerly Butler Street) have been given a new lease of life. The Kitchen, one among several in the East End, was opened in 1854 and moved to its present location in 1902. In his opening chapter, Zangwill uses the setting of the soup kitchen to underline the indignities endured by the East End poor. Just over a hundred years later, transformed into a set of desirable private residences, the building embodies the dramatic gentrification of the area that makes its nineteenth-century past ever more difficult to imagine.

A similar story might be told of the dilapidated rooms where Esther's family live in 'Royal Street', a thinly disguised Princes Street (now Princelet Street), just off Brick Lane. The elegant Georgian terraces in this and the surrounding streets have housed three centuries of immigrants to Spitalfields, from their original inhabitants, Huguenot Protestants, to East European Jews in Zangwill's day, to Bangladeshi Muslims in more recent decades. Although the buildings, like the neighbourhood, had fallen on hard times when Zangwill set his novel there, and continued in their run-down state throughout the twentieth century, they are now fully restored to their original grandeur. One Princelet Street house still awaiting renovation is number 19, where a tiny synagogue, originally built over the back garden in 1870, is one of the few remaining traces of the scores of *chevrot* that constituted the vibrant religious life of the Jewish East End at the turn of the twentieth century.

Perhaps the strongest continuity of all with Zangwill's East End is Petticoat Lane market — which remains defiantly ungentrified and unpicturesque. The market is still held in Middlesex Street, Goulston Street and

Wentworth Street, still sells cheap clothing and is particularly crowded on Sunday mornings, with a faint echo of the banter and swagger Zangwill records in his novel. Jews continued to trade here for decades after their communities had decamped to the suburbs: Petticoat Lane was the place where, contrary to Zangwill's fears, the Jewish presence in the East End lingered longest.

Nadia Valman

Henry W. Nevinson
Neighbours of Ours (1895)

ANGELA V. JOHN

In the mid-1880s a well-educated, middle-class couple and their baby daughter moved into six rooms at 252 Brunswick Buildings East in Goulston Street, Whitechapel. Today this is London Metropolitan University territory, close to the City and the modern chic of Spitalfields. Then it was a slum area. But these rooms (two self-contained workmen's flats) had views of the sunset behind St. Paul's and rent was fifteen shillings and sixpence a week. It was an improvement on their Bloomsbury digs and an invigorating experience.

These 'slummers' were Henry Nevinson (1856–1941) and his wife Margaret Wynne Nevinson. Their decision to live 'among bugs, fleas, old clothes, slippery cods' heads and other garbage' was inspired by high-minded thoughts. In Henry Nevinson's case socialism and social reform were paramount. An Oxford graduate, he was, for a time, an early member of the Social Democratic Federation. For Margaret Nevinson, the daughter of a clergyman, the Christian creed was her prime inspiration. Both were attracted by the new experiment in university settlement developed by the Rev. Samuel Barnett round the corner from them in Toynbee Hall and participated in its work.

A decade later Henry Nevinson's collection of what he called 'Thames Stories' was published. Entitled *Neighbours of Ours*, it appeared in Arrowsmith's 3/6d series. This had already produced such classics as *Three Men in a Boat, The Diary of a Nobody* and *The Prisoner of Zenda*. The timing was not perfect: Arthur Morrison's *Tales of Mean Streets* had appeared a few weeks earlier and stole the limelight. A disappointed Nevinson noted that 'mine was praised, and his was bought'. He believed that the 'gleams of brightness' in his book made it more readable than Morrison's but that *Tales of Mean Streets* appealed to people because it 'flatters the bourgeois idea of the working man'.

Nevinson's reviewers were impressed. C.F.G. Masterman called it 'the best volume of tales which ever took as their theatre of action the desolate and fascinating region of the "East End"' and attributed the book's realism to the author's close proximity to his subjects. And although it passed into obscurity in later years, more recently it has attracted attention from literary critics and historians. Peter Keating (who included two of Nevinson's tales in his selection of working-class stories of the 1890s) dubbed him 'the first distinctive writer of the Cockney School'. Assessing nineteenth-century British short stories Wendell V. Harris calls the collection 'a treasure' and Nevinson 'a master of storytelling'. Its delights 'deserve to be much more widely known'.

So what does *Neighbours* offer? At the *fin-de-siècle* the short story was very much in vogue as was writing about London's East End. But stories about London's poor often favoured the sensational and extreme. Writers tended to depict figures prone to violence or totally bowed down by their circumstances. They were vehicles for their creators' moral indignation or revolutionary message. In Nevinson's fiction, however, character matters more than class. Individuality is emphasised as is an acute sense of place. His protagonists don't think of themselves as failures or types to be labelled and analysed by others and are neither caricatures nor reduced to statistics. Rather than being objects of social pity here are folk in a distinct geographical and social community yet their lives reveal subtle gradations and shifting fortunes. In his diary Nevinson had written: 'The people were almost as distinct and individual as in a village'. He did not minimise the harshness of the environment but neither did he elide it with its inhabitants.

There are ten stories linked by a narrator and some characters crop up in several stories. We learn quite a bit about those who live in the remarkably modern sounding 'Millennium Buildin's', which Nevinson locates in Shadwell close to the docks. And the useful device of having the one narrator throughout not only unifies but also guides 'Dear Reader'. Jacko Britton — the working man's John Bull — takes us around his community, encouraging us to observe and share experiences and witticisms with him.

There is plenty of native wit here. For a start there are the nicknames, suggestive of Dickensian richness and wonderfully tongue in cheek. Take Tom Brier: 'we used to call 'im Victoria Park, or just Parky for short, cos 'e was real fond of the country'. Or ragged old Groun'sel who sold bird-food: "E seemed to be never comin' from nowhere, nor yet goin' nowhere else'. Then there is Ned Phillips the Cadet, known as Tentpole.

The collection of stories is shaped by the East End calendar of events, starting with the all-important summer hop-picking and proceeding through Christmas and Easter to August Bank Holiday. As Gill Davies has noted, the stories 'recognise and celebrate popular culture, many years before this became an acceptable view of working-class life'. Both the first and last tales take the Londoners out into the countryside. In the first we see them "oppin" in Kent. Nevinson experienced this, travelling with them on their annual excursion to Marden. The final tale moves from Aldgate to Aldershot and a form of camping that was rather more familiar to him as he regularly took his cadets to military camp.

The tales are all relayed in dialect. Demotic language in fiction often can be off-putting and patronising. But even though it may help to account for the book not selling as well as Nevinson had hoped, the pervasive humour helps to leaven the effects of using dialect. And he was well aware of his credentials as a first hand observer resident in the area as opposed to someone making a rapid foray into the district.

In an unpublished prose account entitled 'Suburbanism and the Poor' Nevinson poured his scorn on do-gooders who uttered platitudes about the problems of poverty but remained secure in their suburban lives. Somewhat smugly he ridiculed those who found the poor 'so interesting', discussed beautiful schemes for the regeneration of mankind and babbled about 'green tea and Schopenhauer' and 'the poetry of the East End'. When he found a young man trying to 'improve' down and outs in an LCC doss house in Silvertown by playing Beethoven and Chopin, he responded angrily: 'If I had been one I should have gone out & spewed at such treatment'.

Nevertheless Nevinson was well-aware of his own ambivalent position and by the time he visited the doss house (1893) he and Margaret had decamped to leafy Hampstead where their son (the future artist C.R.W. Nevinson) had been born. Hampstead was too full of the intelligentsia to qualify for the suburban spirit Nevinson so despised but it was still a world away from the environs of Petticoat Lane. Yet the Nevinsons had spent two years living in the East End rather than making quick forays and they both continued to do work there.

Most importantly, what redeems *Neighbours* is the fact that, despite the seductive literary device of the narrator drawing us in, we are reminded that we are ultimately observers who might evince sympathy but cannot fully empathise. Here was the real 'Abyss'. Nevinson did not underestimate the gulf. He wrote in his diary, 'We can hardly understand the outlook of most of these people, simply dependent for the day's food on the day's work and never knowing whether they may get it'.

Yet at the same time he was better qualified than most of his contemporaries to convey the timbre of this world, albeit refracted through the lens of an Oxford-educated solicitor's son from Leicester. 'Mrs Simon's Baby', a story in which women, the home and neighbourhood networks are paramount may be Nevinson's version of George Eliot's *Silas Marner* but Ellen Ross has noticed that it chimes with a story revealed in Charles Booth's investigation of *Life and Labour of the People of London*. Margaret Nevinson was a rent-collector for a number of years and there is some evidence that her experience informed *Neighbours of Ours* (my emphasis) despite the couple's increasing estrangement. Beatrice Potter (later Webb) was a manager at Katherine Buildings, one of the model blocks of artisans' dwellings where Margaret worked. In 1893 Henry Nevinson also visited Katherine Buildings, collecting stories as well as rent. He still taught classes at Toynbee Hall, sat on the committee of the Whittington Boys' Club and helped to research the building trades for the Industry Series that comprised part of Charles Booth's massive investigation of life and labour in the capital.

Fortunately Henry Nevinson's notes from June 1893 have survived and reinforce the veracity of the pictures he paints. These notes supply names, locations and descriptions of the interiors of homes. For example, the Bates family, a large young family with a grandfather live in one filthy room in Hayden Square in the Minories. It is much decorated with pictures including a portrait of a great-grandfather that had once cost five pounds. In his second story 'An Aristocrat of Labour' we are told how Spotter's father had paid 'a sportin' kind o' sum', all of 'five poun'' for the family portrait. It hung in a big frame 'with flourishes' on the wall in his tiny room — a reg'lar one-and-sixer, and dear at a shillin'' — and was its only item except for a bed and a box. In another story we hear about a man called Zulu because he was so dirty. Nevinson's notes mention a toddler from a filthy Poplar home known as Zulu to the street.

The notes also describe an 'English common-looking woman with three nigger children'. Her husband was a sailor 'long away'. Nevinson asks whether she was 'justified in having a white one before he came back'. Perhaps the most unusual of the *Neighbours* stories is 'Sissero's Return' about an inter-racial romance between Ginger (defined yet not judged by colour) and her black sailor husband Sissero. The explicit and crude language of neighbours who do not know how to deal with one of their own choosing such a husband, along with the story's sexual frankness, make this story remarkable for its time.

The community can only see Sissero as 'Other': 'the thing we've got to deal with is a nigger, and 'e being black makes a difference'. Sissero goes on a voyage — neighbours can cope with him at a distance but when he does not return Ginger is impoverished and sleeps with a moneylender to pay her rent. Sissero eventually returns having missed his ship and worked on a rice plantation in China where he lived with a local woman. In contrast Ginger's infidelity has been prompted solely by financial desperation for her children. But her neighbours choose not to divulge her secret.

The story does reinforce a number of predictable stereotypes. There is the sexual prowess of Sissero the strong stoker and he is always laughing. The Jewish rent-collector is the 'baddie'. But Nevinson is nevertheless making a bold statement. Just a few years later he experienced at first-hand the second Anglo-Boer War (he was in Ladysmith throughout its famous siege). Unlike most of his contemporaries his fiction encompasses indigenous black Africans. One African short story called 'The Relief of Eden' exposes and mocks the ignorance of British colonials who brag of racial superiority.

These earlier London stories reveal a writer unafraid of tackling issues of racism. London had an estimated twenty thousand Indian and African sailors at the turn of the century but most appear not to have stayed and little is known about those who did. Nevinson's writings help to shed light on this elusive and neglected section of society.

Another story in *Neighbours* is remarkable. Peter Keating has described 'The St. George of Rochester' as 'unlike any working-class story that had been written previously'. This is a cross-class romance with a difference. Nevinson recognised the centrality of the River Thames to any understanding of the society he was writing about. He used to enjoy sailing on a barge that left Wapping Old Stairs bound for Rochester. Like his contemporary Joseph Conrad he used north-west Kent as the setting for a river story and also deployed the device of the framed narrative. In Nevinson's story within a story the former captain regales his listeners with memories of his time on a barge and his romance with a lady. A very tender tale is told by the proud winner of the Doggett Badge (the annual sculling race from London Bridge to Chelsea for Freemen of the Watermen and Lightermen's company. This was known as Doggett's Coat and Badge Race after its founder, the eighteenth-century theatre manager and comedian Thomas Doggett). Later Nevinson wondered whether he had been the first to give 'the touch of romance to those beautiful red-sailed barges'.

In 1893 Nevinson had talked to lightermen and noted their excitement about the Doggett's Coat and Badge race. He also learned about their conditions of work. One young apprentice who worked on a

47

lighter told him that he was often out day and night for half a week. He earned about two shillings daily when in work but he and his father found that demand for their labour was irregular and his mother never knew when they would be home.

Few were as well qualified as Nevinson to write about the last two tales in *Neighbours* with their accounts of cadets. For over a decade he commanded a working-class cadet corps, the first of its kind in London. St. George's in the East Company used the quadrangle of Toynbee Hall before moving to Shadwell Basin. It became part of The Queen's Royal West Surrey Regiment with headquarters in Southwark. Nevinson's diaries for the early 1890s are peppered with frequent references to drill in Shadwell, beside the Basin where ships could be seen entering London Dock. Here was one of London's poorest and most overcrowded districts. Nevinson sought, through his Cadet Company, to help what he called 'the enfeebled and undersized youth'. The site of their Drill Hall was later converted into a public garden and playground as a memorial to Edward VII.

As a cadet officer Nevinson had the freedom (as he admitted in his autobiography) to 'visit the fellows in their homes without patronage or pretence at doing them good, but merely in the course of Army Regulations'. Such latitude and familiarity also supplied and authenticated the material that formed the basis of his *Slum Stories of London* (the title of the American edition of *Neighbours*).

When Nevinson wrote these stories he was in his late thirties. He had already published studies of Herder and Schiller and he followed *Neighbours* with *In the Valley of Tophet: Scenes of Black Country Life* in 1896. But although selling more copies than its predecessor, these stories lacked the spirit of *Neighbours*. For *Tophet* was based on just a cursory glimpse of the Black Country. It was not until the following year that Nevinson seems to have found what he had long been restlessly seeking. In the spring of 1897 he was engaged to report for the *Daily Chronicle* on a conflict — that soon escalated into a short-lived war — between Greece and Turkey. A classical scholar who revered anything Greek and was desperate to court adventure, he now embarked on an extremely successful career as a war correspondent. For decades he traversed the world. He continued to write books, producing more than thirty single-authored volumes as well as numerous chapters and many hundreds of newspaper articles.

Yet there remains something irrepressible about Henry Nevinson's fond tales of life in London's East End. They are of immense value to both the social historian and literary critic. And they have a wider appeal too. Nevinson was a keen observer of people and places who knew how to tell spirited, witty stories that show us how Londoners have coped with and triumphed over everyday life.

References and Further Reading

The Henry W. Nevinson diaries are at the Bodleian Library, Oxford University and his 1893 Notes are in Nevinson Manuscript V1 at Shrewsbury School Archives.

H.W. Nevinson, *Neighbours of Ours*, 1895

H.W. Nevinson, *In the Valley of Tophet: Scenes of Black Country Life*, 1896

H.W. Nevinson, *Changes and Chances*, 1923

Arthur Morrison, *Tales of Mean Streets*, 1894

Gill Davies, 'Foreign Bodies: images of the London working-class at the end of the 19th century', *Literature and History*, Spring 1988

Wendell V. Harris, *British Short Fiction in the Nineteenth Century*, Wayne State University Press, 1979

Angela V. John, *War, Journalism and the Shaping of the Twentieth Century: the Life and Times of Henry W. Nevinson*, I.B. Tauris, 2006

P.J. Keating (ed.), *Working-Class Stories of the 1890s*, Routledge & Kegan Paul, 1971

Seth Koven, *Slumming: Sexual and Social Politics in Victorian London*, Princeton University Press, 2004

Ellen Ross, 'Women's Neighbourhood Sharing in London before World War One', *History Workshop Journal*, Spring 1983

Tracking Nevinson's Neighbours

Goulston Street, Nevinson's home for two years in the 1880s, is in that inter-mediate zone where the City edges into the East End. It's in the shadow of 'the Gherkin', but has the look and feel of Whitechapel. There's still a street market — part of Petticoat Lane — but it's fairly tawdry, as is much of the architecture, old and new. Brunswick Buildings, newly built when the Nevinsons moved in, was demolished in the 1970s. Two mansion blocks from about that time remain. There's little else from that period. At the southern end of the street, at the junction with Whitechapel High Street, an East End institution remains (though not from Nevinson's era) — Tubby Isaacs' seafood stall, now standing opposite a halal fast food outlet. Goulston Street had a tangential part in the 1888 Jack the Ripper murders and resulting conspiracies — though by then the Nevinsons had moved on to Hampstead.

From Brunswick Buildings, Toynbee Hall would have been no more than two minutes walk — along Wentworth Street and across Commercial Street.

It's still there and thriving, a centre of community activity, support, self-help and education. It was founded in 1884 by Nevinson's friend, Samuel Barnett — mentioned in passing in *Neighbours of Ours* — who is remembered in Barnett House, an unremarkable block of flats nearby.

Many of the stories in *Neighbours of Ours* are set in Shadwell, a district which Nevinson knew well. His cadets both drilled in and were in part recruited from this area. Shadwell is not more than twenty minutes walk from Goulston Street, but it has a very different ambience. The City seems distant, while the Thames is close at hand. Little of the Shadwell that Nevinson would have known survives. The Hawksmoor-designed tower of St. George-in-the-East is the main landmark. The church's interior was bombed out during the Second World War, along with so much else of the neighbourhood.

There are tiny enclaves of terraced houses on and around Cable Street, and the occasional older block of flats. Most of the area, however, is given over to soulless mansion blocks. In Nevinson's era, the Jewish East End didn't extend as far as Shadwell. The incidental Jewish characters in *Neighbours of Ours* are outsiders to the community. The presence of the docks, though, meant that black and Indian seafarers would not have been an unusual sight.

At first glance, Shadwell seems old East End. There's a pie and mash shop and a boxing gym within a minute's walk of the station. A more leisurely look reveals how much has changed. Most shops and businesses are now Bangladeshi run. The Britannia pub is a halal chicken joint. On the north side of the railway line, the arches are given over to a range of Bengali stores and supermarkets.

Although Nevinson never precisely located 'Millennium Buildin's', many of the streets he mentioned can still be found: Pennington Street in Wapping, Dora Street in Limehouse, Johnson Street in Shadwell (with the railway arches by which a character in his tales is found dead). There was, and is, a Shadwell Basin and a Pier Head, just as Nevinson related — though with the docks long gone, both seem becalmed backwaters, in sharp contrast to the buzz of activity evident in Nevinson's era.

Andrew Whitehead

Arthur Morrison
A Child of the Jago (1896)

SARAH WISE

'The original of the Jago has, it is admitted, ceased to exist. But I will make bold to say that as described by Mr Morrison, it never did exist.' So wrote critic Henry Duff Traill in his review of Arthur Morrison's novel, *A Child of the Jago*, in the January 1897 edition of the *Fortnightly Review*.

'The Jago' of Morrison's title was the scarcely disguised 'Old Nichol' slum, which stood, until the mid-1890s, just behind Shoreditch High Street, on its eastern side. Published in November 1896, *A Child of the Jago* caused an instant furore. Few reviewers of the novel had failed to be impressed by the power of Morrison's fiction — the savagery of the depiction of street violence, the pathos of neglected, diseased infants, the scathing attack on high-minded philanthropic interventions; what many refused to accept, though, was Morrison's insistence that his book had been based entirely on fact.

Traill had continued his assault upon Morrison's claims to reportage with the words: 'He invites the world to inspect [the Jago] as a sort of essence or extract of metropolitan degradation... It is the idealising method, and its result is as essentially ideal as the Venus of Milo... the total effect of the story is unreal and phantasmagoric.' But over the past 100 years, it is Morrison's vision of that square quarter-mile of east London that has prevailed: his mythic location ('a fairyland of horror', in Traill's view) has usurped the historical fact of the Nichol, which was entirely mundane in its awfulness; and from 1896 onwards, many east London residents have used the words 'Jago' and 'Nichol' interchangeably. When historian Raphael Samuel came to record days' worth of cassette tapes with Arthur Harding, who had lived the first ten years of his life in the Nichol's final ten years, Harding spoke of his childhood in the Jago, as often as he called it the Nichol. This has been one of the most impressive literary re-brandings of a district.

Morrison stated that his intention in writing *A Child of the Jago* had been to show the gradual corruption of a basically decent boy, Dicky Perrott, by the slum in which he was born and grew. 'It was my fate,' wrote Morrison in his preface to the third edition of the novel, 'to encounter a place in Shoreditch, where children were born and reared in circumstances which gave them no reasonable chance of living decent lives: where they were born foredamned to a criminal or semi-criminal career.' No matter what good impulses Dicky has, no matter any kindnesses shown to him by an outsider, nor any stroke of good luck — he cannot evade the destiny that awaits all who are bred within the filthy streets and noxious moral atmosphere of the Jago.

The Old Jago was a direct, street for street, copy of the Old Nichol. Old Jago Street was Old Nichol Street, Jago Row was Nichol Row, and so on; Morrison's Honey Lane was the real Mead Street; Edge Lane was Boundary Street; Meakin Street was Church Street; Luck Row was Chance Street, and Jago Court was Orange Court. Bethnal Green Road, Shoreditch High Street and The Posties (the narrow alley that connected the Nichol to Shoreditch High Street) all starred as themselves.

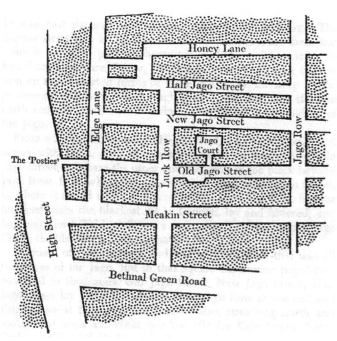

The novel's action spans nine years; in the first section, Dicky is eight years old; in the second he is thirteen; and in the third and last, he has reached seventeen. He grows no older. Inspired by hearing of the real-life killing of seventeen-year-old Nichol boy Charles Clayton, in July 1892, Morrison has Dicky fatally injured during a gang fight. Clayton, a hawker, of 2 Sherwood Place, had been stabbed in the groin, back and arm, on the night of 25th July, and died four days later, of peritonitis, in the London Hospital, refusing to answer questions about the cause of the brawl or the likely identity of his attackers.

The novel's thirty-seven chapters are short, snappy scenes (some are barely five-hundred words long) that drive the plot along at high speed. Meaning never emerges from the story or the characters — the book's theme is always hammered home, like a Jago fist on a baby's face.

Dicky's father, Josh, had been a skilled worker, a plasterer, and has fallen into drink and thieving by the opening of the novel. Dicky's mother, Hannah, had been born 'respectable', outside the Jago, the daughter of a boilermaker; but through flabby inertia and snivelling timidity she has dwindled into Jago life as her husband's prospects narrow. Dicky is told by an ancient Jago resident, Old Beveridge, that for a child like him, there are only three ways out of the Jago: gaol; death on the gallows; or to join the 'Igh Mob — the swankily dressed master criminals who have worked their way to the top of the ladder of East End iniquity.

At eight, Dicky attempts his first major theft; he removes the gold watch of a rotund bishop who is taking tea and cake at a self-congratulatory celebration at the East End Elevation Mission & Pansophical Institute (a bitter attack on the real People's Palace, at Mile End, where Morrison himself had once worked). But instead of a reward, Dicky is badly beaten by his father for attempting such an audacious, unwise 'click' (theft) from a toff. This is the first of several instances in the novel of Dicky's bafflement at the mixed moral messages that press in on him. His mother has told him that 'You must alwis be respectable an' straight... an' you'll git on then'; his father has taught him that 'straight people's fools', while the example of the 'Igh Mob suggests that the only Jago people who find any reward on this earth (in fact, the only ones who can keep themselves fed and adequately dressed) are villains. And yet he is larrupped by his father when he pulls off a lucrative click.

Dicky begins to steal for Aaron Weech, an unctuous, hymn-singing Jago shopkeeper who is also a prolific fence. When High Church Anglican vicar Father Sturt (the single influence for good in the Jago, and a portrait from life of the real Reverend Arthur Osborne Jay) spots the potential within Dicky, he arranges for him to start work for a decent, 'straight' shopkeeper, Mr Grinder. Dicky proves to have all the makings of a good worker; but Weech, keen to retain his services as a street thief and worried that a reformed Dicky might reveal his fencing activities, engineers Dicky's sacking. Next, Weech betrays Dicky's father to the police regarding a theft and assault case, and with the head of the household in jail, Dicky has to steal more and more in order that he, Hannah and his young sister and new baby brother can eat and try to keep warm in their verminous one-room lodging.

Upon his release from prison, Josh hunts down Weech and murders him; Josh is executed, and this completes the work of destroying Dicky's chances of redemption. After his father's death he determines that he will 'spare nobody and stop at nothing... He was a Jago and the world's enemy.'

Dicky's story is regularly sent spinning on to a new course by the continual outbursts of faction fighting in the slum. The two clans that dominate the Jago, and to whom all others must pay allegiance (for being neutral is provocative to both sides), are the Ranns and the Learys. Whenever a period of uneasy truce can no longer hold, the entire Jago engages in street battles:

> The scrimmage on Jerry Gullen's stairs was thundering anew, and parties of Learys were making for other houses in the street, when there came a volley of yells from Jago Row, heralding a scudding mob of Ranns. The defeated sortie party from Jago Court, driven back, had gained New Jago Street by way of the house passages behind the Court, and set to gathering the scattered faction. Now the Ranns came, drunk, semi-drunk, and otherwise, and the Learys, leaving Jerry Gullen's, rushed to meet them. There was a great shock, hats flew, sticks and heads made a wooden rattle, and instantly the two mobs were broken into an uproarious confusion of tangled groups, howling and grappling... Down the middle of Old Jago Street came Sally Green: red-faced, stripped to the waist, dancing, hoarse and triumphant. Nail-scores wide as the finger striped her back, her face, and her throat, and she had a black eye; but in one great hand she dangled a long bunch of clotted hair, as she whooped defiance to the Jago. It was a trophy newly rent from the scalp of Norah Walsh, champion of the Rann womankind.

Sally Green may have been inspired by the Nichol's Mary Ryan, whom Father Jay described as 'a virago... a person greatly feared and dreaded in the locality'. But Ryan may also have been a model for Morrison's character Mother Gapp, owner of the Jago's most foetid pub, The Feathers — itself based on the real Prince of Wales pub, at 52 Old Nichol Street.

Additional excitement arises from the role that the streets of the Jago themselves play. The maze-like configuration of the Jago/Nichol street plan appears both to influence behaviour and to reflect emotional states. The topography of the Jago induces a cunning, furtive mentality; the possessor of that mentality, in turn, learns to make use of the Jago's intricacies to evade hostile 'outsiders' in pursuit. In Morrison's book, knowledge of Jago geography is knowledge of evil.

The Jago is first shown impeding Dicky's movements. As he strolls into view, in the opening pages, he is bumped into by two Jagoites hurtling round the corner of Jago Row, having robbed an unconscious man, just after midnight. Dicky then has to fumble his way carefully along the dark passageway of a tenement so that he doesn't tread on any aggressive drunk who might be lying there. Physically, as well as morally, Dicky, in several episodes, finds himself hemmed in by the Jago, his actions severely circumscribed. Later on, he must be 'careful in his lurkings', avoiding routes used by the Dove Lane (Columbia Road) Gang, who will attack a Jagoite on principal for straying too close to their territory. Dicky's mother, meanwhile — despised in the Jago for the vestiges of respectability that still cling about her — plans a safe route from her home to a nearby grocery shop. (But Hannah and her baby are viciously assaulted by Sally Green as soon as they leave their door.) Dicky also travels along his own private pathway through the slum when he is in need of emotional solace, to the tiny yard where his only confidante lives — an exhausted old donkey, so famished that it has taken to gnawing the wood of the yard's palings.

Time and again in *A Child of the Jago*, characters crash into each other as they burst into the slum, or dash round a corner, or erupt into a court. We also see Dicky expertly negotiating the Jago labyrinth (the 'foul rat runs, these alleys, not to be traversed by a stranger') in full flight whenever he has committed a theft. This underlines his ambivalent relationship to the place: Dicky's worse nature knows how to exploit the streets; his better nature is confounded by them.

The thirty or so streets, courts and alleys of the real slum had been built on a tiny scale on a grid system; most of the Nichol had been thrown up speculatively at the turn of the nineteenth century, although there were some survivors of the original wave of development in the late 17th century. These dwellings were holding up better than the dross that was built circa 1800, with its sagging walls, non-existent foundations, treacherous ceilings and pervasive damp. By the late 1880s, there were no maps that could account for the Nichol's illegal sprouting of sheds, workshops and stables — slung up without parish surveyors' say-so in courts, yards and any remaining free space. The last Ordnance Survey had been undertaken in the early 1870s, and with no cartographers interested or motivated enough to chart this parallel world, the Nichol had certain routes through it that were known only to some of its residents.

The Perrotts' room overlooks Jago Court, a fictionalisation of the Nichol's Orange Court — 'the inner hell of this awful place', as Morrison described the latter, in a defensive interview with the *Daily News* a year after the novel's publication. Orange Court comprised broken-down two- and three-storey houses clustered around a yard that was accessible only through a narrow tunnel that passed beneath the first storey of a house fronting Old Nichol Street. The court appeared to the casual observer to be a cul-de-sac; but the passage-ways of some of the Orange Court houses gave access on to other streets, and once a suspected thief had dashed into the court, police officers knew that they were vulnerable: in one locally notorious inci-dent, a fire grate was hurled down on to the head of a policeman as he emerged from the tunnel into Orange Court (Morrison included this tale in his novel). Orange Court was the site of bare-knuckle prize fights and illegal street-gambling, games such as Pitch & Toss. When the court was torn down in 1888 for the building of Reverend Arthur Osborne Jay's Holy Trinity Church, a tangle of illegal brick sewers and a leaking brick cesspit were found beneath its flagstones.

The reports made by the parish vestry's medical officer concerning conditions at Orange Court (as well as the other most foetid examples of the Nichol's physical fabric) form a catalogue of perfectly common-place nastiness. In Morrison's version, the squalor is given an infernal, Hieronymus Bosch cast. The Jago on a summer midnight has a 'coppery glare' in the glow of a nearby warehouse fire; it is hot, and the houses are verminous, and so 'contorted forms... writhen and gasping' are attempting to sleep out on the pavement under 'a lurid sky'. Here in 'the blackest pit in London... slinking forms, as of great rats' pass doorways that are 'a row of black holes, foul and forbidding'. The Jagoites are described as 'swarming' and 'teeming', and are frequently referred to as rats; even little Dicky is a 'ratling'.

Part of the reason for this fantasticalisation of a dully awful place is the influence of *Oliver Twist* upon *A Child of the Jago*. Morrison never acknowledged Dickens's 1837 masterpiece as an inspiration, though a number of contemporary critics picked out the parallels in their reviews. In both tales, a rather fetching boy falls under the sway of a master thief and corrupter of youth; is rescued and falls again because of his wicked associates and a past he can't seem to shake off. Morrison angrily denied that Aaron Weech was intended to be a Jewish fence and suborner of lost boys; and indeed, Weech has none of the diabolical power — and allure — of Dickens's villain (Weech also has more than a touch of *Bleak House*'s Mr Chadband about him, and touches of Uriah Heep plus *Bleak House*'s Krook). The passages concerning Josh's mental state while on trial and going to the gallows are copies of those that describe Fagin's trial and death-cell experience; and after the murder of Weech, Josh clambers up on to a rooftop and gazes down at the crowd, Bill Sikes-style. Dicky is entrapped by the dark, daedalian streets of the Jago in much the same way that Oliver's descent into Saffron Hill and Fagin's hideout near Field Lane (towards the end of chapter eight of *Oliver Twist*) appears to be a slow physical and spiritual strangulation.

In its old-fashioned melodramatic notes, *A Child of the Jago* is atypical of Morrison's work. Either side of its publication, Morrison enjoyed success within the detective/mystery genre (with his *Martin Hewitt Investigates* series) and with historical fiction with a mystery flavour (*The Hole in the Wall* and *Cunning Murrell*); he had also attempted supernatural tales — *The Shadows Around Us* was published in 1891. But his reputation within literary circles was established by his short stories of ordinary poverty, most notably the collection *Tales of Mean Streets*, published in 1894. In such pieces, Morrison was a new voice within the slum fiction sub-genre; it was he who brought into focus the monotony and mediocrity of perfectly respectable poverty. The 'mean' in Mean Streets referred to the littleness, the lack of aspiration, the lifelessness of hundreds of thousands of upper-working-class East London lives. These tales had none of the hopefulness of Walter Besant's working-class romances, where redemption can come from education and gradual cultural 'improvement'; and there is none of George Gissing's emphasis on the struggling, ambitious hero being slowly crushed by quotidian metropolitan awfulness.

So *A Child of the Jago* is an oddity within his oeuvre. Writing in the late 1960s, Morrison scholar P.J. Keating stated that Morrison's horror and loathing of the Jagoites was probably attributable to some personal source, and that it was this, Keating believed, that 'raises the novel so far above his usual output'. Morrison remains a rather mysterious figure. Interviewers failed to winkle much background information from him; and, as she had been instructed, Morrison's wife, Elizabeth, burnt all his private papers upon his death, in 1945. Recent, diligent scholarship has failed to put much flesh on the bare bones of his biography. He was born in John Street, Poplar (today's Grundy and Rigden streets), on 1 November 1863, in respectable poverty. His father was an engine fitter who died (after three years with tuberculosis) when Morrison was eight; his mother, with three children to support, then opened a small haberdashery shop in John Street. At fifteen, Morrison started as a clerk in the London School

Board's architects' department, and subsequently worked as a clerk at the Beaumont Trust, which administered the People's Palace, and then became a sub-editor on *The Palace Journal*, in 1889, where he impressed Walter Besant. He began to write short stories for the *Journal* and upon leaving his full-time post in 1890, contributed poems about bicycling (his craze of the time) and short stories on a number of themes to various publications, most significantly to the *Strand* magazine (the journal that nurtured so many writers, not least Arthur Conan Doyle) and to W.E. Henley's *National Observer* (Henley was also at that time encouraging the young Rudyard Kipling). *Tales of Mean Streets* was a big success for Morrison, and he was able to move from lodgings in the Strand to rural Chingford, and by 1896 was living in some comfort in Loughton, Essex. It was here he invited some of the men of the Old Nichol so that he could observe their accent and demeanour: 'Sometimes I had the people themselves down here to my house in Loughton. One of my chief characters, a fellow as hard as nails... came several times and told me gruesome stories and how the thieves made a sanctuary of Orange Court.' This was the chap who had dropped the fire grate on a copper's head.

During the 1890s, Morrison began collecting Japanese and Chinese prints, and in 1913, he stopped writing to devote himself to the study of, and dealing in, Oriental artworks. It was art, rather than literature, that brought Morrison both social respect and financial security. His upward trajectory can be traced in his moves to a house in High Beech, near Epping, then to a mansion flat in Cavendish Square, and finally, in 1930, to High Barn, Chalfont St. Peter, Buckinghamshire. His only child, Guy, died of malaria in 1921.

The sketchiest of biographical material appeared in his lifetime, and the 1904 *Dictionary of English Authors* described Morrison as born in Kent and educated at private schools; his father was now an 'engineer', not an 'engine fitter'. Can we surmise that this upgrading of his past was evidence of how Morrison felt about poverty? Was shame part of the creative impulse behind the arch, sneering hostility to the Jago and all who lived in it? It is tempting to view *A Child of the Jago* as a record of a clever, ambitious young man putting a lot of distance between himself and the humble Poplar origins that had balanced Morrison precariously on the edge of Jagoism: for all his claims that Jagoism was an inherited taint, the novel's plot reveals instead the fluidity between respectable indigence and membership of the 'lowest class, vicious, semi-criminal' (Charles Booth's 1889 description of the outcast poor). Hannah Perrott, after all, was born respectable but is seen slowly sinking into Jagoism; daft, squalid but kind prostitute Pigeony Poll gets redeemed at the end of the novel through marriage to Kiddo Cook, a criminal costermonger who has decided to go straight, and prospers.

Personal history aside, there is another factor that could account for Morrison's bleak portrait of the Nichol. The novel was, in a sense, commissioned. In 1894, Reverend Arthur Osborne Jay, vicar of Holy Trinity Shoreditch, in Old Nichol Street, had written to congratulate Morrison on *Tales of Mean Streets*. If, however, Morrison wanted to write about a wholly different type of East End poverty, Jay would be happy to introduce him to the people of his own parish. This invitation was accepted, and in 1895, Morrison began to visit the Nichol daily. Why did Morrison call the Nichol 'the Jago'? As historian David Rich has pointed out: because it's where Jay goes. Father Sturt, the hero of the book, is Jay.

Jay had been the incumbent of Holy Trinity since December 1886; in 1891 he had published an account of his pastoral work in the Nichol entitled *Life In Darkest London, A Hint to General Booth*, which was partly a manifesto for the type of slow, steady parochial relief work that Jay believed in; partly a plea for funds so that Jay's pastoral work could increase; and partly a bashing of William Booth's Salvation Army, whose success at fund-raising appeared to be diverting charitable donations from the Church of England's poverty relief programmes. In 1893, Jay published a second book, *The Social Problem: Its Possible Solution*, in which he retailed further tales of Nichol iniquity, in among another plea for funds; and here he also introduced a new eugenicist note. Among his flock, Jay wrote, were a number who 'by inherited defects and taints of blood, by mental, physical and moral peculiarities, by surroundings and training and circumstances, have no fair chance of being anything but bad. We do not need statistics to prove this. "I should like to turn honest," said a friend of mine to me one day. We were in the street, and I lifted his hat off. "Let me look at your head." He burst out laughing, thinking it was a joke. To me it was none at all. I am no phrenologist, but anyone can tell what that sad, sloping forehead, those shifty eyes, those heavy jaws mean... We have with us a large, miserable and costly class: by our own folly they increase daily...'

Jay's third book, *A Story of Shoreditch*, appeared shortly before *A Child of the Jago* was published, and the crossover between the two is notable, both in the use of specific Nichol incidents and the bleak despair at the notion of ineradicable, biologically transmitted criminality and indigence. The parallels were not lost on the unsigned reviewer of Morrison's novel for the *St. James's Gazette*. In this piece, 'How Realistic Fiction is Written: The Origin of *A Child of the Jago*', which appeared in the *Gazette's* 2nd December 1896 edition, the critic described *A Child of the Jago* as 'an illuminated version' of Jay's *Life in Darkest London*; where Jay's account had been 'cold and colourless', the reviewer stated, Morrison had brought to the same scenes 'warmth and vitality'. In the following week's edition, Jay angrily denied there had been any interference from him in Morrison's work, stating that his own books and Morrison's novel were dissimilar.

At about the same time, Arthur Morrison demanded that H.D. Traill 'trot out his experts', if Traill wanted to prove that the novel was a distortion. Perhaps to Morrison's surprise, Traill did exactly that. He found people who knew the Nichol very well who were willing to go on record to refute Morrison's vision. Woodland Erleback had been a manager at the Nichol Street Board School for thirty years and stated that 'the district, though bad enough, was not even 30 years ago so hopelessly bad and vile as the book paints it. The characters portrayed may have had their originals but they were the exception and not the rule'. J.F. Barnard, meanwhile, told Traill that he had carried cash to and from the Nichol Street Penny Bank since 1874 and had never once been robbed. The textiles firm of Vavasseur, Coleman and Carter, whose warehouse in New Nichol Street stored bolts of valuable silk, had never had a break-in. Two more Board School managers, a pastor at the non-denominational London City Mission, a Poor Law guardian who had been resident in the Nichol for several years, and two women who ran local Mothers' Meetings came forward to Traill to defend the people of the Nichol.

Just over a year later, Reverend Robert Loveridge of St. Philip's, Mount Street, in the east of the Nichol, told one of Charles Booth's *Life and Labour* researchers that the Nichol had been 'painted much too dark, simply on the word of one man [Jay]'. Loveridge said that the area had been 'no worse than several other poor places. He knew it well and visited from house to house, going from "cellar to ceiling". He admits it was bad, but objected to the district being gibbeted as *the* bad spot.'

Morrison said that he knew east London as no other writer did; he pointed out that he had spent eighteen months visiting the Nichol before starting to write *A Child of the Jago*, in April 1896. At the time of its publication, in the November of that year, a number of reviewers wondered why Morrison had decided to write about a spot that, rather famously, no longer existed: in 1891, the London County Council (LCC) had decided to demolish the Nichol in its entirety for the provision of new model dwellings for the working-classes. But what the commentators of the day hadn't grasped was that by the time Father Jay had invited Morrison into the Nichol to study its inhabitants, one-fifth of its population had already been evicted for the demolitions; during Morrison's eighteen months of research in the slum, the final closure notices were being served to locals, and ne'er-do-wells from across the capital came to squat in the vacated properties, living rent free and in the hope that the LCC would have to pay them weekly-tenant compensation. In January 1893 — twenty months before Morrison turned up in the Nichol — the local newspaper, *The Eastern Argus*, proclaimed the area 'The Land of Desolation', declaring: 'Half the houses are now closed by the orders of the County Council, and the dark and deserted alleys afford a likely sanctuary to the burglars and garroters of who we hear so much lately.' Mounted policemen now patrolled the streets of the Nichol, and there were reports of working men being dragged off the Bethnal Green Road and being robbed. But this was not being done by the people of the Nichol; they had been sent elsewhere by the time of Morrison's field trips — October 1894 to April 1896.

Morrison's had not been an eyewitness account but a faithful regurgitation of tales told to him by Father Jay, some of which, what's more, had come to Jay at second hand. 'Typical facts were all I wanted,' Morrison had protested to his critics. Instead, he had retold atypical, and legendary, Nichol events, from which he constructed his fairyland of horror.

References and Further Reading

On the Nichol:

Arthur Osborne Jay, *Life in Darkest London*, 1891

Arthur Osborne Jay, *The Social Problem*, 1893

Arthur Osborne Jay, *A Story of Shoreditch*, 1896

John Reeves, *Recollections of a School Attendance Officer*, c1915

Raphael Samuel, *East End Underworld: Chapters in the Life of Arthur Harding*, Routledge & Kegan Paul, 1981

Montagu Williams, QC, *Later Leaves: Being Further Reminiscences*, 1891

Sarah Wise, *The Blackest Streets: the Life and Death of a Victorian Slum*, The Bodley Head, 2008

www.sarahwise.co.uk for further information on the Old Nichol and the Boundary Street Estate

On Arthur Morrison:

P.J. Keating, *The Working Classes in Victorian Fiction*, Routledge & Kegan Paul, 1971

P.J. Keating's biographical introduction to the 1969 MacGibbon & Kee edition of *A Child of the Jago*

Stan Newens, *Arthur Morrison: the Novelist of Realism in East London and Essex*, Loughton & District Historical Society, 2008

Slum Fiction:

Walter Besant, *All Sorts and Conditions of Men*, 1882

Walter Besant, *Children of Gibeon*, 1886

George Gissing, *Demos*, 1888

George Gissing, *The Nether World*, 1889

George Gissing, *In the Year of Jubilee*, 1894

Rudyard Kipling, '*The Record of Badalia Herodsfoot*', 1890

Somerset Maugham, *Liza of Lambeth*, 1897

L.T. Meade, *A Princess of the Gutter*, 1895

Arthur Morrison, *Tales of Mean Streets*, 1894

Clarence Rook, *The Hooligan Nights*, 1899

Richard Whiteing, *No.5 John Street*, 1899

A Disappeared Neighbourhood

The LCC's Boundary Street Estate was a complete reconstruction of the area and today, little remains of the Old Nichol.

The LCC did not demolish the two Board Schools, built in the 1870s — they stand at the north-west and south-east edges of Arnold Circus.

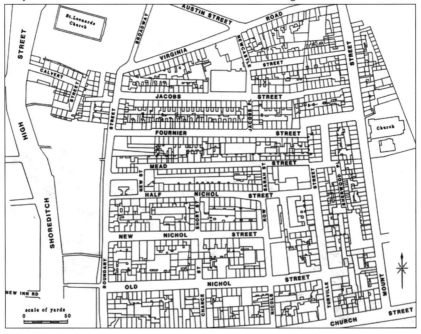

Meanwhile, Boundary Street (Edge Lane in Morrison's novel) still features a few original buildings at its southern end, on the western side; and 'The Posties' — the narrow alleyway that connected the Nichol to Shoreditch High Street — is still there, although the Posties themselves have been upgraded (local legend had it that the posts had been made from upturned cannons from a ship in Nelson's fleet).

The south side of Old Nichol Street did not become part of the LCC estate; similarly, Redchurch Street (formerly Church Street/Morrison's Meakin Street) and the southernmost part of Club Row feature buildings that Morrison would have known. Ebor Street, Chance Street and Turville Street were not part of the LCC reconfiguration and the former two retain their cobbles, while the latter has some early 19th-century buildings.

Orange Court became the site of Holy Trinity, Shoreditch, which was itself destroyed by a direct hit in May 1941; today, a children's playground/sports court is on the spot. Another local rumour has it that the foundations of Father Jay's edifice lie beneath.

Today, the estate is a largely harmonious home to three communities: traditional white Bethnal Greeners; families of Bangladeshi/Sylheti origin; and young (or at least 'kidult') professionals/entrepreneurs. The now middle-aged Young British Art scene of the Blair years has colonised the area, its activities echoing the Nichol tradition of tiny, artisan trades; many of the LCC-constructed workshops at the back of the flats are home to film-editing, post-production and digital industries. In their wake have come high-end restaurants, fashion outlets and an exclusive members-only club, whose outdoor swimming pool overlooks the area in which formerly, running water had been an impossible luxury.

Church Street ('the Champs Elysees of the Nichol,' as Arthur Harding called it) is now a stylish mix of tiny galleries, cafés and funky interiors shops, having been re-branded Redchurch Street by the LCC over 100 years ago. On Great Eastern Street, the title of Morrison's novel has been appropriated for fashion emporium '*A Child of the Jago*'. Terence Conran's food empire, meanwhile, has expanded to Boundary Street, with the Albion restaurant, while the Rochelle School foundation (in the former infants school) provides studio space and facilities for experimental art-workers of many kinds. One such, Thor McIntyre-Burnie, created a site-specific art installation called Rubble Music in 2008 upon Arnold Circus's raised garden with bandstand atop, which lies at the centre of the Estate (a little piece of Walmington-on-Sea in the heart of Shoreditch). Rubble Music sent microphones down into the soil and recorded strange rumblings and vibrations. No voices of the lost Nichol population, alas; just the noises of the trains and traffic that roar around the perimeter of this oddly *rus-in-urbe* spot.

Eighteen months later, the Museum of London archaeological team excavated a trench on the Arnold Circus mound and were at last able to

Boundary Passage ("The Posties") E1

part-confirm a century-old local rumour — that the LCC hillock had been created using the detritus of the Nichol. Prominent among the finds were bricks and other spoil, tiles, crockery, clay pipes, buttons, oyster shells, and all sort of household rubbish of the late-Victorian working-class home. One of the Nichol's major trades — shoe-making — was well represented in the Museum's finds, with uppers, heels, soles and buckles, and a kitten-heel slipper, thought to date to the 18th-century. Plenty of animal bone came to light, too, and a mysterious single human metatarsal was found: the most likely (and dullest) explanation for this is fox or dog activity in a nearby grave-yard.

In 2010, a full refurbishment of the Grade-II-listed bandstand and its gardens was completed. But the area is under persistent threat from devel-opers unhappy to stay within the Corporation of London's limits. Although the residents of Shoreditch (the pressure group's name, 'Jago Action Group') have won many of their fights against immensely unsympathetic buildings planned for Norton Folgate, Shoreditch High Street and Bethnal Green Road, the war against the big and the banal appears to have no end. Already, monstrous mega-projects are looming over the estate, and the latest cathe-drals of capitalism are about to throw the shabby-chic little streets into permanent shadow — a metaphor for the battle for London's soul, if ever there was one.

But while the sun still shines, the Friends of Arnold Circus and the Tenants' & Residents' Association work hard to maintain and make full use of the communal spaces, and to keep alive the fascinating social history of this spot. Many who live or run their businesses in the former Old Nichol have read *A Child of the Jago*, and some of them actually believe it.

Sarah Wise

Thomas Burke
Limehouse Nights (1916)

ANNE WITCHARD

London was my city. It was in my bones and my blood, and part of my work, I knew, would be an attempt to re-present its life.
Thomas Burke, *Son of London* (1946)

In 1914, as war broke out, the London publishing firm, George Allen and Unwin, was offered a manuscript which it very much wanted to take on but which represented 'too startling a departure' from the character of its list. Looking back on his career in *The Truth About a Publisher* (1960), Stanley Unwin considers with regret 'how frequently the most attractive proposals come one's way at the moment when it is impracticable to accept them.' The manuscript in question was a collection of short stories by a relatively unknown writer, Thomas Burke, entitled *Limehouse Nights: Tales of Chinatown*. 'It must be remembered,' writes Unwin, 'that the attitude towards books was much more squeamish and puritanical in 1914 than it has been since 1918. But we were so impressed by the book that we at once commissioned him to write *Nights in Town*, which we published with success.'

Nights in Town: A London Autobiography (1915) was conceived in the tradition of urban guide for the armchair tourist, a collection of personal vignettes of the capital's districts by night. Burke is the seasoned habitué of dark side-streets that lead 'to far countries or to secret encampments of alien and outlaw.' In the chapter 'A Chinese Night: Limehouse' he conjures up the remote dockside byways of the East End as a place of adventure, contrasting the 'corpse electrified' of Piccadilly Circus where 'dreary bands' play 'bilious waltzes' in beer cellars, with the thrilling possibilities to be afforded by boarding an East-bound omnibus for Limehouse Causeway.

Nights In Town earned its author critical acclaim for its originality and lyrical prose style, meanwhile Burke continued to try and place his collection of 'Chinese' tales. When eventually *Limehouse Nights* was accepted by Grant Richards it had been refused by twelve publishing houses. All thought it too shocking. William Heinemann blamed the 'constrained condition of mind' indicated by the recent suppression of D.H. Lawrence's novel, *The Rainbow* (1915), which had been prosecuted under the Obscene Publications Act because of its likelihood to undermine the nation's moral health in a time of war. 'I think that was much to be regretted,' Heinemann wrote to Burke, 'but it is a good illustration of the tendencies just now, and an indication that the interest in the psychology of the pervert is not likely to appeal as long as the war lasts.' Andrew Melrose pronounced unequivocally that he wanted 'nothing to do with books about white girls and chinks.' However, Grant Richards (whose authors included George Bernard Shaw, G. K. Chesterton and Arnold Bennett) made up his mind that 'Thomas Burke and *Limehouse Nights* were just too good to let go,' even though he did anticipate 'trouble' from the book. Richards took the precaution of soliciting letters of support and encouragement from eminent literary figures, among them Ford Madox Ford who dutifully read the book in France to the sound of 'Bosche shells.' As for the immorality Ford commented, 'I never thought about it, so that it cannot be so *very* immoral,' unless, he joked, 'the shell shock which has since sent me home was accentuated' by the stories.

On publication, *The Times* reviewer took a more serious view of *Limehouse Nights*. Burke was condemned as a 'blatant agitator' for his evocative portrayal of a hybrid East End: 'In place of the steady, equalised light which he should have thrown on that pestiferous spot off the West India Dock Road, he has been content... with flashes of limelight and fireworks.' The book achieved instant notoriety by being banned by the circulating libraries, Boots and W. H. Smith. Arnold Bennett (who had just been appointed to the Ministry of Propaganda by press baron, Lord Beaverbrook) warned Burke that the possibility of securing a conviction was being seriously discussed at 'headquarters', and that he himself feared the worst. All this of course was excellent for sales and the book quickly went into further editions.

But what was it, exactly, that 'occasioned the pother'? Some thirty years and another war later John Gawsworth found it difficult to imagine what it was, exactly, 'that occasioned the potter... when James Joyce's *Ulysses* is issued, and reissued in London,' that 'the accouchement of *Limehouse Nights* — surely some occasion in modern literary history? — was, attended by acute anxiety both for the author and the publisher.' In his preface to a posthumous edition of Burke's Best Stories (1950) Gawsworth wonders was it 'the sadistic motif underlying so many of his themes? No I do not think so: but would suggest, rather, that it was the novel, and to most unsavoury, implication that Yellow Man cohabited with White Girl in that East End of an Empire's capital surrounding Limehouse Causeway.'

In 1916, the fact of relations between Chinese men and white women had become an issue of critical national concern. The opening story of *Limehouse Nights*, 'The Chink and the Child', about the devout love of a Chinese man for a white girl was attacked on the grounds that it 'threw a sentimental glamour' over the relations between white women and yellow men and 'might have the harmful effect of encouraging the growth of a tendency that was likely to have disastrous consequences.' In the face of war the very existence of foreign quarters threatened the idea of a nation wishing to believe itself socially and ethnically homogenous. Most worryingly, the fact of co-habitation in Chinatown undermined the hierarchical structure of race that upheld Britain's imperial status quo. Burke's tales of Limehouse love troubled concepts of 'purity' and 'pollution' that had become insistent undercurrents of early twentieth-century thinking. Eugenicists, social scientists and psychologists maintained that Britain was in a state of physical and moral decline. Now the country was engaged in a war that was welcomed in conservative quarters for its 'purifying fire', Royal Academy sculptor W.R. Colton published an essay in *The Architect* magazine in 1916 expressing the hope that England might finally rid itself of degenerate foreign influence disseminated by the likes of Oscar Wilde, Aubrey Beardsley, the futurists, cubists, and 'the whole school of decadent novelists'. The association of Chinese immigrant populations with vice, narcotics, prostitution and gambling (a fear imported from America) prompted increased restrictions of the Aliens Act under the Defence of the Realm Act of 1914 (DORA). Newspapers targeted foreigners living in Britain as 'the enemy within' and foreignness was linked to treason, espionage and subversion. The individual's moral health was considered interdependent with racial fitness and national well-being, crucial both to Britain's defence capabilities and her status as a world power. In 1916, stories about white women and Chinese men in Limehouse vividly symbolised the degeneration of British society.

The 'problem' of interracial alliances among the Chinese in Limehouse was accounted for, not as it conceivably might have been by the almost total absence of Chinese women, but by the giddy susceptibility of a certain 'type' of white woman to 'Oriental' vice. In 1915,

69

a series of addresses by the Bishop of London was published in a collection entitled *Cleansing London*, a patriotic call that linked the home front with the front line. Concern with the moral battles that must be won if the war was to be a true victory was focused on the behaviour of women. It was the task of all the women of London, commanded Bishop Ingram, to 'purge the heart of the Empire before the boys come back.' The usual newspaper reports of gambling raids, opium smoking and hatchet fights in Chinatown, now combined with accounts of English girls being 'inveigled in the meshes of Chinese sorceries' for example, or 'made to serve as votaries at the altars of their gambling hells', stories which would escalate wildly with the onset of war.

It was at the end of the 1890s that the reading public first became aware of Limehouse as London's Chinatown. Operations between England and the Far East had been established since the 1860s by British merchant steamship companies. These employed hundreds of men signed on in China's treaty ports. Whilst soldiers and entrepreneurs set sail from Limehouse Reach to defend and extend Britain's interests in China and the Far East, the capital's East End became cosmopolitan with an influx of Indians, Malaysians, and Chinese. Along the dockside streets, Limehouse Causeway and Pennyfields, there developed a tiny Chinatown. Settled Chinese opened grocery stores, association halls, restaurants, laundries and lodging rooms that catered for seamen, culturally isolated by language and the transience of their stay. At its peak, in 1921, the census returns for the Chinese population of Limehouse was only 337, and while this was an increase on 101, in 1911, and while the Limehouse Chinese accounted for half of London's total 'alien-Chinese' presence, the figures were negligible. The Chinese were a scapegoat for what were considered major social ills, yet the force of this negativity bore no relation at all to the size of their presence. The myth of Chinese Limehouse was always far greater than its actuality.

In Sax Rohmer's best-selling stories of Dr Fu Manchu, Limehouse is a place of shuttered hovels, mysterious passages, 'dark narrow streets and sinister-looking alleys,' home to Rohmer's arch-criminal mastermind, 'the yellow peril incarnate in one man.' The first three Fu Manchu books, published between 1914 and 1917, were a straightforward exploitation of current anxieties which makes the Chinatown fiction of his contemporary, Thomas Burke, appear all the more remarkable. While Rohmer's tales of Fu Manchu reinforced contemporary fears with his evil 'Chinamen' whose interest in white women is part of their fiendish yellow plot to destroy the West, Burke's collection of stories invests London's Chinese Quarter with romance, however spurious. Burke's Limehouse is as alluring as it is forbidding: 'The glamorous January evening of Chinatown — yellow men, with much to spend — beribboned, white girls, gay, flaunting and fond of curious kisses — rainbow lanterns, now lit, and swaying lithely on their strings.' In this depiction of Chinese New Year in Limehouse Causeway, readers are invited to suspend their moral judgement and forgive the girls 'if they love on such a night and with such people.' *Limehouse Nights* contrasts a played out West End with a robust East End bohemia, where the people are 'sick perhaps with toil; but below that sickness there is a lust for enjoyment that lights up every little moment of their evening.' West End theatres might be dazzling audiences with displays of orientalist exoticism but 'saturnalias' and 'true Bacchanales' were being performed in the East End streets.

While *Limehouse Nights* capitalised on contemporary concern about miscegenation, Burke did not temper the romances he spun between white girls and their 'yellow' neighbours with the high moral tone and distaste that was taken by the establishment press with regard to such transgressions. Reviewers registered these lurid tales of Limehouse love on a sliding scale of shock value, 'some too terrible for thought, some cheaply startling,' yet what startles today is their erotic focus on the underage girl that went quite unremarked. As the 'Chink' rescues the 'Child' from the perils of the opium den whence she has fled her brutal father, the 'midnight chimes of the clock above Millwall docks echo the number of little Lucy's years': 'Twelve... Twelve.' Cheng Huan 'had claimed her' we are told, 'but had not asked himself whether she was of an age for love... It may be that he forgot that he was in London and not Tuan-tsen.' The moral standards of Chinese Limehouse are those of the genial rogue, restaurant-keeper Tai Ling, first portrayed in 'A Chinese Night'. He is not immoral, 'for to be immoral you must first subscribe to some conventional morality.'

Burke's Chinatown stories were constructed around an Orient of the mind, a twilight world of exotic ports and red-light districts. Sexual possibilities inhere in the very idea of a Chinese quarter, a Pekin Street or Amoy Place, insinuating that anything might be possible. *Limehouse Nights* partakes of the late nineteenth-century system of highly fantasised imagery that conflated the dark and barbaric East End with the mysterious Orient. The white girls of the stories are the lost or betrayed girl-children of late-Victorian cultural desire, reinvented as objects of Oriental lust. The feverish fascination of the late-Victorian aesthete with child whores and stage waifs reached its height of artistic devotion amongst Ernest Dowson and other Decadents in the 1890s. *Limehouse Nights* demonstrates the continuing cultural strength of the erotic child, but marks a shift from

71

obsession with the child as icon of 'purity' to the new century's fixation on the juvenile delinquent: 'You might have seen her about the streets at all hours of day and night'.

Burke is always most insistent regarding age. Often it is twelve, occasionally fifteen, but mostly it is the 'magic age of fourteen years' that preoccupies. There is poor little Lucy Burrows and the tragic poet Cheng Huan; pretty prostitute Marigold Vassiloff and good-natured Tai Ling who live happily ever after; treacherous Gracie Goodnight who murders her nasty boss Kang Foo Ah and gets away with it; the sordid psychodrama of Daffodil Flanagan and her lover, Fung Tsin; Jewell Angel, the aerialiste (as trapeze artists were rather grandly known), fatally sabotaged for snubbing 'half-caste' Cheng Brander; and Beryl Hermione Chudder and her pimp, Wing Foo, in a story inspired by the siege of Sidney Street in 1911. There is the Cantonese-speaking copper's nark, Poppy Sturdish, and duped Sway Lim who gets his revenge. There is the evil Tai Fu and Pansy Greers who gets her revenge. Their social hub is the Blue Lantern pub. Here, 'in an underground chamber near the furtive Causeway' gather all 'the golden boys and naughty girls of the district' and here the little dancer, Gina of the Chinatown, sometime Casino Juvenile or Quayside Kid, is generally to be found standing on a table 'slightly drunk, and with clothing disarranged, singing that most thrilling and provocative of rag-times: "You're here and I'm here/So what do we care?"'

Grant Richards managed to secure New York publication 'overnight' with Robert M. McBride, whilst in the meantime, he recalls, Burke fretted about the possibility of prosecution at home: 'Being of a more temperamental and more nervous nature he would not rest until I had agreed — for a consideration, I had better frankly confess — to cancel the clause in our contract which would have made him financially responsible for the costs of defending any action brought against me as the book's publisher and for the payment of any losses or financial penalties incurred.' The absence of moral censure regarding what H.G. Wells characteristically referred to as 'rather horrible... "sexual circulation"', contributed towards the book's enormous impact in the States where you were utterly behind the times if you were not intimately acquainted with Burke's stories of Limehouse. American interest was whipped up by racy reviews: 'Amid erotomaniacs, satyrs and sadists — and if the full meaning of these terms escapes you, be thankful — he seizes scraps of splendid courage, beauty and pathos... do not miss *Limehouse Nights*' urged the Boston Transcript. At the prompting of Mary Pickford, D.W. Griffith paid the massive sum of one thousand pounds for the film rights. The fog-bound dockside streets of Burke's stories, the frowsy opium dens and illegal gambling parlours, haunts of his displaced Chinamen and ringletted Cockney waifs, are vividly realised in Griffith's silent adaptation, *Broken Blossoms* (1919) which set a celluloid precedent for the imagery of Limehouse.

Other directors were keen to film Burke's world. A homesick Charlie Chaplin credited *Limehouse Nights* as the inspiration for *A Dog's Life* (1918) in which his character befriends a young dance-hall prostitute: 'I got a feeling from reading Thomas Burke's *Limehouse Nights*... There is beauty in the slums! — for those who can see it despite the dirt and sordidness. There are people reacting toward one another there — there is LIFE, and that's the whole thing!' and Chaplin should have known as he was a London slum kid himself. In 1924, British director, Maurice Elvey (who had made London's Yellow Peril, 1915) exploited Burke's Limehouse scenario by combining a number of his plots in *Curlytop* (1924). Charles Brabin directed *Twinkletoes* in 1926, for which Colleen Moore, the 'screen's first flapper' disguised her iconic bob under blonde ringlets to play the heroine: 'Miss Moore shatters precedent and more than makes good as the little slum child of London's Limehouse district,' commented Variety.

While public reaction to *Limehouse Nights* was dramatic and divided, no prosecution was brought. By the 1920s it was no exaggeration to state that audiences knew every dark and dangerous alley of Limehouse as well as they knew the way to their corner grocery. To the annoyance of Limehouse residents, charabanc trips were put on by Thomas Cook for readers eager to search out the originals of Cheng Huan, Tai Ling and Marigold, and to stare at those real-life 'children with sallow faces and un-English eyebrows', whose existence, commented Rev. Birch, the rector of Limehouse, 'one would regret were it not that they are often none the less delightful enough little creatures. At the same time Birch warned: 'that those who look for the Limehouse of Mr Thomas Burke simply will not find it.'

Throughout the 1920s, novels, plays and films were notable for their offensive stereotypes of Chinese people. If we want a first-hand account of what life was really like for the shopkeepers, transient seamen and restaurateurs that made up the major part of London's Chinese community in London during these years, we only need turn to Chinese writer Lao She's marvellous novel, *Er Ma* (*Mr Ma and Son*, 1929). Lao She came to London in 1924 to take up a post teaching Chinese at the School of Oriental Studies (now the School of Oriental and African Studies) then at Finsbury Circus. The novel, drawing on his own experiences of life in London, takes issue with the popular cultural sinophobia of the Limehouse genre and its pernicious effect on the attitudes of Londoners to the Chinese amongst them.

Thomas Burke's star rose and fell along with the cultural resonance of Limehouse. Throughout his life and despite subsequent successes in diverse genres, his books would carry the hook 'by the author of *Limehouse Nights*'. The 'wretched book' he would complain, has been 'strung around my neck as a literary badge.' During his later years, Burke expounded a belief in writing as an occult process, particularly in defence of the 'ridicule to which I have been subjected for giving a falsely melodramatic picture of Limehouse life.' It was certainly true that the notoriety of Chinatown exploded after the publication of *Limehouse Nights*. Burke needed to explain his part in this as magical rather than malign. Writing about 'The Chink and the Child,' Burke now owned that the location of the story and its Chinese element was quite arbitrary. It 'had no origin as far as I know in China or Limehouse,' it was only when casting about for a setting that the 'West India Dock Road and the two Chinese streets... rose in my mind as exactly fitting.' Here in the Chinese streets was 'a whiff of something odd,' here, he decided, 'was a territory for a certain kind of story.' Disingenuous perhaps, but for the complex and contradictory ways in which he upset social orthodoxies, Burke's *Limehouse Nights* makes compelling reading.

References and Further Reading

Thomas Burke, *Nights In Town: a London Autobiography*, London 1915

Thomas Burke, *Limehouse Nights: Tales of Chinatown*, London, 1916

Thomas Burke, *Out and About: a notebook of London in wartime*, London, 1919

Thomas Burke, *Whispering Windows: Tales of the Waterside*, London, 1921 (published in US as *More Limehouse Nights*, 1921)

Thomas Burke, *The Wind and the Rain: a Book of Confessions*, 1924

Thomas Burke, *East of Mansion House*, London, 1928

Thomas Burke, *The Pleasantries of Old Quong*, London, 1931 (also published as *A Tea-shop in Limehouse*, Boston, 1931)

Thomas Burke, *City of Encounters: a London Divertissement*, London, 1932

Thomas Burke, *Night-Pieces: Eighteen Tales*, London, 1935

Thomas Burke, *Son of London*, London, 1946

Thomas Burke, *Best Stories*. London 1950

Ng Kwee Choo, *The Chinese in London*, Oxford University Press, 1968

Marek Kohn, *Dope Girls: the Birth of the British Drug Underground* (2nd edition), Granta, 2003

John Seed, 'Limehouse Blues: Looking for Chinatown in the London Docks, 1900-1940', *History Workshop Journal*, 62, Autumn 2006

Lao She, *Er Ma*, new translation forthcoming in Penguin Modern Classics

Anne Witchard, *Thomas Burke's Dark Chinoiserie: Limehouse Nights and the Queer Spell of Chinatown*, Ashgate, 2010

Limehouse Today

When Burke wrote *Limehouse Nights*, Pennyfields was almost entirely inhabited by Chinese. Chong Ching, Chong Sam, Wong Ho, Yow Yip, Choi Sau, Ah Chong Koon, Pong Peng, and Cheng Pong Lai, are a few names taken at random from a collection of application forms for ration books during the First World War. By 1934, the Register of Electors shows that of twenty-seven houses listed in the street only one was inhabited by a Chinese family. The combined pressures of the Alien Restriction Acts of 1914 and 1919, together with police harassment were responsible for the decline. Limehouse Causeway was widened in 1934 and a maze of alleys, courts and side streets, including several occupied by Chinese shops and lodging houses, were demolished to make way for blocks of flats. Slum clearance, together with the effects of the Depression and a slump in international trade, further diminished the Chinese population. Thomas Cook's suggested route for an 'East End Drive' no longer made an 'attraction' of Limehouse. The myth declined along with the reality and newspaper stories about the 'dwindling population' of Chinese Limehouse sympathised with 'the sensational writer bereft of one of his more thrilling scenarios.' Census figures from the 1930s indicate an acceleration of movement of Chinese to the West End and the outer suburbs. The Blitz helped finish the work begun by the LCC clearances.

In 1955, even more projected demolition prompted a letter to the editor of *The Times* from the avant-garde Situationist group:

> We protest against such moral ideas in town-planning, ideas which must obviously make England more boring that it has in recent years already become... The only pageants left are a coronation from time to time, an occasional royal marriage which seldom bears fruit; nothing else. The disappearance of pretty girls, of good family especially, will become rarer and rarer after the razing of Limehouse. Do you honestly believe that a gentleman can amuse himself in Soho?.. Anyway, it is inconvenient that this Chinese quarter of London should be destroyed before we have the opportunity to visit and carry out certain psychogeographical experiments we are at present undertaking.

London's Chinatown as we know it today began to take shape at this point. Encouraged by seedy Soho's cheap rents and already established reputation for cosmopolitan dining, a few Chinese restaurants set up in the streets to the north of Leicester Square. Demand from West End theatre and clubbing crowds ensured their popularity, attracting more Chinese not just from the East End but from Hong Kong and the New Territories. Thanks to Docklands regeneration, London's first Chinatown is now all but erased from the physical site of Limehouse Causeway and Pennyfields, The 'Old Friends' restaurant on Commercial Road offers a distant echo of the old Chinatown. It's one of the oldest Chinese restaurants in London, though dating back only to the 1950s, so well after the dissolution of Limehouse's Chinese community. Only the evocative street names — Canton, Pekin, Amoy, Ming, Mandarin, Nankin — and a metal dragon sculpture coiled above the Limehouse exit of the Docklands Light Railway, remind us that once this district vibrated to a distinctly Chinese rhythm.

Anne Witchard

Virginia Woolf
Mrs Dalloway (1925)

HEATHER REYES

As one of *the* great London novels, *Mrs Dalloway* not only takes us on a delicious tour of some of the capital's major attractions, it also conveys better than any work of fiction I can think of the enhanced sense of 'being alive' stimulated by the energy, variety, and complexity of city life. Near the beginning of the novel Clarissa Dalloway declares, 'I love walking in London... Really, it's better than walking in the country,' and we, too, are drawn into 'that divine vitality which Clarissa loved.'

A few editions of *Mrs Dalloway* have included maps so that the reader can follow the routes taken by the cast of the novel but, for me, it is the way that London 'maps' the characters — creates their individual minds and attitudes — that is as important as the locations they visit.

The tour begins and ends at the Dalloways' residence in Westminster and is haunted throughout by that landmark London sound, the chimes of Big Ben (more on those later). Like James Joyce's portrait of Dublin in *Ulysses* (1922), *Mrs Dalloway* (1925) can be said to observe two of the three Classical unities — of time and place: both books concentrate on a single location and both take place on a single day (and both in June). In both, we meet a range of inhabitants from the respective cities, moving in and out of their varied minds as they experience and respond to the world around them.

Clarissa Dalloway, something over fifty years old, is not an exceptional woman: some dismiss her as 'shallow' and nothing more than a 'perfect hostess' (possibly quite a useful attribute for the wife of an MP at the time). But she is the perfect companion to start us off on a walking tour of the city she loves so much, leading us, on that

77

glorious June morning, through St. James's Park to Piccadilly and Bond Street to buy flowers for the party she is to give that evening. Her party will assemble most of the people we will have encountered in the course of the day and wind together various thematic strands we have been following during our city tour. And it's a celebration of London life.

Although we are handed over to various of her friends and family for much of the day, it is when we are with Clarissa herself that we experience the most heightened pleasure in all the sights, sounds, and general atmosphere of London.

> In people's eyes, in the swing, tramp and trudge; in the bellow and the uproar; the carriages, motor cars, omnibuses, vans, sandwich men shuffling and swinging; brass bands; barrel organs; in the triumph and the jingle and the strange high singing of some aeroplane overhead was what she loved; life; London; this moment in June.

My own theory is that this intensified feeling for 'life' springs from a sharpened sense of her own mortality. A severe case of influenza (one can assume she was a victim of the pandemic of 1918) has left her with a weakened heart, and there is nothing like a brush with death or the diagnosis of a potentially fatal condition to magnify one's sense of life and push one to live more intensely. In a broader version of the same phenomenon, one might compare it to the frantic pleasures of the 1920s that followed from the horrendous and continual presence of death during the four years of the First World War, the long shadow of which falls across London and Clarissa Dalloway's party.

It's true that, even as a young woman living in the country, Clarissa 'loved life' — loved flinging open the French doors to feel the fresh, early morning air on her face. But the ageing Clarissa knows that her thirst to have as much life as possible, while there is still time, is best met by the complex physical, historical and social structures of a great city. It is human life in its most concentrated form. 'Like the pulse of a perfect heart, life struck straight through the streets,' muses Peter Walsh, the suitor Clarissa rejected in her youth and who, returning from India, is himself struck afresh by the sights and sounds of London.

But back to more details of the tour. We step out from the Dalloways' Westminster house and, even as we are waiting to cross Victoria Street, we hear Big Ben strike, reminding us of the passage of time. At first the sound is 'musical', suggesting joy and lightness. But as the hour strikes, it becomes 'irrevocable', the sound of 'leaden circles'. They are as heavy as the memories of the recent Great War. The sound reminds us that, while London is a place of beauty and stimulation, it is also the site of Parliament which decides the fate of millions with decisions such as whether or not the country should go to war. (The institution is brilliantly described by Woolf in 'This is the House of Commons', one of the essays collected in *The London Scene*.) Yet the heavy sound of Big Ben — tolling rather than ringing — 'dissolved in the air'. The inevitability of death and the tragedy of war dissolve in the bustling details and variety of this glorious London morning.

As Clarissa takes us through St. James's Park (the first of three great London parks we visit in the novel), we bump into her old friend Hugh Walpole. Dismissed by many as pompous and slightly ridiculous, Clarissa sees beyond his irritating behaviour to his essential goodness and unselfishness. Her generosity of spirit, her awareness of the complexity of people (Hugh can be foolish but good, Peter can be intolerable but 'adorable to walk with on a morning like this') seems to spring from her immersion in the complex nature of city life itself. At the very moment when she is reflecting on the contradictory qualities within Hugh and Peter, we are also given her awareness of the energy and many simultaneous 'goings on' within London.

> June had drawn out every leaf on the trees. The mothers of Pimlico gave suck to their young. Messages were passing from the fleet to the Admiralty. Arlington Street and Piccadilly seemed to chafe the very air in the Park and lift its leaves hotly, brilliantly, on waves of that divine vitality which Clarissa loved. To dance, to ride, she had adored all that.

The only time we see a less generous response to others by Clarissa is in the case of Ellie Henderson and Miss Kilman — both 'life-deniers' in their different ways. As well as being dull, they evoke the duty of pity, Miss Kilman guilty of the additional sin of trying to influence Clarissa's daughter to adopt the constricting sort of Christianity that is anathema to Clarissa's appetite for life.

In the same way that London is many things at the same time, so each person is many-layered and contradictory, and cannot be dismissed as merely 'this' or 'that'. And this is how we come to perceive Clarissa herself: by the end of the book we know her to be far more than a superficial, poorly educated, well-heeled little wife of a fairly mediocre MP. Immersion in city life can teach us about people, can make us more profound, broad-minded, perceptive. The city is an educator of the human spirit and is the place where Clarissa likes to think her spirit will linger after death — 'in the streets of London, on the ebb and flow of things, here, there... part of people she had never met.'

Walking along Piccadilly, we pause at the window of Hatchard's bookshop, and find a fittingly eclectic mix of books on display: Shakespeare's *Cymbeline* (open at the lines 'Fear no more the heat of the sun', prompting thoughts of the young men lost in the war) is alongside *Jaunts and Jollities, Soapy Sponge* (!!??), the memoirs of Mrs Asquith and *Big Game Shooting in Nigeria* — an odd collection but one that humorously sums up Britain at the time.

One does not usually associate Virginia Woolf with shopping.* In the course of this novel we visit three more London 'retail outlets'. Clarissa herself moves on from Hatchard's to Mulberry's, a high-class florist on Bond Street (we are treated to a sumptuous description of the flowers). Later we visit a Mayfair jeweller's with Richard Dalloway and Hugh Walpole, and also purchase a petticoat at the Army and Navy department store in Victoria, in the company of Clarissa's daughter, Elizabeth, and her tutor, Miss Kilman, before taking afternoon tea with them in the store's tea room.

While we are in the Bond Street florist, a sound like a pistol shot in the street outside (just a car back-firing) provides the occasion to switch the focus to Clarissa's dark shadow in the novel, the shell-shocked Septimus Warren Smith. His experience of horrific deaths in war have intensified his vision of 'life' to the point of madness — a hideously magnified version of what has happened to Clarissa.

Our tour continues as we follow the car (containing, it is suggested, the Prince of Wales) down St. James's Street and towards Buckingham Palace, the usual crowd at the gates, the flag flying and the monument to Queen Victoria 'billowing on her mound'. Though they had hoped to glimpse royalty, the crowd is momentarily distracted by an aeroplane sky-writing an advertisement and the royal car slips past them, unnoticed, into the Palace. We return to Buckingham Palace later with Clarissa's husband, passing by on his way from Green Park to his Westminster home. He compares the Palace to 'an old prima donna facing the audience all in white' (having once read that comparison it's hard not to think of it whenever one sees the palace), and although it has acquired dignity from what it has come to symbolise to millions of people, architecturally it is disappointing — 'a child with a box of bricks could have done better'. We are also given a second viewing of the statue of Queen Victoria in front of the Palace, 'its white mound, its billowing motherliness'.

The sound of the plane which had distracted the Palace crowd is heard, we are told, by everyone in the Mall, Green Park, Piccadilly, Regent Street, and even in Regent's Park and we are whisked *par*

*But see her delightful account of the activity in her 1930 essay *Street Haunting: a London Adventure.*

avion, as it were, from Buckingham Palace to Regent's Park, to a seat in the Broad Walk. Here we join Septimus Warren Smith and his Italian wife, Lucrezia, passing the time in the sunshine before going on to a consultation with Sir William Bradshaw in London's most famous medical location, Harley Street. The intense, anguished visions conjured by the park in the mind of Septimus are in contrast with our later visit to the same location with Peter Walsh who dozes on a bench next to an elderly grey nurse with a baby asleep in a perambulator.

The third royal park we visit is Green Park — in the company of Richard Dalloway, MP. His walk home through the park is used by Woolf to reveal more of his character and values as he observes, with pleasure, how 'in the shade of the trees whole families, poor families, were sprawling; children kicking up their legs; sucking milk'. Even the resulting rubbish doesn't bother him as 'paper bags thrown about' could easily be picked up by 'one of those fat gentlemen in livery'. Richard has social conscience and general kindness enough to believe that 'every park, every square, during the summer months should be open to children'.

Of the great London churches, three are only mentioned in passing — Westminster Cathedral, St. Margaret's and St. Paul's (for a Woolfian visit to St. Paul's, turn to Chapter Five of *Jacob's Room*, a novel which contains many delightful observations on London), but a visit to Westminster Abbey takes place in the company of Miss Kilman, tutor to Elizabeth Dalloway. We watch the people shuffle past the Tomb of the Unknown Warrior, reminding us again of the shadow of war still hanging over the capital. And not far away is Lutyens' new monument, the Cenotaph, erected in Whitehall in 1920. Peter Walsh watches a company of young cadets marching up Whitehall to lay a wreath there, and we pause, with him, in Trafalgar Square, to notice a handful of London's many statues to great military figures who helped forge the country's history.

There are many other London locations mentioned in passing — streets known to any Londoner or frequent visitor to the city: Brook Street, Great Portland Street, Regent Street, the Strand, Cockspur Street, Bedford Square, Russell Square, Tottenham Court Road, Conduit Street, Dean's Yard, Chancery Lane, Fleet Street, Haymarket... and there are references to Greenwich, Regent's Park Tube Station, Hampton Court, the Tower of London, the Victoria and Albert Museum, Somerset House, and Caledonian Market. One of the key locations Woolf doesn't take us to is the British Museum, but she had already done so, unbeatably, in *Jacob's Room*. Neither does the Thames really feature — but do see the description of the Frost Fair on the Thames in *Orlando*.

81

It is, I suppose, very much 'tourist' London that we are given —
we aren't taken south of the river, don't venture further west than
Kensington, never make it as far north as even Hampstead (but read
her description of Keats's Hampstead house in the essay 'Great Men's
Houses' in *The London Scene*) and certainly don't stray further east
than the City. It is prosperous London that we visit, perhaps a deliberate attempt to dispel the Dickensian fogs and poverty of much
nineteenth-century writing about the city. It is also a pleasant interlude before the dour, bomb-scarred, post-1945 literature on the city.

Woolf gives us joyous London, and it is a London we can still recognise today. In both *Mrs Dalloway* and *Jacob's Room* we find delightful
descriptions of travelling through the centre of the capital on the top of
a bus — a mode of transport that then, as now, brings together a fair
cross-section of the city's inhabitants (though in Woolf's day the upper
deck would have been open). If buses of the 1920s lacked the diversity
of languages we hear today, the experience remains entirely recognisable. The Dalloways' seventeen-year-old daughter goes on an
'adventure', taking the bus from Victoria to Chancery Lane. We are told
that, even though she had no intention of queue-jumping, once the bus
arrived she suddenly 'stepped forward and most competently boarded
the omnibus, in front of everybody'. The top of a London bus is still no
place for those unwilling to suffer a good deal of jerking and swaying.
Elizabeth had to 'hold the rail to steady herself' and compares the bus
to a pirate ship, 'dangerously, boldly snatching a passenger, or ignoring
a passenger'. And *Jacob's Room* gives us an all too recognisable traffic
jam in Oxford Street: '... all the red and blue beads had run together on
the string. The motor omnibuses were locked'. The closeness of the
buses going in opposite directions gives the passengers the chance to
stare, with impunity, into each other's faces. It is to *Jacob's Room*, too,
that we must turn for a brief descent into the Underground, the station
names lodging in Londoners' minds as the 'large letters upon enamel
plates... eternally white letters upon a blue ground'.

The London tour offered by *Mrs Dalloway* is mainly conducted on
foot, however — still the best way to see a city and get to know it. It
is only on foot that we have the opportunity to observe the buildings,
the people, the natural world, the statues and myriad details of a city
that stimulate the intellect and educate the spirit.

At the end of a day's sight-seeing, what better than to step into the
Westminster house from which we had set off with Clarissa in the
early freshness of the June morning and have the whole, rich day
brought back to us in the company of those who have revealed the city
to us and have, in turn — and perhaps more importantly — been
revealed to us through the city.

We may be a little nervous (like Clarissa) when the Prime Minister himself puts in a brief appearance and will be deeply saddened (like Clarissa) when the news of Septimus' suicide casts a shadow over the party, the effects of the Great War continuing to echo, along with the subject of ageing and approaching death. Yet the conclusion that three of the main characters come to is that age intensifies the power of feeling — 'one feels more passionately every year', about people, about the world, about the whole experience of living.

Woolf herself was a great lover of London (though she sometimes had to be 'protected', for the good of her fragile mental health, from the heightened stimulation it provided) and this love is clear in every page of *Mrs Dalloway*, in much of *Jacob's Room*, and in the five essays collected in *The London Scene*. But *Mrs Dalloway* above all is her love song to London and anyone who has read it surely cannot walk through that part of London mapped by the novel without feeling the exhilaration of the city — especially if it happens to be a sunny morning in June.

References and Further Reading

Virginia Woolf, *Jacob's Room*, 1922
Virginia Woolf, *Orlando*, 1928
Virginia Woolf, *The London Scene*, 1931

There are so many books on Woolf that it's very hard to create a manageable reading list. Better than reading commentaries is to read and re-read the books themselves. We should visit London with them in our pockets, do what Woolf did and use all our senses and powers of observation and our life will be enhanced. And be alive to her sense of humour! But if you want more than the texts themselves, the biographies of Woolf by Hermione Lee (*Virginia Woolf*, Knopf, 1997) and by her nephew Quentin Bell (*Virginia Woolf: a Biography*, Harcourt Brace Jovanovich, 1972) are a good place to start.

Mrs Dalloway's London, Then and Now

Hatchard's bookshop is still thriving. It's still possible to find a portrait of the present in the books to be found in the window, though today publishers usually have to pay for their books to be promoted in a window display, so it will probably be a portrait of the publishing industry rather than the country.

Westminster Abbey can no longer be casually 'popped into' in the way that Miss Kilman does. An outrageously high fee has to be paid to enter the Abbey. (If you 'only want to pray', there is an insulting side-room reserved for you.) It is criminal that such an important part of our national heritage is not state-funded. One doesn't pay to enter Notre Dame or Sacré Cœur (at least, not the last time I was in Paris).

The Royal Parks are happily recognisable. Like much else in *Mrs Dalloway*'s London, they help us to map ourselves in history, as well as geographically and socially. A few monuments have been added to the parks since Woolf's time, of course, and one wonders whether the smell from hot-dog stands in St. James's Park ever waft over to Buckingham Palace.

The River Thames might have featured if Woolf was writing today. The function of the river has changed radically since the twenties: the London docks were among the busiest in the world, and Woolf gives a wonderful portrait in her essay on them in *The London Scene*. Today, of course, the river and the docks have been taken over by leisure activities and residential accommodation.

Heather Reyes

Pamela Hansford Johnson
This Bed Thy Centre (1935)

ZOË FAIRBAIRNS

*T*his Bed Thy Centre is a novel about sex in a south London suburb in the years between the two world wars. At its heart is sixteen-year-old Elsie Cotton who wants to know all about intercourse, without actually having it. Her boyfriend Roly would be only too happy to give a practical demonstration, but Elsie's fears hold her back. Their struggle interweaves with other lives, some public, some intimate, many both.

The exact area of London in which the story unfolds — down-at-heel, but up-and-coming — is not specified in the book, only referred to as the Neighbourhood, and the Locality. But the author Pamela Hansford Johnson (1912–1981) made clear in her introduction to the 1961 edition that she had in mind the Clapham Common area where she grew up.

In Johnson's youth, Clapham Common consisted of 'vast fields above which the stars were clear and the lovers lay in the dark.' (All autobiographical quotations from Pamela Hansford Johnson in this article come from her collection of essays *Important To Me, a Personal Record*, unless otherwise indicated.) In the novel, parts of the fictionalised Neighbourhood are similarly rural, and close enough to the river that you can see boats going by with red sails.

The riverbank in *This Bed Thy Centre*, like the Common, is a place for trysts: in an early scene, Elsie is invited there by her beloved lesbian art teacher Miss Chavasse, for a spot of private tuition. But Miss Chavasse doesn't show up.

> Elsie walked along the shore, kicking the pebbles into the water... As the sunset faded into the strong yellow of a late summer night, she

85

climbed the steps to the embankment and walked away in the direction of her home. Crossing the Common, she stared up into the still leaves and saw new colours there. A boy and a girl, kissing under a tree, parted hurriedly as she passed them by.

Later, the Common is the location of Elsie's first date with Roly.

He put his hand on hers. This time she did not draw it away. She was unbelievably happy. The evening was quiet, and so delicate that a single word might break it in two pieces. The sun faded down to the ragged edges of the Common. There was a watery light on the church spire, far away over the trees, and the lamps were lit on the path to the railway station.

You don't get that sort of peace and quiet on Clapham Common these days. Traffic thunders through on the South Circular, and the Common's determination to be all things to all people (with its ponds and playgrounds, bandstand and bowling green, cafés and cricket nets, all-weather pitch and athletics sprint track) keeps the casual walker in a constant state of alertness, lest she be mown down by the vigorous activity of someone more purposeful.

On the north side is Holy Trinity Church where, says the sign, 'William Wilberforce and members of the congregation worshipped and campaigned against the slave trade up to and beyond its abolition in 1807. Remember: reflect: respond. 1807–2007.' And there's a drinking-water fountain installed by the United Kingdom Temperance and General Provident Institution in 1884, with a sculpture of a woman giving water to a beggar.

The fountain no longer works, but what I did find there, on the afternoon when I went walking on the Common in the hope of retracing the footsteps of Pamela Hansford Johnson and some of her characters, was an abandoned and much-used plastic shaving razor. It brought to mind a busker I was once entertained by on a train passing through nearby Clapham Junction. His face was a bit stubbly, for which he apologised, explaining that although he usually tried to smarten up before performing, on this occasion he had been ejected from a public toilet on Clapham Common for shaving, a practice which is forbidden. And he sang a song which he had penned in honour of the official who had made this rule:

If you can't have a shave in a toilet,
where can you have a shave?
Think of all the other things
that people do in toilets

Whether or not the temperance fountain is now the shaving-place of choice for buskers banned from toilets, I can't say; I don't even know if the no-shaving-in-toilets rule still stands. But contemporary Clapham Common has plenty of others. They come at you from all sides: This is a Controlled Drinking Zone. Carp Anglers Must Be in Possession of a Landing Net. No Cash on Rides on Inflatables. No Person Shall Throw or Strike with a Bat a Cricket Ball Except in a Designated Area for Playing Cricket. No Person Shall Without the Consent of the Council Erect a Tent.

Someone had erected one on the afternoon I was there, by Eagle Pond, a favourite spot for anglers. There wasn't a lot of angling going on, only a strong smell of cannabis wafting from the tent's interior. A voice floated after it, telling me to piss off, so I did.

The afternoon was freezing cold — it was January — and I was starting to feel I had had enough, and would come back another day. I caught a bus along Battersea Rise and got off to walk towards Clapham Junction station.

Shops in Pamela Hansford Johnson's fictionalised 1930s suburb include Woolworths, a draper's, a hairdresser's offering 'Perms from One Guinea', a café where you can enjoy 'a hearty meal of kidneys on toast', and a newsagent's where, for those in the know, a copy of *Lady Chatterley's Lover* is available for hire at sixpence per day, disguised as *Robinson Crusoe*. These days, retail outlets in the area include Cleavers Free Range Butchers, Southern Foam (soft furnishings), Under the Greenwood Tree (books, toys and a café for children), a bakery with a window display of chocolate meringues so huge you would need both hands to pick one up, and bars and restaurants with names like Le Bouchon Bordelais and Tsunami. That's in addition to the usual chains: Body Shop and Waitrose, Starbucks and Waterstones.

'May we pray for you?' asked a man outside Starbucks.

'We'll pray for anything,' added his female companion.

You can't win with an offer like that, I find. Say yes and you're signing up to the value of prayer, which may or may not be a core belief for you; say no and you're rebuffing someone's kindly-meant gesture of good will. I muttered noncommittally and continued my journey.

'We are not asking for money,' they called after me. 'We just want to pass on God's blessing.' And I just wanted to get out of that freezing cold. Nevertheless, after a few steps I turned back, having remembered Mrs Godshill.

A minor but disproportionately noisy character in *This Bed Thy Centre*, 'Oly 'oly Godshill, as her neighbours call her, is a Christian evangelist, and as such perhaps the spiritual foremother of the couple outside Starbucks. But whereas they seem low-key, polite and non-threatening, Mrs G is loud, rude and violent, swiping dissenters with her umbrella, and bullying one of her teenage children into alcoholism, the other into suicide. On Sundays, Mrs G heads for the Common where she sets up a rostrum, from which, flanked by corn-plaster sellers and communist agitators, she casts aspersions on people's private morality, and sings 'A Sinner Coming Home At Eventide'. To many she is a spectator sport, a weekend entertainment, with hecklers taking particular pleasure in reminding her about her son's drunkenness.

Back in the real world, I explained to the couple outside Starbucks that I was not seeking their prayers, but researching an article on a local author of the 1930s, and differences between Clapham then and now. 'She wrote about street preachers,' I told them. 'They sometimes attracted hostility. What about you?'

'We get a good response,' said the woman. 'There have been healings,' said the man. 'Jesus heals, he really does. I notice you're shivering. Do you have a trembling disorder?'

'Yes. I'm cold. Do people ever give you a hard time?'

'Not really,' said the woman. 'They sometimes roll their eyes, or say 'No!' very crossly when we offer to pray for them. Or they're like you, they say they're not Christians but they want to talk to us anyway. May we pray for you?'

'Thanks, but you don't need my permission, do you?'

The man pressed a leaflet into my hand. 'Will you tell us your name?'

'Why would you need that?'

'We'll pray for your book,' said the man, and I hurried away before he could ask for the ISBN.

The leaflet revealed that the pair were from St. Mark's church on Battersea Rise, which Pamela Hansford Johnson attended as a child with her mother, so I went to take a look.

St. Mark's is built of brownish Victorian brick with red brick arches over the doorways, a tall spire and four crosses of different shapes. In her essay 'St. Mark's and Mr Russell's', Johnson recalls how she 'revelled in Broad Church ritual... There was a real male choir in those days, and I would wait breathless for the great basses to come in with "the holy company of the apostles praise thee".' She also liked 'the springlike unbudding of the Benedicite.'

But young Pamela was lured away from St. Mark's by an aunt who preferred the more unconventional ways of the Congregational

Church in Grafton Square, Clapham Old Town, where intellectuals and homosexuals gathered, and where communion wine was served in tiny glasses rather than the 'common cup' favoured by the Church of England. Pamela's mother dubbed this practice a 'Nippy' service, a reference to Lyons' waitresses. One can only speculate as to what she would make of the angular modernist annexe round the back of today's St. Mark's, with its offerings of Messy Church (arts and crafts days for children), Alpha courses, and debt counselling.

***

Pamela Hansford Johnson was born in 1912, the daughter of Amy Clotilda *née* Howson, an actor and singer with the D'Oyly Carte Opera Company, and Reginald Johnson, a colonial administrator based in what is now Ghana. He was frequently absent, and Pamela grew up among her mother's theatrical relatives in Battersea Rise, in 'a large brick terrace house bought by my grandfather sometime in the 1880s, when it looked out on fields where sheep might safely graze.' By the time Pamela was born, the railway had come, and 'houses had been built up right over the hills between it and us. Not pretty, I suppose.' But she was still able to 'create an Arabian Nights fantasy about anything', and found the 'smoky sunset between the spires of St. Mark's and the Masonic School magical to contemplate.'

Part of the magic of Battersea Rise came from her relationship with her father who would come home on leave from his overseas postings every couple of years: 'we would stand waiting in the drawing-room window for his appearance on the Rise. And sure enough he would appear in the sunset — bronzed as a sea captain, bearing some extraordinary gift such as a Benin mask and once a canary in a cage.'

Less magical were the financial difficulties which followed Reginald's sudden death in 1923. In an essay entitled 'A Sharp Decline in Income', Johnson describes the embarrassments, inconveniences and disappointments of a once comfortably-off family learning to do without.

She and her mother had to move out of their flat at the top of the house and share a bedroom in the basement; Pamela left school at 16, to train as a stenographer and work in a bank. Her family remained class-conscious, referring to the area of Battersea Rise in which they did not live as 'the other Battersea Rise' and recoiling in horror from the idea that one of their number might 'marry into trade'. But to the young Pamela, a low-paid office worker saving up her pennies to buy her lunch, things were not so simple: 'I have often thought that we had no recognisable class at all.'

This 'come-down' was, she acknowledged, 'a wretched thing for my elders, but a stimulus to me.' To earn extra cash, she started writing stories and poems; she won a poetry competition in the *Sunday Referee*. She joined a writers' group that met at the house of journalist Victor Neuburg, and had a romance — briefly an engagement — with Dylan Thomas. When at the age of twenty-two she conceived the idea for *This Bed Thy Centre*, she wrote it in two months, sometimes resting her work-in-progress on top of packing cases as she and her mother were moving house at the time.

She described the book as 'an attempt to tell the truth about a group of people in a London suburb, whose lives were arbitrarily linked'. It's a mixed neighbourhood: the working poor push barrows, pull pints or work shifts in the candle factory, while the unemployed go job hunting, and the idle rich sleep late before checking what is on at the pictures and deciding what to have for tea. Those in between struggle to keep up appearances, borrowing money to pay their gambling debts, or heading off to the big city to buy a new autumn coat (with a not-quite-crêpe-de-Chine lining and 'two whole foxes' in the collar) before coming home to their terraced houses with cramped bathrooms and pomegranate-motif wallpapers.

Sexual politics are alive and well in the Neighbourhood, even if they are not yet called that. 'The main cross the unmarried woman has to bear is not that she has no husband, but that she is unnecessarily pitied by the women who do' remarks Rose, an older single woman. A younger one, the sexually experienced and enthusiastic Patty Maginnis, advising Roly on how to get away with infidelity, points out double standards: 'It isn't jealousy of another woman that makes a girl upset when a fellow confesses an affair, it's envy that he can do what she can't.'

Financial and social inequalities are noted, resented and/or enjoyed. Roly uses family connections to get himself a managerial job at the town hall, where he earns £3 per week; Elsie, with no strings to pull, answers an advertisement and gets 25 shillings working as a clerk in the same place. She is quick to pull rank over Mrs Godshill's daughter Ada, who after three years as a shop assistant at the draper's is still only on 22 shillings and sixpence.

Hearing about this, Ada is 'conscious of a slight stirring that she did not recognise as class hatred'. That's how it is in the Neighbourhood: the wider political world rarely intrudes, except perhaps when Roly comes up with what he hopes is a clinching argument on why Elsie should have sex with him: 'it's the whole social system that's at fault... When a man loves a woman, he ought to be able to sleep with her right away, and then there would be no repressions or inhibitions or anything.'

Elsie remains unconvinced. Approaching her wedding day and night with her virginity intact, her head full of questions and her gut churning with desire and fear, she goes to the Common for reassurance:

> Perfect love casteth out fear, she thought, as she walked through the little hills to sit alone by the pond. When we have loved each other for the first time, everything will change and I shall be able to feel myself alive again.
> The surface of the pond bloomed with coming summer. Anyhow, I'm not going away from all this. It will be here, near me, all the time. I'm going to Roland whom I love, whom I must love, and not to a stranger. I am not going to a strange house. We will lie together as we lay under the trees last year, only we shall not lie as we lay then.
> Oh God, I don't want to get married.

But she does. On the day itself (the chapter describing it is entitled 'The Bitter Paradox'), 'the morning, drawing within itself, moved in sun and shadow over the Common and through the pond, till it came to settle in dust over the room where Elsie had lain wakeful all the night through.' Elsie begs her mother to sit with her while she has her bath, as otherwise 'I shall look at my body and know that it is mine no longer.'

The wedding goes smoothly, and the novel ends with Elsie lying alone in bed, awaiting her bridegroom. It is for the reader to supply what happens next.

This lack of explicitness cut little ice with some reviewers. 'Words like "outspoken", "fearless", "frank" (dirty words, the lot of them) flashed out of my headlines,' Johnson wrote, in her preface to the 1961 edition. 'I was shocked and terrified... I was given to understand that I had disgraced myself and the entire area of Clapham Common.'

But it survived (albeit without a copy of *This Bed Thy Centre* in Battersea Rise library, which refused to stock it), as did Pamela Hansford Johnson's literary career. She went on to publish short stories, plays, books of non-fiction and journalism, as well as twenty-seven other novels.

One of these, *Here Today* (her third, published in 1937) contains a cameo appearance by the sexually joyous Patty Maginnis, which is odd because she committed suicide about three-quarters of the way through *This Bed Thy Centre*, rather than face cancer treatment. The reader of both books may wonder whether this part of *Here Today* started life as a prequel, or whether Patty is a ghost, dropping into a pub in a neighbouring suburb called Wadley to make trouble by flirting with the barmaid's husband. Patty reflects on how the suburbs of the same city can differ from each other:

> As the men of Brixton differed from the men of Clapham Junction, their mental bludgeons being larger or smaller as the case might be, so did Wadley men differ from the familiars of her own neighbourhood where all was sweet, rough and guileless.

However sweet and guileless the neighbourhood, Patty's destiny remains the same: cancer and suicide, the underside of her glorious physicality. Meanwhile newlyweds Roly and Elsie approach an equally physical threshold, and a future equally unknown.

Nearby, Patty's last lover is mourning for her, and for the money she used to give him to buy cigarettes. And Mrs Godshill is preparing to go out on the Common to preach.

References and Further Reading

Pamela Hansford Johnson, *This Bed Thy Centre*, 1935, republished by Five Leaves, 2012, with an introduction by Zoë Fairbairns

Pamela Hansford Johnson, *Here Today*, 1937

Pamela Hansford Johnson, *Important to Me*, 1974

Ishrat Lindblad, *Pamela Hansford Johnson*, Twayne Publishers, 1982

Love in the Library

In *This Bed Thy Centre*, Pamela Hansford Johnson charges the workaday public library with all sorts of erotic opportunities. Roly has a fling with the older, more experienced Patty Maginnis which springs from an encounter among the library book cases, where she had gone in search of 'something with lots of love in it'. Later, Roly rushes in to the library to escape Mrs Maginnis, and straight in to the embrace of Gwenny, 'the library girl' ('"That library cat", rails Mrs Maginnis, "... All scent and dirty neck, she is"').

Battersea Rise was well endowed with nearby public libraries, products of late Victorian civic-mindedness. From 53 Battersea Rise, still Pamela's home when she started writing her first novel (it now has a coffee bar on the ground floor), Battersea Public Library on Lavender Hill was just five minutes' walk away through the back streets. Built in 1889, it's still there, refurbished, imposing, and with the high ceilings, internal arches and sweeping staircase which give a feel of its original grandeur. This locality

Battersea Rise SW11

close to Clapham Junction is more 'neighbourhood', and less gentrified, than much of this corner of south London. Next door to the library, a solicitors' office stoutly proclaims: 'criminal defence specialists'.

Head in another direction from Battersea Rise and you come to Clapham Library, on a far corner of the Common, opposite Holy Trinity and alongside the elegance of Clapham Old Town. This too was built in 1889 — there must be a back story of municipal rivalry here, and the local government fault line persists, for Clapham is now in Lambeth and Battersea in Wandsworth. Clapham Library is the more compact and pleasing to the eye. And it was here, on the centenary of Pamela Hansford Johnson's birth, where her daughter and others gathered to open an exhibition about her life and writing. The day the exhibition closed was also Clapham Library's last day, after 123 years. It wasn't clear whether the building would be given over to top-end flats or a community arts centre.

Andrew Whitehead

Simon Blumenfeld
Jew Boy (1935)

Rachel Lichtenstein

When *Jew Boy* was first published in 1935 it caused a sensation. There was an enormous amount of controversy about and interest in the book, partly because of its deliberately provocative title and forceful political message but predominately for its gritty depiction of working-class Jewish life in Whitechapel.

Back then the majority of the population knew little about the religious practises and daily lives of the poverty stricken Jewish community who occupied much of the area. The Jewish East End was an entirely closed world to outsiders, and one which had not been written about in British fiction since Israel Zangwill published his bestselling novel back in 1892, *Children of the Ghetto*. It was a revelation to people to learn about the place and its inhabitants through reading *Jew Boy*. They were intrigued by the detailed descriptions of the Jewish festivals and celebrations. Amazed to learn about the complex network of self-supporting interconnected Jewish societies, clubs, theatres and institutions. Shocked to hear of the terrible working conditions in the tailoring sweatshops where thousands toiled up to eighteen hours a day. *Jew Boy* became an instant bestseller, which was widely reviewed and highly praised. For most readers it provided a window into an unfamiliar and exotic milieu.

For Simon Blumenfeld there was nothing mysterious or strange about the pre-war Jewish East End. It was a place he knew intimately and many elements of *Jew Boy* are undoubtedly autobiographical. Much like Alec, the protagonist of his novel, Blumenfeld was a second-generation immigrant Jew who had been born and raised in Whitechapel. He was a bright student, who dreamt of becoming a writer but like most young Jewish men living there during this period, his career choices were severely restricted by the depressed economic environment around him. After managing to win a coveted scholarship to the local grammar school, Blumenfeld then had to leave before completing his studies to help provide for the family. His first job was as a cap-maker (like his father), then later he became a presser, in the sweatshops he portrays so vividly in *Jew Boy*.

The East London of the 1930s was not the same place described by Zangwill half a century before. The younger generation were a completely different breed to their Yiddish speaking orthodox parents. They had an entirely different set of concerns. Many were dissatisfied by the confines of the Jewish ghetto. They didn't want to become tailors, furriers, cap-makers, pressers, cabinet-makers or taxi drivers. They dreamt, like Blumenfeld, of other more satisfying careers. I imagine Blumenfeld felt resentful towards his parents about having to leave school early and abandon his dream. There is a great deal of anger expressed in *Jew Boy* about the limited opportunities available to poor Jewish and gentile working-class young people during that period. There is also a realistic portrayal in the novel of the integration of different communities that was taking place in the area during that time, predominately between young Jews, gentiles and Irish migrants. My own father is typical of this generation. He was born in Whitechapel, to first generation immigrant parents, married a gentile woman, anglicised his surname and moved away from the area.

Another central feature of the novel, radical left-wing politics, was part of the landscape of Blumenfeld's early life. In Harry Blacker's 1993 film *Eastendings,* Blumenfeld reminisces about the furious debates he regularly witnessed on the pavements of Whitechapel as a child: 'there were more Communists and anarchists outside the synagogue arguing about the state of the world than there were inside praying. The activity was all out there, with these people milling around talking politics.' This energetic street-life has been perfectly captured in *Jew Boy* in a number of engaging and lively chapters that focus on Alec's fervent attachment to Communism.

I have recently discovered members of my own family were heavily involved in socialist politics during the same period. My grandfather's uncle, Yisroel Lichtenstein, was a prominent member of The General Jewish Labour Bund (in Lodz, Poland), a secular Jewish socialist party, which sort to unite all Jewish workers in the Russian Empire. Yisroel came to visit my grandparents in their Whitechapel home in Brick Lane in 1931, whilst on a fundraising tour for the party. My grandfather asked him if he would like to go and see the sights of

London; Big Ben, the Tower of London. 'Take me down to the docks,' he replied, 'I want to see how the workers of England live.'

This response could have been lifted directly from the pages of *Jew Boy* — which is a truly proletarian novel and the first literary work to depict in detail the radical, turbulent, politicized and divided Jewish East End of the 1930s.

Many of the scenes described in *Jew Boy* would have been familiar to my paternal grandparents, who met, married and settled in Brick Lane, after arriving from Poland as refugees in 1925. Much like Alec in the novel, they were poor Jews, who weren't particularly observant but had rich cultural and social lives. My grandfather (who was also called Alec) was one of the founding members of the *Literarishe Shabbes Nokhmitogs,* The Friends of Yiddish literary group, which had been established in 1936 by the Yiddish poet Avram Stencl. My grandparents attended the Yiddish theatres, frequented the dance halls, cafés, libraries and societies which are so personally described in *Jew Boy* and mingled with the poets, radicals, artists, boxers, musicians, politicians and workers who lived in the area at the time.

After the war, like many others from that community, they moved from the bombed out streets of east London to Westcliff, or Whitechapel-on-sea as many called it. Their new home in Essex became a refuge and meeting place for the characters they had met in the former Jewish East End. Half remembered details about meeting these lively people when I was a child, along with hearing my grandparent's stories about the artistic and vibrant atmosphere of Jewish Whitechapel, fuelled my fantasies about the place.

I moved there aged nineteen, filled with romantic notions about the past. I spent years living and working in the area, tracing and recording the stories of the rapidly diminishing Yiddish speaking community who still lived there. I met extraordinary characters, like the great east London historian, Professor Bill Fishman, and the tailor and Yiddish singer, Majer Bogdanski, who both looked back at a disappearing world with some nostalgia and longing. I devoured the literature that described the former Jewish quarter; the novels of Israel Zangwill, Wolf Mankowitz, Alexander Baron and Emanuel Litvinoff along with the plays of Bernard Kops and Arnold Wesker. Although these works do not shy away from talking about the tough living and working conditions that existed in the area before the war, they all have nostalgic or romanticised elements, which are almost completely missing from Simon Blumenfeld's hard hitting debut novel *Jew Boy*.

The tone of the book is set within the opening page, where we find Alec, a twenty-three year old tailor, being roughly awakened by his mother, who is screaming at him to get out of his 'stinking bed' and into the workshop. She is not the stereotypical doting *Yiddishe momma* of East End folklore but a furious, disappointed woman, who 'shouts violently all the time.'

After dressing hurriedly, Alec gulps down some tea and leaves the rundown flat for a windowless basement five minutes walk away, where he is confronted with the familiar and depressing scene of 'a dozen automata bent over the garments, sewing, machining, pressing, at top speed.' The relentless physical working day is described in minute detail, as are the cramped and unhygienic conditions 'with the steam and the sweat and the boss shouting like a madman.' After years spent hunched over the benches, Alec feels his mind has been ruined by the 'unrelenting drudgery' and physically he has become 'almost like a cripple, a limp, screwed-out rag'. Returning early from work he catches his mother fooling around with a heavy set middle-aged man and after a violent argument Alec abruptly leaves the family home and finds new lodgings nearby.

Although *Jew Boy* is often described as the definitive east London Jewish novel of the period, much of the action takes place in other parts of the metropolis and some of the central characters are not Jewish. The strongest and most rounded character is a working-class gentile woman called Olive, who is introduced to readers whilst on a date with Alec's womanising former school friend, Dave, in one of a number of scenes in the book set in Hyde Park. After canoodling with Dave in dark corners, Olive starts to panic when she realises the late hour and rushes back to her lodgings in Edgware Road. After knocking repeatedly on the door of the 'dirty little dwelling' where she lives, a 'savage toothless bitch' eventually opens the window and throws the contents of a chamber pot over Olive, whilst calling her a slut and telling her to come and collect 'her filthy rags in the morning.' Feeling terribly alone and dejected, Olive takes the night bus with Dave back to Whitechapel. They turn up at Alec's bedsit and persuade him to let Olive stay the night.

The next chapter opens in Stepney Green where thousands of Jewish protestors are massing for a demonstration to Hyde Park remonstrating against the persecution of Jews in Germany. During the 1930s there were numerous anti-Nazi demonstrations in London. The largest took place on 20th July 1933, when 50,000 Jews marched from the East End to Hyde Park. Blumenfield dedicates a whole chapter to this event, which is portrayed from Alec's perspective at the back with 'the reds'. As the Jewish demonstrators pass through the city, anti-Semitic and anti-communist abuse is hurled at them from bystanders: 'Damn Jews! They're all Communists, reds — revolutionaries!'

When the march eventually reaches Hyde Park 'another thirty thousand Jews' are waiting for them. Exhausted, Alec retires to a Lyons' teashop nearby where he bumps into another old friend, Sam. As the two men walk back towards the park, 'the dark masses of people thinning out behind them', they swap stories, discovering they now share the same political orientation along with a great passion for high culture. Alec is delighted to have found someone with whom to attend lectures, concerts and meetings.

The plot of the novel weakens slightly from this point onwards, as a series of highly unlikely meetings on West End streets occur. On his way home from the march, Alec bumps into Dave, who tells him Olive is now working as a live-in daily at his family home. Despite the low wages of most east London Jewish families at the time, having a gentile live in maid was a common occurrence, particularly for observant Jews who needed a *Shabbas goy* to light the fire for them and perform other menial tasks they were not permitted to complete because of religious restrictions.

On the morning of *Yom Kippur*, Olive rises early to help Mrs Bercovitch (Dave's mother) prepare the feast to be consumed after the *Kol Nidre* service. 'When the sun was down low at the end of the day, she had to put the soup on the stove, the roast in the oven. On the table, the decanter of spirit and kummel, one Dutch and one pickled herring, green olives, bread and the horseradish sauce.'

Mr and Mrs Bercovitch leave for synagogue, dressed in their finest clothes but Dave stays behind, claiming to be unwell. Worried about her son, Mrs Bercovitch returns early to find Olive 'crying bitterly in the corner.' Her clothes have been torn and there are 'red marks like scratches across her chest.' After being the victim of an attack, possibly a rape, Mrs Bercovitch calls Olive 'a whore' and throws her out of the house.

In the meantime Alec and Sam walk to the Workers' Circle (*Arbeiter Ring*), which was the central meeting place for working-class left wing activism in east London during the 1920s and '30s. The Circle had originally been formed as a socialist friendly society in 1909 by Russian immigrant cabinet-makers, to protect those in the community who were sick or unemployed. Over the years it developed into a cultural and social club as well, with an emphasis on self-improvement and socialist politics. In 1924 the society took over two buildings in Great Alie Street (just off Commerical Road), which became known as Circle House. It consisted of a large clubroom, meeting rooms and a concert hall. Blumenfield paints a wonderful portrait of the political make-up and great range of activities available there in the 1930s. When Alec enters the crowded clubroom 'the air was thick with steam from the urn and a bluey-grey fog of tobacco smoke.' A few old men were playing chess and dominoes in the corner and at the back of the room sat a man with a beard reading the Jewish anarchist paper *Freiheit*. Alec ordered some supper at the canteen; herring, black bread, lemon tea, and sat amongst the other Marxists, poets, Communists, writers, Labour Party members, anarchists, Bundists and Zionists gathered there.

Later in the evening Alec attends a classical concert in the building where a 'beautiful blonde' in the audience distracts him. During the interval he buys her a cup of tea, which she snottily accepts from the 'penniless, skinny little Jew tailor.' Alec fantasises about her during the second half but she leaves before the end. Sexually frustrated and consumed by desire he wanders alone around the West End, tempted by prostitutes, angry and dejected.

Dave (who has moved into Alec's bedsit by this time) continues to date numerous women, with semi-disastrous consequences, before being forced into an arranged marriage with a wealthy older Jewish woman. The wedding scene takes place in a typical, overcrowded Whitechapel synagogue. Blumenfeld intimately describes the different characters of the community, from the 'jabbering' women sat in the balcony, to the 'greybeards' arguing about 'what rabbi Akiba said' to the youngsters discussing boxing, dogs and horse racing. Throughout the service 'the throbbing dynamo of conversation rose above the organ.'

Alec's luck temporarily changes when he meets a nice sensible Jewish girl called Sarah on a Sunday ramble in the countryside. The most affectionate description of the former Jewish East End occurs when he visits her Whitechapel home for Sunday lunch. Inside the small flat he listens to Sarah sing Hebrew melodies around the piano, eats a wonderful home cooked kosher meal and plays chess in the parlour with her brothers. By the end of the evening he has decided Sarah is 'just the girl for him'.

Soon after Alec accompanies Sarah to visit her sister in the suburbs of Barnes, where she lives in a 'clean semi-detached villa' with a 'tall and fair' gentile college professor. A comical scene follows as Alec becomes determined to 'out' Sarah's sister in front of her posh gentile lunch guest and 'let the whole neighbourhood know she is Jewish.' Although Alec is more than aware of the limitations of Jewish east London, with all 'its faults, its turbulent excitable people and habits,' he cannot understand how 'any intelligent person could exchange that for the anaemic narrow-minded dreariness of suburbia.'

As the relationship between Sarah and Alec progresses he pushes her into coming away with him for the weekend but she fails to turn up. After sobbing into his pillow, Alec argues with a poet and his cronies at the Workers' Circle then wanders around the West End again like a lost soul. On the street he bumps into Dave and Olive. Then in a very hard to believe double coincidence, Dave's new brother-in-law also appears on the same street corner and Dave quickly dumps Olive on Alec. By now Olive is earning a living as a West End prostitute, which is told to the reader in a very matter of fact way. Olive invites Alec back to her flat, where he loses his virginity and after that he continues to see Olive 'pretty frequently.'

Alec regards Olive as 'another who had never had a decent break from life' like him. Soon they move in together, finding a bed-sit 'on the top floor of a dirty three-storeyed house in north-east London.' Olive starts waitressing in a café and Alec continues to work as a tailor in Whitechapel.

After saving for months, the couple treat themselves to a day trip to Southend-on-Sea. Disembarking from the train they breathe 'in the keen salty air' and take a stroll along the pier. Alec tells Olive he hasn't felt so fit and well for years. After hiring some deck chairs, Olive happily exclaims, 'If there were a heaven, it must be some place like this, where you could just lounge about... and do nothing for hours, and hours and hours.' They spend the last of their savings on fish and chips, a ride on a trolley bus and a cruise on the *Mary Ann*: 'Out to the ocean-going liners, and back for sixpence.'

I expect my own grandparents took a very similar day trip from Whitechapel to Southend in the 1930s. I remember my grandfather saying to me that he still felt like he was on permanent holiday, even after living there for over forty years.

Back in Whitechapel life is worse than ever for Alec after the controversial Bedaux system is introduced to his workshop, forcing the workers to 'work twice as hard for the same money.' Alec instigates a strike, making his boss determined to lay him off as soon as an opportunity arises.

Life continues in an unchanging pattern. Although they can barely afford the rent, Alec is desperate for culture and encouraged by Olive, he attends a symphony concert in the West End. Standing happily amongst the chattering crowd, 'drunk' with the 'wealth of unaccustomed beauty' he relishes every moment. In the bar he bumps into the blonde from the Workers' Circle and although he feels terribly guilty, he leaves with her. She takes him to Perelli's — a cellar bar filled with 'bohemians, tobacco smoke and the clattering of plates.' Alec is nauseated by the place with its 'fake intellectuals, fake Communists and fake artists.'

The girl invites him back to her beautifully furnished flat nearby. Alec cannot believe the size of the place and soon becomes filled with jealousy and a repressed hatred for the girl and her privileged lifestyle. They start to argue and she accuses Alec and 'his people of only being guests here.' Fuming he tells her about his father, 'an emigrant running away from the Czar's hell' who came to London a pauper, slaved for twenty years in the workshops, ruined his health and died before he was fifty. The girl only laughed at him. Feeling murderous towards 'the beautiful bitch' he 'kissed her fiercely, biting her lips wildly, trying to dominate her, to make her feel him and accept him; and she submitted, yet he felt that aloofness all the while.'

He returns home, smelling of perfume and poor Olive sobs herself to sleep, begging him not to leave her. Soon after she falls pregnant. Determined not to drag 'another soul into this filthy world' she tries to get rid of the baby by taking boiling hot baths and lifting heavy weights but 'the seed still flourished in her womb.' Eventually she has an illegal abortion. Much like the sex scenes in the book and the probable rape scene, all details are left to the reader's imagination. Olive stays in bed for three days, 'her face drained of blood' before returning to work. She doesn't mention the baby or the abortion to Alec.

In November, Alec is given notice to quit the workshop and fails to find another job. 'He had no head for books now, the problem of living took up all his time, worrying about the future; the terrible, uncertain, ever darkening future.' Grim scenes follow as Alec joins the 'long grey line' of men at the Labour Exchange, with 'tired pale faces, stooping shoulders and threadbare coats.'

As the weeks of Alec's unemployment drag on Olive tries to get him interested in working the markets. He visits an old friend who has a stall in Petticoat Lane but after spending a day helping out: 'rolling and unrolling fabrics, arranging and re-arranging, all for a lousy few pence' Alec returns home tired and dejected with 'all his hunches pricked flat.'

The next day he returns to Whitechapel, for the first time since he moved in with Olive. After a trip to the reference library he wanders aimlessly towards Aldgate, passing the Odessa Yiddish restaurant, where he is drawn inside by an 'overpowering gust of appetizing smells.' Inside a matronly woman serves him a Russian Jewish feast. Feeling nostalgic he makes his way towards his mother's house but finding her to be out he returns to Whitechapel High Street, 'the broadest pavement in the world' where he reminisces about promenading there in his smartest clothes, 'chasing girls, snatching kisses.' He stops outside Gardiners Corner and talks to a group of taxi drivers about potential work, only to find the taxi business is 'all played out' as well.

Driven nearly to the point of despair, Alec wanders aimlessly around the city, eventually making his way to Speakers' Corner in

Hyde Park, where he listens to a black activist called Jo-Jo speak about the problems affecting workers all over the world. Jo-Jo helps Alec see that his miserable situation is part of a wider global problem, he talks about the persecution of blacks in Africa, the murder of the Chinese, the abuse of women in the South of America. With his 'eyes lit up, as if a flame had suddenly crackled into life,' Jo-Jo tells Alec about his recent visit to Russia, where he was treated as an equal, 'like a comrade.'

In the most romanticized domestic scene in the whole novel Alec visits Jo-Jo's flat, in 'a tall, dark-grey block of tenements.' Inside the welcoming front room he sees 'a broad negress' with a face that radiated 'warmth and life' sat beside a fire, with a chubby baby on her knee and a small boy playing on the floor nearby. Alec plays with the children and for the first time contemplates how nice it would be to have one of his own.

Walking home, inspired by Jo-Jo, Alec decides to emigrate to Russia. The ever patient Olive reluctantly agrees to accompany him there but the dream, like so many others, is 'pricked flat' when the Russian consulate rejects his application.

The final scene in the book takes place back in Hyde Park, during another anti-fascist demonstration. During the march Jo-Jo is arrested and Alec is 'violently brushed into the gutter by the powerful impact of a horse.' At this moment Alec decides it is 'criminal to stay out [of the Party] any longer.' The book ends with the rallying cries, 'freedom for the oppressed' and 'No Peace until the disinherited regain the Earth!' Alec seems to finally find salvation in revolutionary politics.

This ending seemed most unsatisfactory to me as a modern reader until I was reminded by the writer Ken Worpole (who has written a brilliant introduction to the new edition of *Jew Boy*) of the dangers of having a condescending attitude to the past in the present. He pointed out that 'we really do not know what it feels like now to have lived in that time, to feel the very real threat and danger of fascism. There was a great pressure both close to home and on a global scale. People really did feel that passionate about Russia and Communism.' This sentiment is backed up by Rabbi Lionel Blue, who also appears in the film *Eastendings,* where he talks about how idealistic the majority of young Jews were about communism before the war, describing the depths of their passion as being akin to 'a religious movement'.

In my opinion *Jew Boy* is not as strong a novel as Blumenfeld's next book *Phineas Kahn: Portrait of an Immigrant* (published in 1937), which is a marvellously written fictionalised account of his wife's family's story of migration from Russia to East London.

There are weaknesses in the plot of *Jew Boy*, but despite this the novel is extraordinarily rich and there is still nothing else quite like it. The Jewish Whitechapel of the 1930s Blumenfeld describes, with its communists and anarchists, sweatshops and theatres, cafés and libraries, slaughterhouses and concert halls, has completely disappeared. I for one feel immensely grateful that Blumenfeld took the time and care to write about the place, which for all its problems, 'had life and colour and throbbed with vitality.'

References and Further Reading

Simon Blumenfeld, *Phineas Kahn: portrait of an immigrant*, 1937, republished by Lawrence and Wishart, 1987

G. Black, *Jewish London — an Illustrated History*, Breedon, 2003

Harry Blacker, *Just Like It Was: Memoirs of the Mittel East*, Vallentine Mitchell, 1974

William J. Fishman, *East End Jewish Radicals 1875–1914,* Duckworth, 1975

East End 1888, Duckworth, 1988

Willy Goldman, *East End My Cradle*, Faber and Faber, 1940

Joe Jacobs, *Out of the Ghetto — My Youth in the East End: Communism and Fascism 1913–1939,* Janet Simon, 1978, republished by Phoenix Press, 1991

Tony Kushner and Nadia Valman (eds), *Remembering Cable Street: Fascism and Anti-Fascism in British Society,* Vallentine Mitchell, 2000

Rachel Lichtenstein and Iain Sinclair, *Rodinsky's Rooom,* Granta, 1999

Emanuel Litvinoff, *Journey Through a Small Planet,* Michael Joseph, 1972

Phil Piratin, *Our Flag Stays Red,* Thames Publications, 1948, republished by Lawrence and Wishart, 1978

Raphael Samuel, *East End Underworld: Chapters in the Life of Arthur Harding,* Routledge & Kegan Paul, 1981

H. Srebrnik, *London Jews and British Communism 1935-45,* Vallentine Mitchell, 1995

Arnold Wesker, *Chicken Soup With Barley,* (play first performed Coventry, 1958)

Jerry White, *Rothschild Buildings: Life in an East End Tenement Block 1887–1920*, Routledge & Kegan Paul, 1980

Ken Worpole, *Dockers & Detectives*, Verso, 1983, republished by Five Leaves, 2008

Ken Worpole's introduction to new edition of *Jew Boy* published by London Books in 2011

East London Today

The only visible sign of a former Jewish presence in Whitechapel High Street today is a large Star of David above Albert's clothing store at no.88, which marks the site of a former Jewish daily newspaper. The last kosher eatery in the area *Blooms* (the location of the film *Eastendings)* closed in 1996 and relocated to Golders Green. In 2005, the Whitechapel Library, formerly known as the University of the Ghetto, where anarchists, poets and artists would meet, shut down. It has since become a part of the gallery next door. The last overtly functioning Jewish business in the area, A. Elfes Monumental Stone Masons, closed their showroom on Brick Lane in 2010. There are not even enough Jewish dead in east London to warrant them being there any longer. A. Elfes have since moved to Ilford and have branched out from making Hebrew inscribed headstones, which had been their core business since 1894, to producing Muslim memorials and granite and marble kitchen worktops.

I recently visited Alie Street (formerly Great Alie Street) to see if any remnants of the Workers' Circle remained. Crossing Leman Street, where the Jewish Temporary Shelter was once based, I made my way down Alie Street, passing a Halal restaurant, two strip clubs and a number of anonymous looking modern office blocks. I knew the original Circle House building had been destroyed in the blitz (the Workers' Circle moved to Hackney in the '50s before dissolving completely in 1985) so I didn't expect to find much. I found the White Swan pub, which used to be a synagogue and later became the Half Moon Theatre. I went inside and spoke with the Australian landlady who had been running the bar for about ten years. She had no idea a synagogue had ever existed on that site and was surprised to learn that a sizeable Jewish community had once lived in the area.

Back on the street I called the historian David Rosenberg, to see if he could help me find the location of the former Workers' Circle. He told me it was listed in old trade directories as being based at 15 Great Alie Street. Walking further down the street, I came across a large new development at 14–20 Alie Street. The hoardings outside the as yet unfinished building advertised 'luxurious apartments for sale,' whose primary selling points were their proximity to the City and Canary Wharf and the galleries and restaurants of Brick Lane.

Rachel Lichtenstein

John Sommerfield
May Day (1936)

JOHN KING

olitical, experimental, essential — *May Day*, first published in
1936, is a work of fiction so sharply written its prose still excites,
so relevant it could be describing events in modern day Britain.
The core of the book is straightforward and familiar. The owners of
an east London factory are bullying their workers into speeding up
production, cutting corners to increase profit margins. The union is
doing its best to fight back, considering strike action as it looks to the
wider movement for inspiration. Beyond the factory gates a broader
rebellion is brewing, the events that follow taking place across a three-
day period leading to industrial action by busmen and a march into
central London on May 1st.

Driven by author John Sommerfield's youthful communism, *May
Day* is clearly anti-capitalist, but it is also honest enough to look at the
inner feelings of rich as well as poor. In literature, and the arts in
general, then as now, the common people are stereotyped or belittled,
or, if they are lucky, treated as curiosities before being dismissed to
the margins. So when a novel is written from a more sympathetic position it is natural for the author to want to reverse the prejudice.
Sommerfield resists the temptation. This is important, as it shows the
truth that selfishness isn't confined to capitalists, while empathy
doesn't always belong to socialists. Even so, capitalism remains the
enemy, and working-class characters dominate, but by considering the
foibles of human nature the author earns the trust of his readership.
Sommerfield believes the system is bad for everyone, that it damages
exploiters as well as the exploited.

May Day's strongest figures believe in the work ethic, that earning
what you have is healthy for mind and soul. This stance is shared by

107

the working-class Seton brothers and Sir Edwin Langfier, owner of the Carbon Works. The first to appear is James Seton — communist and seaman — who is on a ship anchored off Gravesend, waiting to return to London. Soon after this we meet his brother John, sister-in-law Martine, their child and dog, sleeping in a house near the Harrow Road. John works at Langfier's, his boss Sir Edwin a decent man who has lost his real power in a deal with Amalgamated Industrial Enterprises, a big organisation driven solely by a desire to increase profits. The paternal factory owner is being replaced by a different sort of entrepreneur. Capitalism is changing, expanding, moving towards future models.

London is present from the start: 'The sky oozes soot and aeroplanes and burns by night with an electric glow. Railways writhe like worms under the clay, tangled with spider's webs and mazes of electric cables, drains and gaspipes. Then there are the eight or nine million people.' There is an almost filmic quality about many of the novel's descriptive passages, a spliced montage of images and interaction. The industrial landscape is stark and at times brutal, but it is also beautiful, tunnelling out of human inventiveness, the creation of men. All the while spring pushes through the stone and bricks of the city. Bulbs sprout. Blossom appears on trees. Nature won't be crushed. Hope fills the pages, as the future promises new life. *May Day* crisscrosses the city, moving from the docks and terraces of the East End to the bustling market on Portobello Road to the green spaces of Hyde Park — and back again. Following the book's initial release *Left Review* said: 'Sommerfield gives us the true London — smelled, seen, understood'. And the story always returns to those eight or nine million souls. London is its people.

This belief in the individual shows itself in the large number of characters who make up *May Day*. No single voice dominates, no central character is in control. The political is made very personal as a series of smaller sketches connect to form the bigger picture. Scenes shift and faces change, but the links are neat and effective — some complementary, others adding contrast and conflict — and they always push the novel forward. This approach could easily have collapsed in on itself, the book left weak and lacking focus, but the threads are tight and can allow deviation, the final result a complex yet easy-to-read slab of true rebel fiction. John Sommerfield is brave, takes risks with his structure and prose, and it pays off. Reading the book today is like watching a disappeared London through a cut in time, standing at the bar of a grand old gin palace as familiar faces in thirties' clothes pass by outside, the windows turned into a flickering silver screen.

108

Much political fiction is dull and dogmatic, but *May Day* insists this doesn't have to be the case, the experimental structure and fluency it encourages giving the book a dynamic that comes out of the author. Sommerfield lived the life — losing teeth in political punch-ups on the streets of London before going off to fight with a Republican machine gun unit in the Spanish Civil War. His friend and fellow writer John Cornford was killed in the conflict, but on his return he found that *he* had been reported dead, his obituary appearing in two newspapers. Sommerfield's *Volunteer in Spain* was published in 1937 and dedicated to Cornford, but he felt that he had been rushed in writing it, despite mainly positive coverage.

During the Second World War, he served as an armour fitter for a Spitfire squadron, based first in Burma and then India, and while stationed near Karachi taught himself Urdu. An incident occurred at this time which shows the impression *May Day* had made. As a corporal and communist, Sommerfield was chosen by the other men to complain about the food being served. The officer he went to see listened and then stood up and walked over to a filing cabinet, pulled out a file and dropped it on the desk in front of him. Sommerfield was clearly known to the authorities.

He kept writing for John Lehmann's *New Writing* during the war, and a new book, *The Survivors*, appeared in 1947. A collection of short stories that drew on his time in the RAF, it was followed by more novels in the post-war years — *The Adversaries, The Inheritance, North West Five* and *The Imprinted*, while *May Day* was republished in 1984. He also wrote for the Mass Observation movement, the Ministry of Information's film unit and for various advertising companies, but *May Day* stands out as his greatest book.

Some readers might find *May Day*'s massive cast of characters and open-minded approach odd, given that Sommerfield was a member of the Communist Party when he wrote the book, but these were different days and the story captures the optimism many idealists living in Britain felt during the 1930s. The idea of a classless society seemed a real possibility in those pre-war years, while the perversions of communist rule were as yet unknown. Writing later, in 1984, Sommerfield described *May Day* as 'communist romanticism' rather than 'socialist realism'. He goes on to call it 'enthusiastic, simple-minded political idealism'. This is true, but idealism has to be better than cynicism, and the book *is* socially aware and realistic, whatever the author's post-Stalin feelings.

When the book was republished in 1984, John Sommerfield compared living conditions with those experienced in 1936, commenting that the 'truly rich and powerful' carried on regardless, as if nothing

109

had changed apart from 'electronic improvements in the means of selling goods and bending minds'. This was long before the arrival of the internet and the digital blitzkreig, the casual doling out of easy credit and the massive levels of personal debt that followed.

To understand London and the politics of the city in the 1930s, *May Day* is a great place to start. The first day dawns, and the Thames is heaving with ships, the great dockyards of east London throbbing with activity, and soon we are inside the Carbon Works where 'two hundred and forty girls in ugly grey overalls and caps live, breathe and think, their fragile flesh confused with the greasy embraces of steel tentacles'. They are on piecework rather than proper pay, and the bosses are demanding a 'speed-up'. These young women are kept on until they are twenty-one and then let go, as their rate would have to be increased. The conditions are cramped and dangerous, and the girls are tired. Machines roar and hands are mangled.

As trouble brews, Martine is anxious about her husband, John, who — after a spell without work — has a job as a carpenter at Carbon Works. (Sommerfield also worked as a carpenter and spent periods unemployed.) Martine worries about what a strike will mean for her family. It is fine for her husband to stand up for what he believes is honourable and right, but how is she expected to feed her family? How will they live if the strike fails and he loses his job? These same arguments are prominent today. Idealism faces the realities of food and shelter, the power of the bosses and those on their payroll. *May Day* was written at a time of high trade union membership, before unions were hobbled by smears and legislation, and yet despite their power in the 1930s those same human concerns were obviously a factor in the life of workers. Then there is the union boss whose nest has been nicely feathered, a working man who has been corrupted and refuses to rock the boat, frustrating and alienating his members.

The fourth estate is present and correct. Long before Rupert Murdoch and Fortress Wapping, a fictional sub-editor on a leading newspaper — Pat Morgan, a former comrade of James Seton — makes his mark. Pat's workmate is Vernon (the name of John Sommerfield's father), a journalist — and through their work Morgan sees what the newspaper's owner is planning to write about the busmen and their May Day protest. He visits a printer called Jackson, an older communist, and we are left with the impression that justice will be done by this man, who is a living ghost inside a propagandist's machine.

May Day belongs to a British rebel fiction that rises up every so often before being dismissed and/or belittled — books such as Simon Blumenfeld's *Jew Boy*, Robert Tressell's *The Ragged Trousered Philanthropists* and Alan Sillitoe's *Saturday Night and Sunday*

Morning. This is ambitious, honest fiction from writers drawing on their own lives and beliefs, an English language tradition mirrored across the Atlantic in the writing of Americans such as Upton Sinclair, Hubert Selby Jr, Charles Bukowski and Thom Jones.

The 1930s were a golden period for this sort of literature, and Sommerfield was one of several young men making their mark. Just as important was the presence of publishers willing to print fiction that dealt with working-class life in a realistic and honest way. These authors refused to self-censor and, for a while, reached the public in dramatic fashion. Today the likes of *May Day* might be regarded as 'cult' fiction, a term that can easily convert to kitsch and lead to casual dismissal, but this is an important book, part of a canon beyond the one inflicted on us by academics, marketing departments and the usual array of media lackeys. These writers were excited by life. Contemporaries of Sommerfield include the likes of James Curtis, Gerald Kersh, Alexander Baron and Robert Westerby.

It's likely John Sommerfield knew Kersh and Curtis, who both drank in the Fitzroy Tavern, in north Soho, as this was one of Sommerfield's haunts when he was in the West End. Kersh was a larger-than-life character from west London — born in Teddington, living in Shepherd's Bush, with family links to Soho — while Curtis was from a wealthier background, his fierce socialism meaning he turned his back on the easy life, working as a hotel porter after the war. Both died broke, Curtis living alone in Kilburn, Kersh married to Flossie and dodging creditors in upstate New York. Sommerfield was more fortunate, living in and around Kentish Town after the war with his second wife Molly Moss, an illustrator who designed several of his book covers, by all accounts happy, content, optimistic. Blumenfeld, meanwhile, became a leading theatre critic for *The Stage* and was working until his death at the age of 97.

John Sommerfield was a pub man, the sort of character who liked a pint and chat, the company of other human beings, with firm beliefs but an open-mind. *May Day* comes out of the public house, the common ground where society used to meet irrespective of age, class, politics. The novel was published at a time when the General Strike of 1926 was still fresh in the collective memory, and this is referred to several times in the text, while the nature of the Carbon Works, with its female workforce stirs memories of the match girls' strike of 1888, which took place in Bow, east London — not too far from Sommerfield's fictional factory.

When tragedy hits the Carbon Works, it is Ivy Cutford who steps forward and finds her voice, mobilising the other girls in a doubly brave move given the position of working girls at the time. Some of the most downtrodden members of the workforce stand up and fight back. The May Day march is passing the Carbon Works... flesh meets machine... the factory gates are locked... mounted police fight the marchers... a truncheon is raised in the air. It is one of the most symbolic and dramatic passages in the book. The great workers' posters of the period appear in the reader's mind.

Another young woman, Jenny Hardy, has escaped the factory floor through a relationship with Amalgamated Industrial man Dartry, who has set her up as his mistress in a nice flat in a wealthy part of London. She is given money and jewellery and keeps a secret boyfriend, but Sommerfield undermines the initial dislike we feel for this married exploiter with a glimpse of his inner loneliness. Jenny wants the good things in life, lacks the dignity and morals of Ivy and her friends Molly Davis and Daisy Miller, and so the clear lines of life are blurred once more. There is a longing sitting between the lines of *May Day*, a realisation of the emptiness people feel when they are alone. There is a lack of love in the lives of several of the rich characters, as if a trade-off has somehow been made, and yet, interestingly, there is this same sadness in James Seton, a free spirit who has separated himself from the masses in order to fight for his beliefs.

May Day tells us about our own lives. It shows London as it was in the mid-1930s, and London as it is today. For anyone who believes in the unchanging drives of humans, the repetition of events and the lessons that can genuinely be learned from history, there are clear warnings. The book ends in an ongoing conflict between controllers and controlled on the streets of the city. The last line reads: 'Everyone has agreed on the need for a big change.' Those words could easily have been written today, and yet *May Day,* against the odds, still manages to leave us with a feeling of optimism for the future.

References and Further Reading

John Sommerfield, *May Day*. 1936. Republished in 1984 with an introduction by Andy Croft and an author's note by Sommerfield. This note is also included in the 2010 London Books edition, which has an introduction by John King.

John Sommerfield, *Volunteer in Spain,* 1937

John Sommerfield, *Trouble in Porter Street,* 1939

H. Gustav Klaus, *The Literature of Labour: 200 years of working-class writing*, Harvester Press, 1985

David Smith, *Socialist Propaganda in the Twentieth-Century British Novel*, Macmillan, 1978

A Toast to *May Day*

The London of *May Day* is as much about flavours as specific locations, and yet the book captures local characteristics that linger to this day. The story has its roots in working-class east London, but it also shows the bosses in and around Hyde Park before dipping back into the humble streets of west London. One of the joys of fiction is that the reader gets to create their own imagery, so for a version of the Carbon Works I would take a stroll around Silvertown and end up spending some time looking at the Tate and Lyle factory. Relatives of mine lived across the road long before *May Day* was published, their descendants then shifting into Canning Town and East Ham, and it is from these areas that the author created the factory and its workers.

There is no better place to connect with that tougher, magical London of the past than in a pub, but it has to be one that hasn't been turned into a EuroBar and stuffed full of cloned trendies. For a taste of the old East End why not try the Salmon and Ball in Bethnal Green, across from the library and Barmy Park. This pub is friendly and down-to-earth, while many years ago it was a meeting place for Mosley's Blackshirts, around about the time *May Day* was first published. John Sommerfield may well have known about this pub. Another decent choice is the Pride Of Spitalfields, just off Brick Lane.

The march in *May Day* heads for Marble Arch, but why not stop off for a rest on the way? The Fitzroy Tavern, just north of Oxford Street, was one of John Sommerfield's favourites, as mentioned above. With Martin Knight, I met John's son Peter here following the London Books publication of *May Day*. We arranged it for midday when the pub is quiet and after a while it felt as if John was there with us — which in a way I suppose he was.

Following the First World War there seems to have been a big shift of people from east London into the new houses being built in west London. I found this in the stories of older people I knew growing up, who were born in Hounslow in the 1920s, their parents coming from Hackney, Poplar, East Ham. So maybe east and west London aren't as far apart as they have seemed in my lifetime, and this is reflected in the fact that one of the main characters in *May Day*, John Seton, lives near the Harrow Road but works at the Carbon Works. It is only really the power of the West End that divides these two sides of London.

West London comes alive on the Portobello Road, where Martine is out shopping with her son. I first went here with my father in the late 1960s as a boy, and the book's description feels exactly as I remember the place then, even if it was written more than thirty years earlier. We watched Dave Brock — who went on to form Hawkwind and who played with and knew my dad — busking in the street. Sommerfield grew up here and the Earl of Lonsdale and the Portobello Gold are two spots where it would be worth toasting the man. After a while you might cut through time and see Martine and her son outside, and when you come back inside perhaps you will recognise the lad in the old man sitting nearby, smiling at his own memories, nursing a pint of London Pride.

John King

Patrick Hamilton
Hangover Square (1941)

JOHN LUCAS

'W aiting for the end, boys, waiting for the end.' William Empson included 'Just a Smack at Auden' in his second collection, *The Gathering Storm*. The poem, which is not much more than a casual squib, genially disparages the note of premonitory gloom which Empson takes to characterize the MacSpaunday group of poets — Auden, Spender, MacNeice and Day Lewis. 'Waiting for the end, boys, waiting for the end./What is there to be or do?/What's become of me or you... Sitting in cold fears, boys, waiting for the end.' By the time *The Gathering Storm* came out, in 1940, Auden was, of course, in America, where the waiting would continue. But for the others the wait was over. The war which all foresaw had begun.

A year later Patrick Hamilton's *Hangover Square* appeared. This remarkable novel, set in the period between the Munich agreement and the declaration of war on 3 September 1939, focusses on the doings of a group of Londoners who drift from pub to pub, habitually drunk or hungover, shiftless, hollow, enervate, their poisonous lack of care for anyone or anything diluted by the kind of ennui that would have made even St. Augustine blink, and who are, though they lack the wit to know it, waiting for the end — not merely theirs but the way of life they lackadaisically embody. Among them, though not really of them, is George Harvey Bone, a large, melancholy man, whose innate good feelings are made soggy by drink and a hopeless infatuation for Netta Longdon. Netta has film-star good looks and exudes a tawdry glamour which she uses to exploit Bone's devotion to her in order to get from him what little money he has. She needs the cash in order to buy herself more drink and she needs Bone himself in

115

order to gain an introduction to men he knows, men who may be able to help her in what she occasionally allows herself to think of as her career.

For Netta has an idle fancy that she is an actress. Idle is the right word for it. Netta is beautiful but talentless and she is entirely devoid of commitment, to work, to love, to loyalty. And what is true of her, is true of the others in her circle. Her part-time lover, Peter, is a vicious ne'er do well — Fascination Fledgeby masquerading as Lord Lucan, we might say — among whose dubious achievements are his wounding a man at a fascist political rally and killing another while driving a car, drunk. Peter wears a polo-neck sweater and sports a small moustache as a 'uniform'. By such means he tries to single himself out as an 'ultra-masculine' man, and like Netta and Mickey, another of her hangers-on, Peter regards the Munich agreement, which we hear of at the beginning of the novel, as providing the licence for a stupendous drinking orgy. 'They went raving mad, they weren't sober for a whole week after Munich. — it was just in their line. They *liked* Hitler, really: they didn't hate him, anyway. They liked Musso, too. And how they cheered old Umbrella. Oh yes, it was their cup of tea all right, was Munich.'

Bone *doesn't* like Hitler. On the other hand, caught in the net of his would-be lover's graceless charms, without a job — his erstwhile friend and business-partner Bob Barton has taken off for Canada — and lacking much by way of a purpose in life, George Harvey Bone seeks a variety of refuges from the existence he neither wants nor understands. One way out is to believe that the worst — that is, war — might never happen. In this, he is not alone. The novel, which charts with aplomb the calendar from winter through to late summer 1939, shows how with spring may come hope. George's school friend, Johnnie Littlejohn, a now-successful business man attached to a theatrical agency, whom he encounters by chance and with whom he renews a friendship, allows himself to think as he strolls through Leicester Square on a warm day early in the year, that all is fine:

Fine for the King and Queen in Canada...
Fine for the salvaging of the *Thetis*...
Fine for the West Indian team...
Fine for the I.R.A. and their cloakrooms...
Fine for Hitler in Czechoslovakia...
Fine for Mr Chamberlain, who believed it was peace in our time — his umbrella a parasol!...
You couldn't believe that it would ever break, that the bombs had to fall.

This is a good deal subtler than may at first glance seem to be the case. Johnnie's benign view of even the contemporary disaster of the

116

Thetis (a submarine sunk in the Mersey in which all those on board in fact died) is not so much a way of whistling in the dark as a sudden irrational but understandable surge of optimism. The IRA's campaign of bombing cloakrooms and postal stores (one went off at Nottingham's Midland Station) was aimed at property rather than people. Why, even Hitler's march into Czechoslovakia — that 'far-off country' as Chamberlain called it — might be no bad thing if it ended his desire to over-run Europe. And the fact is that many readers coming across this passage in 1941 would be bound to shift uneasily as they digested its implication. For as C.L. Mowat points out in his splendid *Britain Between the Wars, 1918–1940*, probably a majority of Chamberlain's countrymen supported his 'triumph' at Munich, even if Hitler's subsequent invasion of Poland caused them to denounce it. From the autumn of 1938 until the spring of 1939, the illusion that there could be Peace in Our Time was widely shared. Perhaps the end might not come, might be endlessly deferred. Or it may be more accurate to say that most people, especially those with memories of the years 1914–18, fervently hoped that another war might still, somehow, be averted. And who can blame them?

II

Not Bone, certainly. What separates him from his 'chums' — as Peter calls the wretched group of soaks and leeches who infest Earl's Court — is that he actually wants to like people. Bone is a man of peace. And so, having at one point gone into a bank in order to cash a cheque, he thinks as he walks up Earl's Court Road that the bank clerk with whom he has done business has treated him as an equal, which is certainly not how he is treated by Netta and the rest of her vicious set. 'He believed that this bank clerk was one of those few, warm-hearted, indiscriminate, easy-going people, who were naturally unaware of any superiority or inferiority in individuals, or who, even if they were aware of such things, were not impressed by, or at all interested in them.' This belief isn't put to the test. We never meet the bank clerk again. But it's of no consequence. Bone's view of the clerk matters not because it's a right estimation — for all we know it could be wrong — but because it reveals his own capacity to think well of others, especially as the others he thinks well of have one thing in common: an indifference to 'any superiority or inferiority in individuals.' At some instinctive level, Bone is a person whose innate decency is expressive of a democratic impulse. Call it comradeship.

That said, who exactly is George Harvey Bone? Or to put the question differently: why does Hamilton make this amiable, ineffective,

117

insecure, warm-hearted but hapless man the protagonist of his novel? George of England, but apparently no slayer of dragons. This George is more of a Dobbin. In some respects he is quite like George Bowling, the protagonist of the almost exact contemporary *Coming Up For Air* by "George Orwell". I put Orwell's name in quotes merely to remind us that Eric Blair's choice of pseudonym could perhaps be read as a token of his desire to be a kind of spokesman for England. George speaks for itself. And Orwell is the name of a small river that runs into the sea near Southwold, where Eric Blair's parents retired after years in the Colonial Service. The opening of *Hangover Square* is set at Hunstanton, Christmas time 1938, where George is staying at the house of an aged aunt. Same sea-coast, though this time Norfolk rather than Suffolk. But neither, surely, much to do with England in the late 1930s.

Which is Hamilton's point. Or rather, because novels don't exist to make a point, it's what we can infer from all that Hamilton shows us. George's aunt embodies old-style decencies. Her washed-out kindliness is a world away from the rootless, amoral decadence of Hangover Square. Bone belongs to the Square but he is not really of it. At the beginning of the novel we are even told that he would prefer to be a countryman. 'He wanted a cottage in the country — yes, a good old cottage in the country — and he wanted Netta as his wife. No children, just Netta — and to live with her happily and quietly ever afterwards.' In your dreams, as the saying goes.

But it was, as it still is, a dream widely shared by his countrymen. In the country, there you feel free. Hunstanton is one version of the dream. Another, to which Bone is repeatedly drawn, lies in reaching Maidenhead. There, he keeps reminding himself, he had for a brief period of his childhood been happy, living with a sister now dead, before he was sent away to public school. Maidenhead is his vision of the paradisal place where he can recover innocence and happiness. This is very like George Bowling's dream of Lower Binfield in *Coming Up For Air*. And not this novel alone. The yearning away from the corruptions of the city aligns Bone's dream vision of Maidenhead with a number of novels reaching back at least as far as *Our Mutual Friend*, and taking in Margaret Harkness's fine novel *Out of Work*, and, admittedly more teasingly, Sylvia Townsend Warner's *Lolly Willowes*. In all these novels — the list could be greatly lengthened — the main characters, trapped in city life, imagine that the rural alternative will guarantee their better health. But for all, disillusionment awaits. You can't escape history, you can't escape yourself.

This of course prompts the question, who is 'you'? Trying to answer this will lead us to understand just how original a novelist Hamilton

118

is. Much fiction of the 1930s, especially that written from what can be called a radical left-wing perspective, endorses a kind of drab socialist realism. It is manacled to a heavy weight of exact description, of individuals and their circumstances. It's not so much mass as massy observation. At its best, which is probably Walter Brierley's *Means-Test Man*, such observation is redeemed from tedium by an account of particular lives which through sheer accumulation of details gives a sense of the actuality of day-to-day existence. At its worst, it's a bit like being button-holed by the pub bore determined to tell you in remorseless detail about how he found true love and saved the world.

Bone might be one such bore. He certainly bores Netta. He dreams of inviting her to Brighton for a weekend. Brighton in the 1930s stood for a seedy bohemianism, as it did for long years afterwards. Netta agrees to go, not because she likes Bone but because she needs him to 'lend' her money for her rental and other sundries. Bone, poor Bone, is delighted. He goes down to London-on-Sea ahead of her, plays a round of golf while waiting for her to join him — a good golfer, and how Edwardian is that (shades of Sassoon) — he imagines his score of 68 will impress her. He tries not to drink too much and then, sober and wearing his best suit, goes to meet her at the station. She turns up late, escorted by Peter and a drunken hanger-on with whom, as it turns out, she plans to spend the night. Bone protests feebly that he thought she would be coming on her own. "My God," said Netta. "You didn't think I could stand you alone, my sweet Bone, did you?" And at this they all laughed.'

It says much for Hamilton's way of writing that we are likely to feel for Bone's exquisite embarrassment and hurt at Netta's treatment of him. It has become a habit for some commentators to suggest that at such a moment Hamilton betrays misogynistic tendencies. This is about as sensible as asserting that Peter is unfairly represented as a fascist sympathizer. No. Peter *is* a fascist. Netta *is* a bitch. These people are *types*. Hamilton writes a kind of black comedy which owes far more to Dickens, and behind him Jonson, than it does to the proponents of literalistic naturalism. Whether Hamilton had read Kafka, I don't know. I doubt it and yet there are connections between Joseph K and George Harvey Bone which allow us to identify both of them as the grotesquely comic victims of forces over which they have no control. In passing, I should note that at about the time Hamilton was writing his novel, Georg Lukács was championing realism against naturalism by arguing that the former made use of the 'average' hero, someone who isn't a romantic exception but whose very ordinariness makes him available as a model for all. The triumphs of the average hero in surmounting opposition is how society moves forward. Given that nobody in England in the 1930s was familiar with the work of Georg Lukács, Hamilton is very unlikely to have been aware of the distinction Lukács made between what was for him the key to realism — the agency of the average hero — and naturalism, a reactionary form which promoted through its determinism a denial of human agency. Nevertheless, it's reasonable to see in Bone a version of this 'average' hero, though in his case one more wedded to defeat than victory.

Except, that is, for his schizophrenia. '*Click!*... Here it was again. He was walking along the cliff at Hunstanton and it had come again... *Click!*...' This is how the novel opens. Bone is, temporarily, out of his mind. Or is he? When his mind goes click, as it does throughout the novel, and with increasing frequency and violence, the shutters come down on his day-to-day glumly polite timidity, his drinking, his irresolution. He knows what he has to do:

> He had to kill Netta Longdon...
> Why must he kill Netta? Because things had been going on too long, and he must get to Maidenhead and be peaceful and contented again. And why Maidenhead? Because he had been happy there with his sister, Ellen. They had had a splendid fortnight there, and she had died a year or so later. He would go on the river again, and be at peace... But first of all he had to kill Netta.

In the best sense of the word, Bone's schizophrenia is a gimmick. ('A tricky or ingenious device' O.E.D.) It is Hamilton's non-naturalistic way of dramatising a split identity, though not, I should emphasise, the kind of doppelganger much favoured in late nineteenth-century fiction and typified by Stevenson's great novel *The Strange Case of Dr Jekyll and Mr Hyde*. There, light and dark represent what Freud would later come to identify as the opposing forces of Id and Ego. The split that rends Bone is between acquiescence in the intolerable and — *Click!* — a determination to destroy it. As long as we don't put too much pressure on the term we can say that Bone represents a type of modern everyman: his liberal decencies immobilise him, much as liberal western governments found themselves immobilised in 1936 when Franco invaded Spain. But Bone's other side gives him access to a strength by means of which he can destroy the forces that otherwise will destroy him.

It goes without saying — it *should* go without saying — that a dystopic vision underlies Hamilton's novel. His modernist vision of London gives us the city as a quasi-phantasmagoric place of atomistic, separated, even alienated lives. Yes, there can be friendships, even wider alliances; but for the most part, while London may bring people together geographically, grouping them into communities, it separates them emotionally, socially, humanly. The Dantean allusions of Eliot's *Waste Land* — 'I had not thought death had undone so many' — are implicitly echoed in all of Hamilton's work.

They are there, for example, in *Twenty Thousand Streets Under the Sky*, that trilogy which tells from different perspectives three stories about the same individuals, among them a barman, a prostitute, a pub bore, each story showing us the incomprehensions, the misunderstandings, the exploitation of offered love and friendship, which characterise the rootless population of Fitzrovia. As with the Earl's Court of *Hangover Square,* this is a society without a true sense of mutuality. There is a telling moment in *Our Mutual Friend* when Bradley Headstone meets Rogue Riderhood and thinks 'Here is an instrument. Can I use it?' Many of the protagonists of Hamilton's novels think the same way. 'Chums' are to be (ab)used and discarded, the charivari of pub talk and apparently inconsequential chatter contains a ground-bass of contempt, loathing, and of disgust directed both outwards and inwards. In such a society there can only be victors and victims.

Or is this too glib, too reductive an account of Hamilton's presentation of London? History to the defeated may say alas, but cannot help, nor pardon, Auden famously wrote. But not all were defeated, not all were immobilised. Some tried to change history. And though by the time Hamilton sat down to write *Hangover Square* the Republican cause in Spain was clearly lost, the possibility for change remained. Previous philosophers have only interpreted history. The point, however, is to change it. Whether Hamilton was at this time a paid-up member of the Communist Party of Great Britain, I don't know. I do know, because the writer and Communist Party member Arnold Rattenbury told me, that in the immediate post-war years, Hamilton gave money on a regular and generous basis to the Party. And in the way it notionalises change, *Hangover Square* is surely a Marxist novel. The society it depicts — although 'evokes' or even 'ghosts' might be the better word for a technique that refuses to stick to the literalistic — is sick almost to death. The denizens of Hangover Square, a place which is as much a state of mind as a physical location, are dying of inanition.

Nor are they alone. There is a brilliant moment in the Seventh of the Ten Parts into which the novel is divided, this one called 'End of Summer', where Bone reads a newspaper account of Gracie Fields arriving at Broadcasting House. Under the headline LOOKING EXHAUSTED, the singer tells the waiting crowd that she is delighted to be released from hospital and she offers to sing to them.

Click!...
     Click... Here it was again. He was sitting in a damp, stuffy, third-class compartment, reading his newspaper, and it had happened again.
     He tried to read on.
     She sang, 'I Love the Moon...' At the end of her song she said, 'Thank you, Mr BBC. Good night and God bless you...' Miss Fields will leave for Capri today. It is expected...
     But he couldn't make sense of the words. He could only think of what had happened in his head.

Poor Gracie Fields. Her illness and her mechanically uttered, vacuous words have the effect of shaking Bone out of his torpor. (I've no doubt Hamilton is accurately reporting a newspaper account of this event.) And so — *Click!* At the fag end of the English summer, 1939, as war comes closer, Bone remembers yet again what he must do. He must kill Netta.
     Each of the novel's Parts carries at least one epigraph. This is the epigraph for the Seventh Part.

> They, only set on sport and play,
> Unweetingly importuned
> Their own destruction to come speedy upon them.
> So fond are mortal men,
> Fallen into wrath divine,
> As their own ruin on themselves invite.
>   J. Milton. *Samson Agonistes.*

These lines (1679–1684) are spoken by the Chorus near the end of Milton's great work, after Samson has pulled down the temple, in the process killing both himself and the Philistines to whom he has for years been hostage, 'Eyeless in Gaza at the mill with Slaves.' Betrayed into captivity by his passion for Dalilah, he avenges himself on her and the society she serves. From now on, Hamilton will supply further epigraphs from Milton's work to each Part of *Hangover Square*. The Tenth and final Part begins with Samson's own words to the Philistines he has been summoned to entertain, as reported by the messenger at lines 1640–1645:

> ...What your commands imposed
> I have now performed, as reason was, obeying,
> Not without wonder or delight beheld;
> Now, of my own accord, such other trial
> I mean to show you of my strength yet greater
> As with amaze shall strike all who behold.

And in a display of what may be God-given strength, he then buries himself and them. This isn't to say that we should regard Bone as a Miltonic hero. The whole point is that, unlike Samson, Bone is not exceptional. Hamilton's regard for his protagonist, while genuine, has a sardonic edge to it. To be sure, as Empson would have said, a question hovers over Samson's final act: was it justifiable or a vain-glorious gesture. Did he save or damn himself? But this isn't what Hamilton has in mind.

Nevertheless, Bone does kill his enemies. He murders both Peter and Netta and in doing so displays the physical strength that goes, Hamilton suggests, with his golfing prowess. Up until very near the end Bone has been a slave to Hangoverians, the object of their sadistic taunts, victim of behaviour calculated to humiliate him. But now, he rises up and destroys them. In what seems to me a masterstroke, neither Netta nor Peter is shown protesting overmuch at their deaths. It's as though, lacking any inner vitality, they are almost content to die. Bone goes round to Netta's flat at the moment she is about to take a bath. He follows her into the bathroom.

> He saw her staring at him, first in surprise, then in terror: he saw that she was trying to speak, but that nothing would come out.
> 'Don't bother!' he said. 'It's all right. Don't be frightened! Don't bother. Don't *bother!*'
> He seized hold of her ankles firmly and hauled them up in the air with his great strength, his great golfer's wrists. Then he grasped both of her legs in one arm, and with the other held her, unstruggling, under water.

Unstruggling! Netta lacks the energy to fight back. And when, soon after, Peter arrives, Bone waits till the man turns his back, then picks up his golf club and whacks him 'just behind his ear where he understood it would kill instantly. Then he went in front of Peter and said, "Are you all right, old boy? I'm sorry. I didn't hurt you did I? Are you all right?"' The insouciance of the question seems to give Peter pause, as though he's considering the courtesy of Bone's question, but then, like a stage actor in search of a cheap laugh, he simply crashes to the floor. After which Bone takes out some reels of thread and winds them round objects until 'All the threads were gathered up. The net was complete.' And while he is doing this, the wireless carries Chamberlain's announcement of war.

> *Now may God bless you all. May He defend the right. It is the evil things that we shall be fighting against, bad faith, oppression and persecution — and against them I am certain that the right will prevail.*
> He turned off that nonsense, and put on his coat.

It's possible, I suppose, to interpret Hamilton's response to Chamberlain's words as prompted by the Communist Party leadership which, after initially supporting the war as an anti-Fascist one, between October 1939 and June 1941 followed the Comintern line that the war against Hitler was an imperialist one and should be opposed. But in his biography, Nigel Jones says that Hamilton never accepted this line and was, for all his Communist sympathies, Churchillian in his patriotism. Not that Jones has anything to say about this moment in the novel. My own view is that Bone is understandably irked by Chamberlain's routine piety. Anyway, by his double murder he has brought speedy destruction on the basically rotten life of which he had for too long been a part and which now requires his own death. For suddenly death is everywhere.

Bone gets to Maidenhead, realises it's no good, and, with the last of his money, buys a bun and cup of tea in a tea-shop where he studies the newspapers. 'They were all about the sinking of the *Athenia*.' (The Canada-bound Cunard liner was torpedoed by a U boat some 200 miles out into the Atlantic on the very first day of war.) He returns to the digs he's booked in at, writes a suicide note, turns on the gas and dies early the following morning. Hamilton comments: 'because of the interest then prevailing in the war [his death] was given very little publicity by the press.' Average to the last.

References and Further Reading

Other especially relevant novels by Hamilton are: *Impromptu in Moribundia*, first published more or less the day war was declared and then lost to sight until Trent Editions re-issued it in 1999, with an introduction and notes by Peter Widdowson.

The Slaves of Solitude, Constable, 1947, reprinted 1972, later reprinted by Penguin. A brilliant, scabrous account of wartime England, using much the same technique as that employed in *Hangover Square*.

There are several biographies of Hamilton, including a peevish one by his brother and a grossly obtuse one by Sean French. The shilling life that gives you most of the facts is Nigel Jones, *Through a Glass Darkly: The Life of Patrick Hamilton*, Abacus, 1991.

Among the critical writings on Hamilton, I recommend especially Peter Widdowson's essay 'The Saloon Bar Society: Patrick Hamilton's Fiction in the 1930s' in *The 1930s: A Challenge to Orthodoxy*, ed. John Lucas, Harvester Press, 1978, and 'Literature, lying and sober truth: attitudes to the work of Patrick Hamilton and Sylvia Townsend Warner', by Arnold Rattenbury, in *Writing and Radicalism*, ed. John Lucas, Longman, 1996.

There are a good many histories of the inter-war years and, in particular, the 1930s, to choose from, but I still think the fullest, most reliable, and best ordered, is C.L. Mowat's *Britain Between the Wars, 1918–1940*, Methuen (revised edn.) 1968. And although I can't bring myself to share Andy Croft's enthusiasm for some of the novelists of the 1930s he writes about in *Red Letter Days: British Fiction of the 1930s*, Lawrence & Wishart, 1990, his comprehensive, generous account of the fiction of that decade makes his book essential reading.

Searching for Hangover Square

'A story of darkest Earl's Court' — the sub-title Patrick Hamilton gave to *Hangover Square*. It's a glancing reference to the 'darkest London' school of writing about the East End, suggesting that despair at least as great can be found within the superficially much more imposing streets of west London.

Patrick Hamilton knew Earl's Court well, and when George Bone saunters up and down Earl's Court Road, crosses Cromwell Road to see if the lights are on in Netta Longdon's rooms, and ventures into pubs and cafés by the station, all this would have been familiar ground to the author.

Walks are often plotted with precision — 'They went past the Post Office and A.B.C. and then turned down a narrow road on their right...' — not that Hamilton suggests any affection for 'the hard, frozen plains of Earl's Court'. Indeed he conjures up one of the most memorable, miserable, sentences in London fiction: 'To those whom God has forsaken, is given a gas-fire in Earl's Court.'

George Bone's residential hotel — the Fauconberg Hotel, a 'large glorified boarding-house' — harks back to the White House Hotel in Earl's Court Square, where Hamilton spent a year in his teens while studying at a crammer close by. Hamilton's sister lived in Earl's Court, and it was while staying with her in 1932 that he was struck by a car and nearly killed. He was permanently scarred and lost the use of one arm — he later suggested that the incident pushed him towards dependency on alcohol.

One of Hamilton's biographers, Sean French, suggests that the novelist locates Netta's flat at exactly the spot of his life-changing road accident — at the junction of Logan Place and Earl's Court Road. Logan Place has been redeveloped, but Lexham Gardens just across the road is largely untouched, terraces of tall late Victorian or Edwardian town houses, now comfortable flats.

After the war, Earl's Court was home to waves of immigrants — first Poles, later Australians. As befits an area adjoining both Kensington and Chelsea, it's now more gentrified. But stretches of Earl's Court Road are still twenty doorbells to the building. Parts of Warwick Road remain determinedly down-at-heel. Some of the streets running between the two are home to small, at best mid-market, hotels. Now as then, much of Earl's Court is given over to people living on their own.

The transient, largely young population of Earl's Court has helped the pubs — they keep changing to fit their clientele, but stay in business. There

Hogarth Place SW5

are still five within a three minute stroll of Earl's Court Station. All would probably have been there in Bone's time.

Although a lot of *Hangover Square* takes place in Earl's Court bars, only two are named. The Rockingham 'opposite Earl's Court station', where Bone first falls in with Netta and her crowd, is the Courtfield. The Black Hart is the gang's main local drinking spot — not located more precisely that 'near the station', but by implication not far from Netta's furnished rooms. The Earl's Court Tavern is the best fit.

An unnamed pub where Bone drinks with his old friend Johnnie Littlejohn can be matched with more confidence. It's described as a small pub on a narrow road leading indirectly from Earl's Court Road to Cromwell Road. That sounds like the King's Head on Hogarth Place, the most comfortable of contemporary Earl's Court's drinking holes.

The square of the title is not a place, of course, but a condition. 'What's the matter — our old friend Hangover Square?'

Andrew Whitehead

Betty Miller
Farewell Leicester Square (1941)

SUSAN ALICE FISCHER

Mention Jewish London, and the East End of a couple of generations ago leaps to mind, and indeed, Brick Lane and environs still hold vestiges of a Jewish past. The importance of the East End in this history can, however, obscure the more varied nature of Jewish London life and culture. Indeed significant novels of earlier periods take place in other parts of the capital. For instance, Amy Levy's *Reuben Sachs* (1888) is located in the upper middle-class echelons of Jewish society, well away from the East End, while Israel Zangwill's *Children of the Ghetto* (1892) shows the tensions between the East End poor (or those of working-class Jewish roots) and those with aspirations of greater assimilation into upper middle-class London society.

Placing its main character squarely at the centre of London, Betty Miller's *Farewell Leicester Square* (1941) explores a similar conflict between Jewish identity and the desire for acceptance. The novel recounts the story of a young man, Alexander ('Alec') Berman, who attempts to enter mainstream culture in the years leading up to the Second World War. Miller uses London locations symbolically to show Alec's experiences of marginalisation in English life.

Betty Miller (1910–1965) was born in Cork to a Jewish family — her father was originally from Lithuania and her mother from Sweden — and the family moved to London in 1922. Miller was not only the wife of psychiatrist Emanuel Miller and mother of theatre, opera and film director Jonathan Miller, but also the author of several novels. *Farewell Leicester Square,* her only title to touch on the 'Jewish question', was originally published in 1941, six years after it had been rejected by her publisher Victor Gollancz. As Jane Miller points out in her preface to the Persephone Press edition of 2000, on which this paragraph draws, Gollancz was 'well-known for his Jewish family's long history of comfortable accommodation to English life and ways', culminating in his own conversion.

The novel is divided into three parts and follows the seventeen-year trajectory of Alec Berman, who leaves his lower middle-class family in Brighton to pursue a career in filmmaking in London, where he makes it big, despite the anti-Semitism he encounters, and who returns at the end of the novel to his family in Brighton with a deeper understanding of himself, his values and his place in the world as a Jewish man. Jane Miller writes that Betty Miller had originally thought of titling the novel *Next Year in Jerusalem* — the closing words of the Passover Seder in the Diaspora — suggests the marginalisation that Alec encounters in England, the land of his birth and the only country he has known, and the ways he feels a stranger in it. Yet the actual title, *Farewell Leicester Square*, is more fitting not only because Alec has no desire to leave England, but also because it highlights the ways space is used in the novel with its circular movement from Brighton to London and return, which characterises the protagonist's experience as a Jew and his aspirations for acceptance by the mainstream culture. The chosen title — also the name of Alec's most important film — firmly locates the novel in London and prophesies Alec's eventual movement away from centre and back to periphery. The title comes from the 1912 song entitled 'It's a long way to Tipperary', which begins with the following lyrics: Up to mighty London / Came an Irishman one day. / As the streets are paved with gold / Sure, everyone was gay, / Singing songs of Piccadilly, Strand and Leicester Square...

The song is derogatory of the Irishman — another outsider — and presents the view of all that London has to offer and that young Alec buys into and seems to acquire. The novel opens at the height of Alec's career with the premiere of his film at the Piccadilly Dome Theatre — described as 'unparalleled anywhere else in London' for its luxury — and then flashes back to his origins in Brighton and his break with his father to pursue a career in filmmaking.

Thus the novel is clearly grounded in specific places as Alec moves from Brighton to London and, after a hiatus in Sweden, back again. Also within London, specific locations highlight both Alec's aspiration towards acceptance and his realisation that he exists in a society where his marginalisation is generally unspoken, though never far from the surface, and where his acceptance is precarious.

The texture of the novel is richly descriptive of the material world that Alec attempts to navigate. Indeed, one of Alec's most obvious characteristics is his intense observation of the physical world around him, born not only of his artistic eye which will serve him well in his chosen profession — something he shares with the author of this acutely observed novel — but also of his experience of being Jewish in a hostile environment, which means that he is always reading people and the world for clues to his acceptance or rejection. We see this with young Alec's desire to move away from his life of the family business punctuated by Sabbath ritual as he seeks out Richard Nicolls, who will provide entry into the world of cinema. This episode takes place in Brighton where Nicolls has a home, described as being potentially walled off to Alec. Looking at Oldwood Lodge, Alec observes:

> the discreetly veiled windows of the house, trying to divine from them the inward pattern of the place; guess something of its life: but window after window returned his scrutiny with blankness. The reserve of the house was not to be penetrated. Its exterior presented a correct formality, unrevealing, which seemed to rebuke his curiosity.

It is thus in terms of space that Miller describes young Alec's attempt to fathom the shape and depth of the largely unspoken societal barriers he experiences as a Jew in 'polite' English society. Alec also first sees Nicolls' son and daughter at this point. While he scrutinises them and the ease that accompanies the insider, Alec is positioned as invisible: 'they had not even glanced' at him. Indeed, the young people's

> gaze passed him over, up and down, idly; without interest or curiosity. Then they continued on their way as though nothing were.... Alec, looking after them as they went, felt down to the roots of his being the contrast which emerged between himself and them: and it was at that precise moment, for the first time, that something new, the sense of racial distinctness, awoke in him.... A sudden knowledge of the difference between these two, who could tread with careless assurance a land which in every sense was theirs; and himself, who was destined to live always on the fringe: to exist only in virtue of the toleration of others, with no birthright but that toleration....

Miller highlights this moment of dissonance as the young Alec gauges his relation to the world in which he lives. Alec will not only gain access to the movie business through Richard Nicolls, but later marry his daughter Catherine and thus seemingly enter the dominant culture. Yet by the end, he will come full circle, back to Brighton and his family once his marriage has dissolved.

131

In the meantime, the London spaces that Alec inhabits illustrate his progression towards the centre, and thus the dominant culture. This is shown in terms of both ethnicity and class. Alec does enter the world of the cinema after a year's internship in Lewisham — not at the heart of London — where he meets another intern, Lew Solomon, who will return at the end of the year with no regrets to his parents, tailoring and the regularity of the Sabbath. Lew functions as a foil to Alec, who seeks acceptance in the mainstream culture, and he also represents Alec's longing for his familial and ethnic connections. Once Alec succeeds in the film industry, he moves to a much more central (and upper-class) London location, living in 'a flat overlooking Regent's Park Canal', and later when he marries he lives near Holland Park. We learn little of the struggle which got him to this point, though we know how much it meant as '[h]e glanced up: remembering, as he always did, how, when he first came to London, the beauty of these dark squares at night had held him transfixed', as they seemed so out of reach. Now at the heart of the capital, Alec is nostalgic for the passion and drive which got him there.

Some of that passion is rekindled when Alec meets Catherine years after his first sighting of her and he falls in love with what she represents. Always 'sensitive to social intonations' and the possibility of being 'discredited at the outset by general prejudice', he is forewarned that their relationship will be no easy journey. During his first meeting with her, his senses are jarred when she refers to someone else as 'some awful dago'. Catherine finds Alec 'attractive with his dark, screened eyes: the matt, foreign skin', and she 'enjoy[s] being with' Jews: 'They were so appreciative, so vital; and at the same time curiously humble. One felt a being apart: ardently desired: no less ardently respected. Taboo gave its mystery, its emotional intensity to the situation. It was, too, an easy, a flattering situation, for whatever one's value to a male of one's own race, with these men one was, at the outset, heavily at a premium....' This acutely observed passage hones in on the ways that members of Jewish and dominant cultures view each other through either idealising or orientalising lenses. Later Catherine claims she cannot understand the difference between being born an 'Englishman' rather than a Jew — something that Alec feels keenly and tries to explain to her as creating a 'perpetual uneasiness', a 'terrifying lack of security'. She ascribes his feelings to what she thinks of as his excessive sensitivity, and she is never really able to grasp his experience of being '[t]olerated; and yet not tolerated by 'polite' English society.'

Alec realises that his place at the centre of London life is precarious, saying of England that 'The concentration camp is only *spiritual,* here'. His sense of alienation comes to the fore in the chapter which takes place in and is entitled 'Piccadilly Circus', where he meets his old friend Lew for lunch. As they walk from Regent Street to the Circus, they encounter a man hawking fascist newspapers: 'Buy the only newspaper not run by Jewish finance!... Clear out the Jews!... England for the English!' Alec and Lew then go to a Chinese restaurant with a sign saying 'No Japanese Served Here' — an irony he comments upon. As they sit upstairs in the restaurant and peer down on Piccadilly Circus, Alec evaluates his position. This metaphor of gaining perspective by literally looking down at something from a different — and higher — angle locates Alec simultaneously at the centre of London and at a distance from it and thus replicates his experience as a Jew in England:

> looking at the familiar scene, he knew a sharp uneasiness. Suppose that his material (the streets and characters and shadows of this city which he loved) were denied to him — even his right to appreciate it questioned? That would be exile, suicide in the midst of his own living. Where then should he turn? To what horizons native to him?

Both he and Lew experience anti-Semitism in London — Lew in more overt ways as he works in his family's tailoring business in the East End, Alec in ways that are generally, as he puts it 'more rarefied perhaps': 'Living in a sort of civilized limbo'. But neither desires to leave England for Palestine, even as they 'imagine for one moment standing on earth that really belongs to you.... *Belonging*'.

It is, significantly, after this pivotal scene at the heart of London highlighting Alec's precarious position as a Jew in England that the entire perspective in the novel shifts. Up to this point, the novel has been narrated in third person through Alec's point of view, yet with the very next chapter, entitled 'Gynaecological', it veers momentarily to Catherine's point of view as she prepares for the birth of their child. The child's arrival will ultimately alter Alec's position in London, literally decentring him as Catherine decides to 'protect' their son, who has been taunted for being Jewish, by leaving London and her marriage and taking their child to live with her in the aptly named Middle Bay on the southwest coast.

Alec learns of this decision as he is on location in Göthenburg, and this space, which is neither London, nor even England, shows Alec's now intense separation from everything, including himself, as he endures an unexplained, yet overwhelming sickness, obviously symbolic of his alienation: 'Alec, still wearing his overcoat, could find no warmth: on the contrary, warmth seemed, with each breath, to flow out of him, leaving him transparent, vulnerable', and he is described as having 'suffered a sea-change of some sort' and as feeling 'remote from himself'. Göthenburg thus represents a hiatus from London in which Alec's sense of alienation as a Jew — and as someone who has tried desperately to gain access to the mainstream life London represents — has reached a crisis.

Alec soon recovers from his illness, and it is significant that after this 'sea-change' he does not return to London. Instead he is met at the plane on the Croydon airfield to be hastened back to his dying mother's bedside. London and all it represents is behind him, and he returns to Brighton alone 'looking about him with excitement, as if he had reached some unimaginable land....' Thus the break and illness in Gothenburg have torn his eyes away from London and allow him to see anew. As Miller writes, 'Space intervened'. As he returns to Brighton, he becomes aware of 'the isolation of his being in space'. Yet, his return home ultimately brings him some solace and sense of belonging.

In this circular journey, Alec comes to recognise 'a moment indescribable and strangely thrilling, in which, after seventeen years, his being recognized again the special tone and familiarity of kindred flesh; the physical warmth, mutuality of *family*, of an intimacy that is amorphous and without frontiers. It was, in that moment, as if he had never been away: as if all his subsequent life since walking out of that door seventeen years ago had been a fantasy, a dream, and this the sole reality....' The number of years — seventeen — is significant as the number eighteen in Hebrew signifies life, and it is as if Alec is about to embark upon another life with a new awareness of who he is.

Thus in this journey, the centre of London represents for Alec the unattainable centrality of belonging — and the moment when he most recognises his alienation is at the city's iconic centre in Piccadilly Circus. It is after that moment that his marriage begins to unravel, despite the arrival of his son, who is described as looking and being much more like his wife's family and thus unavailable to him. Because his family lives there and because it is at the periphery, Brighton represents the authenticity of Jewish identity and at the end comes to signify a place where Alec can be himself. In returning to Brighton, Alec 'permit[s] all sorts of things, hitherto rigorously repressed, to come again into the foreground'. It is here that Alec is finally able to relax; no longer hyper-vigilant he is 'incapable even of thought. In a moment, very gently, his eyelids began to close' and he is able to drift off into a 'delicious drug-like vagueness, lack of definition'. As he sits by his mother's bedside, he feels 'an overwhelming loneliness' because of 'lost opportunity', which speaks not only to the lack of connection with his family of origin for all those years, but also to the loss of his wife and son. Alec continues to believe in the ideal of love surmount-

134

ing differences, but recognises that his marriage has failed to achieve it.

Fortunately, his mother is revived by his presence, and Alec is able to reconnect with his family. By the end of the novel, he feels 'a strange lightheartedness' for the first time in the novel: 'The worst had happened — and now he was free.... He was no longer afraid, because he no longer had anything to lose.... Whatever happened now, spiritual or physical exile, he was ready for it.... He was free: he was invulnerable, he was strong....'

Alec's identity formation has come at the cost of his marriage and his son, yet the novel ends on this hopeful note and with the Sabbath meal, replete with all the foods of his heritage, and Alec is part of this multi-generational family that has grown in his absence. The novel ends with 'The familiar, long unheard words [that] smote sharply upon Alec's awareness' of Psalm 126, the grace after meals, that sums up Alec's journey: 'They that sow in tears shall reap in joy. Though he goeth on his way weeping, bearing the store of seed, he shall come back with joy, bearing his sheaves.'

Farewell Leicester Square is only one example of a novel that puts British Jewish life squarely at its centre and in so doing uses central and peripheral London spaces to delineate the experiences of belonging and not belonging. Amongst contemporary Jewish writers, Linda Grant continues, in *The Clothes on Their Backs*, to see London's public spaces as both desirable and fraught with peril for the person deemed different by virtue of his or her culture or appearance. But using London spaces to highlight this tension is not peculiar to Jewish novels, as can be seen in fiction focusing on other marginalised groups, from Sam Selvon's West Indian characters in *The Lonely Londoners* (1956), whose experiences of exclusion are highlighted by episodes in iconic spaces of central London similar to Alec's, to Hanif Kureishi's Karim Amir in *The Buddha of Suburbia* (1990), who longs to create a life for himself on the north side of the river and who, like Alec, finds that the dominant culture sees him as other.

References and Further Reading

Linda Grant, *The Clothes on Their Backs,* Virago, 2009

Hanif Kureishi, *The Buddha of Suburbia* (1990), Faber and Faber, 2009

Amy Levy, *Reuben Sachs* (1888), Persephone Press, 2001

Betty Miller, *Farewell Leicester Square* (1941), preface by Jane Miller, Persephone Press, 2000

Sam Selvon, *The Lonely Londoners* (1956), Penguin, 2006

Susie Thomas, 'London to Brighton: Round the Bend and Over the Edge', *Literary London: Interdisciplinary Studies in the Representation of London,* http://www.literarylondon.org/ london-journal/september2010/thomas1. html

Israel Zangwill, *Children of the Ghetto* (1892), Adamant Media Corporation, 2001

London Locations in *Farewell Leicester Square*

Despite its focus on a Jewish character, the London of Betty Miller's *Farewell Leicester Square* is not the Jewish East End, with which some readers may be more familiar. Rather the novel's London locations juxtapose periphery and centre, symbolising Alec Berman's struggle as a Jew to break through the 'polite' disdain of upper middle-class English society.

Miller locates British-Alliance Pictures, where Alec directs his movies, in Oxshott, Surrey. On the other hand, Ladywell Studios, where Alec is an apprentice, is set 'between Hilly Fields and what had once been a Bird Sanctuary' in Lewisham. During this time, Alec lodges in a two-storey, semi-detached house at 58, Marsala Road (SE13), with a bow window, replete with aspidistra — and all the connotations of frustrated aspirations from George Orwell's *Keep the Aspidistra Flying* (1936). This is a real address with the sorts of houses described. Alec's friend Lew Solomon, the other Jewish apprentice at Ladywell Studios, lives with his family in Brondesbury Villas Road, which is in Kilburn, NW6.

The novel opens at the heart of London at the 'Piccadilly Dome Theatre' before flashing back to earlier times. This is probably a reference to the London Pavilion in Piccadilly Circus, which was an important cinema between 1934 and 1981. Undergoing various reincarnations from the 1880s to the present, the London Pavilion more recently became part of the Trocadero Centre and has since been reincarnated as 'Ripley's Believe It or Not' (see http://www.arthurlloyd.co.uk/Pavilion.htm)

Later in Miller's novel, in the chapter entitled 'Piccadilly Circus', this renowned location comes to represent a key moment in Alec's recognition of his precarious position as a Jew in London, and indeed England, as he looks down onto Piccadilly Circus from the first floor of a Chinese restaurant. From its location and description, this must be the now vanished Cathay Restaurant, which was on the first floor of a building at the beginning of Glasshouse Street. From the tables at the windows, one could indeed peer down onto Piccadilly Circus. It's in nearby Frith Street that Alec and Catherine go on their first date. They end up at her place 'somewhere in St. John's Wood' but not in 'one of the best parts'.

Once Alec makes it in the film industry, he lives in two London locations: 'in a flat overlooking Regent's Park Canal' where he entertains various lovers, and after he is married, in Addison Road, near Holland Park, which one of his colleagues, Brian, describes as '*Très* upper-middle-class' and 'Ultra-respectable, like Alec himself'. In her use of location, Miller shows a keen awareness of the class connotations of London spaces.

However, just as Alec is located in London's periphery upon his arrival, his last location is even more decentralised as it is the Croydon airfield where he lands upon returning from Göthenburg and other parts of Sweden, where he has been shooting a film; he returns to Brighton directly, without setting foot in London. This underscores the sense that he no longer belongs in London — and indeed, that London does not belong to him.

Susan Alice Fischer

Weymouth Street W1

Elizabeth Bowen
The Heat of the Day (1949)

JANE MILLER

The Heat of the Day is famous for being Elizabeth Bowen's London wartime novel, though she wrote other novels set in London, and several of her best short stories deal, sometimes as ghost stories, with the strange hiatus amid the continuities which characterised London life during and just after the Blitz. There was very little about her times, or the places her characters inhabit, that Elizabeth Bowen took for granted or assumed her readers would know already, and in this novel London is minutely scrutinised and accounted for from the first Sunday of September 1942 to the same Sunday two years later. More than that, though. Place and time are palpable forces in a novel which traffics in rain and sunlight, in the 'tired physical smell' of London, in the total darkness of the Blackout and in the vivid contrasts between night-time bombing and the light-hearted relief people felt during daylight hours, as the substance and temper of its characters' emotional life. Anxiety, suspicion, fear envelop the lovers at the centre of the novel, who are curiously sketchy, despite their moments in bed and their elegant dressing-gowns. Yet they are also believably happy together, in love as neither has ever been before and unexpectedly at ease with one another. So that London is for both of them a place of nightmare, darkness and danger, but also the dodgy home and encourager of love. Bowen apparently found this the most difficult of all her novels to write. She started it as the bombs were still falling in 1944, and it was not published until 1949. The novel is, in some ways, a casualty of war itself, damaged in certain places, the prose often fractured and elliptical, with verbs and articles left out, and odd breaches of idiom: contortions which catch the contortions of the time. It is also capable of

139

inducing precisely the excitement and the anxiety lurking at its heart.

Stella and Robert, the novel's lovers, are 'creatures of history, whose coming together was of a nature possible in no other day.' This is not so much a grand claim for the peculiarity of their situation as a simple truth about how things were in London during the Second World War: 'War time, with its makeshifts, shelvings, deferrings, could not have been kinder to romantic love.' Elizabeth Bowen herself had a passionate affair through most of the war with a young Canadian diplomat called Charles Ritchie, to whom she dedicated the novel. Social and family life became difficult for all Londoners. For the middle-classes there was not only food rationing but very few servants. It was sometimes possible to be private, though, anonymously and anomalously housed, and, at the same time, to communicate outside with people you'd never have known in normal life.

Within its two-year span, the novel shifts nervously back and forth in time, making little forays out of the city as if to escape the bombing, always uncertain of the events it narrates and of their sequence, and returning from its excursions, it can seem, on the orders of some badgering inquisitor, determined to achieve at least a glimmer of clarity, an explanation in the face of all this. 'Ghostly' is a word that crops up a good deal, and 'haunting'. Many of her wartime stories, 'In the Square', 'The Demon Lover' and 'Mysterious Kôr', for instance, focus on the phantasmogorical effect on people of living among bombed houses and an only partly recognisable landscape. *The Heat of the Day* starts in Regent's Park, autumnal, slightly fly-blown, with its bandstand still just bandstanding to an assortment of mostly lonely derelict people. A plump, ungainly young woman, working-class and speaking a form of English derived, it sometimes seems, from a rare variant of dyslexia, makes an awkward friendly pass at her neighbour, who, shifty and unkind, testily puts her down. It is a London of solitary strangers and drifting leaves, a 'tarnished' version of the Regent's Park that glitters in winter sunshine at the beginning of Bowen's earlier, pre-war novel, also set in London, *The Death of the Heart*. This, we quickly realise, is to be a London transformed by the war.

Stella has lived stylishly on the edge of Regent's Park in a Nash terrace house of exactly the kind that figures in the earlier novel and which Bowen herself inhabited until she was bombed out in 1944. Stella's house has been bombed too, just as Bowen's was, so that we meet her first in the elegant, characterless flat she has rented at the top of a high house that empties itself of its doctors at night and at weekends, near to the park and the shell of her old house. Weymouth Street must have possessed the heavy impersonal grandeur in those

140

days that it still does. Stella works all day in a secret branch of government (as Bowen herself did) and here she is on that Sunday evening, in the middle of a querulous conversation with the man we've already met in the park earlier in the day, as he snubbed the young woman who'd hoped to go home with him. He is the one being snubbed now, by this attractive fortyish woman to whom he appears to be offering himself, having surprisingly invaded the bleak refuge her flat provides. He *is* offering himself, it turns out, in exchange for the information that Stella's lover Robert (who is also engaged in secret government work) is selling secrets to the enemy, a fact he is prepared to withhold, or which he might, at least, delay in divulging — in the interest of catching bigger fry — if she accepts him as her lover.

Harrison, as his name turns out to be, is an alarming presence, insistently and disagreeably material, yet ghostly in his comings and goings, so that neither Stella nor the reader can be sure whether he is telling the truth about her lover, let alone about his own role and his ability to intervene as he is proposing to do. The scene gives us our first taste of the novel's jumpiness and terror and of its central theme: love is no guarantee of truth or trust and provides no protection against betrayal. Is it, indeed, ever possible to know whether someone is telling the truth? Harrison, it turns out, is called Robert too. How is Stella to adjudicate between these two Roberts, or, perhaps, even distinguish between them?

She keeps quiet about Harrison's accusation for two months, and the reader is no clearer than she is about whether her lover is really a spy. Her anxiety permeates the novel as we watch her getting on with her life and trying to ignore Harrison's blandishments. We return to the young woman in the park, Louie, and her cannier friend, Connie, and listen, somewhat disbelievingly, perhaps, to their chatter. Connie is a reader of newspapers and is clear about the progress of the war. She has reminded Louie, as Louie later remembers, of 'the advantage I should be at if I could speak grammar'. Louie's husband, Tom, is a soldier in India, and her parents have been killed by a direct hit on their house. She is not a Londoner, and her sturdy, optimistic nature is out of its element in this injured and complicated city. From loneliness and an apparently innocent desire for company of any sort, Louie occasionally approaches men and takes them home with her. She failed with Harrison, as we've seen.

There are glimpses into Stella's life. We are told that she left her husband, and needn't have bothered to divorce him, as he died just afterwards. She has a twenty-year-old son, Roderick, one of Bowen's oddly affectless young men, who spent a futile year at Oxford before being called up. She visits the estate in Ireland he is due to inherit from a cousin of his father's, and Roderick later visits this cousin's wife, who lives in an old people's home. It is this old woman, who may be mad and is certainly unreliable, who reveals to Roderick that Stella was left by her husband for a 'common' nurse he loved and wanted to marry. Stella has misled the world and her son by preferring it to be thought she had callously left her husband, when the truth was that he rejected her as a very young mother for someone else. Her son feels betrayed by this untruth, with its curious mixture of innocence and self-serving denial, which prefigures Robert's possible treachery and Stella's possible reaction to it.

An unsettling visit to Robert's mother and sister in the Home Counties offers some insight into Robert's life. They live in an elaborately horrible house, ugly, demanding and impersonal, perpetually up for sale, and the uncomfortable setting for a family controlled by women and destructively dismissive of men and of sex. Robert's father appears to have died defeated by all this, and 'unstated indignities suffered by the father remained burned deeply into the son's mind'. The bond between Stella and Robert draws on their shared experience of growing up unloved and knowing at first as well as second-hand what it is to be found wanting sexually.

When Elizabeth Bowen's novels were reissued as paperbacks in 1999 to celebrate the centenary of her birth, the rereadings they occasioned were mostly serious and admiring; the savaging she had received earlier from critics like Elizabeth Hardwick, Raymond Williams and Angus Wilson, amongst others, refuted or forgotten. She was not, and would not have wanted to be, received into the feminist literary fold, though she sometimes figured on lists of women writers denied their due. The charges against her were of snobbery, of having 'the moral intransigence of the interior decorator' (Hardwick), of 'special pleading', so that 'the reality of society is excluded' (Williams), and of inhabiting 'the land of the middlebrow' (Wilson). These charges seemed to many of her readers unfair and malicious, and to some extent familiar and typical of how serious novels written by women were often read. It is certainly true that Bowen wrote mostly about middle and upper-class people, that she was perhaps over-exercised by the differences among members of those groups and often clumsy in her treatment of working-class characters. But there was also something direct and honest about her sense of class, so that, for instance, Stella at one point wonders whether her class is perhaps the only thing she has going for her; and when Louie and she are brought together by Harrison, both women are immediately and self-consciously aware of the class differences manifested in their clothes, their speech and their demeanour. Stella notices Louie's crooked

142

seams and 'flimsy gloves', while Louie goes home to ponder the meaning of the word 'refined'. Each woman is intrigued by the other, however, and not in the least repelled.

Bowen's novels are full of servants and other working-class characters, and they are by no means all walk-on parts, though they are sometimes possessors of peculiar speech habits. They often stand in the novels for energy, straightforwardness and a capacity for warmth and feeling that Bowen clearly admired. In *The Death of the Heart*, for instance, the seaside household of the Heccomb family is portrayed as lively, humorous and good at enjoying themselves, in absolute contrast to the repressed and mannered tastefulness of the Quayne family in Regent's Park. Meanwhile Portia, the unhappy orphan at the centre of the novel, relies on the kindness of the housekeeper in a house where she is continually let down by her adoptive family and their friends. The two young working-class women in *The Heat of the Day* are affectionately drawn, and the birth of Louie's illegitimate baby at the end of the novel is a positive, life-affirming moment, strikingly at odds with references throughout the novel to false or phantom pregnancies, which yield questions and secrets rather than living infants.

Bowen, it seems — or at least it is rumoured — was briefly a member of the British Communist Party, like many of her friends and fellow writers, and though this by no means guaranteed sympathy with or knowledge about working-class people, let alone identification with their far greater vulnerability in wartime London, it is not without significance. Bowen was an only child. Her father suffered for many years from a serious breakdown, so that her mother took Elizabeth to England, where she died when her daughter was only thirteen. Thereafter, her life was spent in boarding schools and with an aunt, though she did live with her father in Ireland during the holidays. All this certainly introduced her to one version of social exile, a particular form of rootlessness and homelessness, which is like the experience of many of her heroines. She was also, it has to be said, seduced by grand old houses, and the Irish one in this novel, which Stella's son inherits, is clearly based on Bowen's Court, which the author inherited from her father.

The Heat of the Day is also remembered as a novel about spying. It is sometimes compared with Graham Greene's *The Ministry of Fear* and not always to Bowen's advantage. Readers have wondered why Robert spies for the Nazis rather than the Russians, though it is likely that spying for the Russians would have carried too many distracting ambiguities in 1942. Nor do we know what kinds of secrets he was handing over or to whom. Are we to assume that Robert seriously impedes the war effort and may even have caused the death of friends and colleagues? Bowen wilfully denies us satisfaction on these points and concentrates instead on the dilemma Robert poses for Stella. When she does finally confront him with Harrison's accusation and her own two-month delay in telling him about it, his first instinct is to lie, and he does this convincingly for a moment, and then blusteringly proposes marriage. Stella only knows for certain that he has been spying when Harrison is able to pinpoint the exact moment when she asked Robert if he was a spy: a moment that was followed, just as Harrison had predicted it would be, by instant moves to cover his tracks.

Stella finds herself telling Harrison about the lie she's told about her marriage. They have dinner together in a basement bar off Regent Street, where lights blaze in frantic denial of the darkness outside, and she formally offers herself to him in a last-ditch attempt to deflect him from Robert, only to be turned down by him, as he had been by her. Robert, meanwhile, has mysteriously made off to his mother's hated house, the scene of his father's humiliations, which is suddenly coveted by a real-life buyer: presumably someone in pursuit of Robert, almost certainly Harrison. Robert returns to London and the final reckoning. Stella and he are in bed together for what they know to be the last time when he delivers a mystifying diatribe as explanation of his spying. He is, above all, contemptuous of the language of loyalty, he tells her. Words like 'betrayal' and 'freedom' are part of the 'racket', a 'dead currency' he has learned to immunize himself against. He has longed for 'scale', 'vision', grandeur. Wouldn't she wish that for him too, even expect it of him? Stella is astonished, as the reader is, by his chaotic, vaporous words:

Freedom, Freedom to be what? — the muddled, mediocre, damned. Good enough to die for, freedom, for the good reason that it's the very thing which has made it impossible to live, so there's no alternative. Look at your free people — mice let loose in the middle of the Sahara.

It is possible that Robert's wasted anger, his ranting and generalised 'disaffection', as he calls it, echoes some of the sentiments Bowen harvested while she was in Ireland during the Second World War, when she was required to report on the character of Irish neutrality. Roy Foster, in his *Modern Ireland 1600–1972*, quotes from one of her reports:

The most disagreeable aspect of this official 'spirituality' is its smugness, even phariseeism. I have heard it said (and have heard it constantly being said) that 'the bombing is a punishment on England

144

for her materialism.'... And there is still admiration for Franco's Spain... The effect of religious opinion in this country (Protestant as well as Catholic) still seems to be a heavy trend to the Right.

Robert's disgust with the war seems less principled and even more negative than the testimony of Bowen's Irish men and women, though it is possible that Bowen found his *not* invoking religious or spiritual reasons for the position he has taken up preferable to the Irish versions of it she had listened to. It is also clear that many people Bowen knew (including her lover, Charles Ritchie) felt no enthusiasm for the war, though they may not have expressed this quite as Robert does. His explanation appears arrogant as well as smug, and it is delivered in the voice of an officer and gentleman used to getting his way.

> This war's just so much bloody quibbling about some thing that's pre-decided itself. Either side's winning would stop the war; only their side's winning would stop the quibbling. I want the cackle cut.

We are left to attribute his behaviour principally — as Stella does — to what he thinks of as his father's weakness and humiliations. His work for the enemy, he tells her, 'bred my father out of me, gave me a new heredity.' We cannot know for certain whether his subsequent fall from her roof to his death is an act of suicide or murder, or an accident, nor whether it is to be considered brave, foolhardy or expedient. Stella firmly protects his name and his purpose as she gives evidence at the inquest on his death, and she is regarded as 'a good witness'.

When a telegram arrives announcing the death of Louie's husband, Tom, at the very moment that Connie is writing a letter to explain Louie's pregnancy to him, Bowen declares that 'questions to which we find no answers find their own.' She depicts a world in which lying is ubiquitous and probably unavoidable. She believed, to some degree, in coincidence and in ghosts and haunting, and even more so in the unknown and the unknowable. She may also have believed in doubles. She expected us to make do with what we were given, and to see uncertainty as intrinsic to fiction as it is to life. And it is true that these mysteries are not disappointing. Towards the end of the novel Stella is sitting in a train going out of London and looking into the rooms and houses she passes:

> Sometimes Stella was fortunate in being able to see through railings or over fences not only yards and gardens but right into back windows of homes. Prominent sculleries with bent-forward heads of women back at the sink again after Sunday dinner, and recessive living-rooms in which the breadwinner armchair-slumbered, legs out, hands across the eyes, displayed themselves; upstairs, at looking-glasses in windows,

girls got themselves ready to go out with boys. One old unneeded woman, relegated all day to where she slept and would die, prised apart lace curtains to take a look at the train, as though calculating whether it might not be possible to escape this time.

Stella's watching eye, dispassionate, imaginative, yet restrained in its claims to know the whole story, is a reflection of what Bowen could do as a novelist. She could tell you how things looked and how they seemed and also how it might be possible to extrapolate from that to how people thought and felt. But you could never really know another person, and though love mattered more than anything it didn't help. Bowen's refusal to clear up confusions works especially well in this novel, where London's inhabitants are watched groping for order and understanding in darkness and rubble and dust, and contending, often blithely, with shattering changes to their expectations and habits. Stella's disappointment is that Robert did not share, as she'd thought he had, her sense of there being a peculiar romance to wartime London. She loves the place and the time they've occupied together, with its dangers and horrors and possibilities. Their love affair, passionately sealed off from their earlier lives within the alien enclosure of Stella's rented flat, seemed to protect them from the dangerous world outside, as it pressed clamorously on walls and windows, with thick sooty smells and blinded nights. But she had also believed that it linked them to the destinies of other people in the world outside. So altered were everybody's lives by what was happening that they could feel as if they were all 'inside the pages of a book', or indeed a 'garrison', in which unusual pleasures and company were to be sought and found in compensation for the wreckage outside. Robert has undermined that vision.

Bowen evokes the tangled physical reality of the time, its extremes and opposites, in an awkward, broken language:

> Out of mists of morning charred by the smoke from ruins each day rose to a height of unmisty glitter; between the last of sunset and first note of the siren the darkening glassy tenseness of evening was drawn fine. From the moment of waking you tasted the sweet autumn not less because of an acridity on the tongue and nostrils; and as the singed dust settled and smoke diluted you felt more and more called upon to observe the daytime as a pure and curious holiday from fear.

Stella is haunted by the intense beauty of daybreak and the horrors it can manage to disguise:

> Most of all the dead, from mortuaries, from under cataracts of rubble, made their anonymous presence — not as today's dead but as yesterday's living — felt through London.

146

The novel ends on an ambiguous note of renewal. Stella tells Harrison that she is going to marry a distant cousin, a Brigadier, who has kindly ignored her shaky past and unusual connections; and Louie's baby, Tom, is growing to look more and more like the man who was not his father. It is not a return to normality or peace, but some careful human adjustments and accommodations are being made to this extraordinary time.

References and Further Reading

Elizabeth Bowen, *The Death of the Heart*, 1938

Elizabeth Bowen, *The Demon Lover, and Other Stories*, 1945, includes 'In the Square' and 'Mysterious Kôr'

Elizabeth Bowen, Victoria Glendinning, *Elizabeth Bowen: Portrait of a Writer*, Weidenfeld & Nicolson, 1977

Love's Civil War: Elizabeth Bowen and Charles Ritchie, Letters and Diaries, 1941-1973, edited by Victoria Glendinning and Judith Robertson, Simon & Schuster, 2009

Around Regent's Park

The opening pages of both of Elizabeth Bowen's best known novels are set in Regent's Park. A slow walk round the boating lake constitutes the opening chapter of *The Death of the Heart*. In *The Heat of the Day*, a concert in the park's Open Air Theatre sets the scene for this rendition of a wartime, dis-located, disoriented city.

Bowen has been described as the 'doyenne' of Regent's Park writers. She could see over the park from her sitting room at 2 Clarence Terrace, close to its south-west corner. This exceptional terrace — designed not by John Nash but by the young Decimus Burton — dates from the 1820s, the decade before the park was opened to the public. Bowen was an air raid warden during the war. Her home in Clarence Terrace was damaged in the Blitz of 1940 and again in the summer of 1944, when a bomb brought down the ceilings. She was obliged to move out while the property was rebuilt.

Much of *The Heat of the Day* is set on the southern fringes of Regent's Park, and above all in Marylebone, which Bowen once described as 'my village'. The area is now, as it was then, largely given over to mansion blocks, mews streets and white stucco propriety. Her topography in the novel is imprecise, for she is more concerned to capture a moment than a place — the London of the Blitz and its aftermath. Louie, a factory worker, has 'a double first-floor room in one of those little houses in Chilcombe Street' close to Marylebone station, the last, smallest and nicest of London's mainline stations, where she could hear the 'nocturnal train-sounds, shunting, clanking and hissing, from the network of Marylebone lines'.

Stella Rodney lives in an altogether grander and more austere part of Marylebone, Weymouth Street, which runs east from the bustle of Marylebone High Street, across Wimpole Street, Harley Street and Portland Place before dissolving into the hinterland of Fitzrovia. 'This fairly old house in Weymouth Street, of which her flat took up the top floor, was otherwise in professional, doctors' and dentists', occupation and was accordingly empty at week-ends'. Perhaps echoing the author's own experience after being forced out of Clarence Terrace, Stella — living in a furnished flat — 'had the irritation of being surrounded by somebody else's irreproachable taste'. The street still has the slightly anonymous air of surgeries and smart apartments, and if Stella Rodney strolled down there today, she would find much that is familiar.

Andrew Whitehead

Jack Lindsay
Rising Tide (1953)

ANDY CROFT

They started off from the Fields, some 400 strong, on the five-mile march, with 150 C.S.U. strikers falling in behind. Two lads had borrowed a wooden leg from an old-age pensioner who'd been a stevedore, and had dressed it up on a black stocking provided by the fat girl who worked in a near newsagent's shop. This black leg they then hung from an improvised gallows, an angle of wood with the notice *Blacklegs Beware*; and now they carried it at the head of the procession amid repeated bursts of laughter... The march went on, with slogans and songs, from Burdett Road to Commercial Road, picking up more groups on the way. A grey-headed but stalwart docker, striding in an open blue shirt, with his coat over his arm, struck up a song by William Morris:

What is this, the sound and rumour? What is this that
   all men hear?
Like the wind in hollow valleys when the storm is
   drawing near,
Like the rolling on of oceans in the eventide of fear?
   'Tis the people marching on...

A swing of purpose seemed to move along the line of marchers like a gold ripple of wind over a field of ripe wheat. We march towards our England in a world delivered over to the enemy of man. Now England is ours, and every note of the song, every tramp of the march is the certain pledge of the day when the people are undisputed masters of their earth... Men of Poplar, men of Shadwell, men of Wapping, men of Stepney, coming with banners and placards. *Together in war, Together in Peace. Our Fight is Justice.* The lines extended. The great wind of the song rose higher.

Hark, the rolling of the thunder.
Lo, the sun, and lo, thereunder

Riseth wrath and hope, and wonder,
And the host comes marching on.

There were a thousand and a half men by the end, and some three thousand waiting in the Park to swell the cheer, the unending song. As the marchers came up the shady green path, a voice cried, 'Are we solid?' and the thousands answered in a single shout, 'Yes!'

As this passage suggests, *Rising Tide* is in many ways a classic example of Cold War Communist fiction. As the grammar shifts from the third to the first person, and from the past tense to the present, the crowd of striking London dockers swells on the page, via the heavily staged quotations from Morris and Shelley, to become The People. This is perhaps the kind of rhetorical gesture we expect to find in a Socialist Realist novel — too much socialism and not enough realism.

But there is rather more to *Rising Tide* than this — as there was, in fact, to most attempts in the 1940s and 1950s to Anglicise the claims of Socialist Realism. These dockers may be marching towards the Future, but they are also taking possession of the real East End, as the narrative follows the precise route of their march from Canning Town to Bethnal Green. And for all the Priestley-like sentimentality of these jolly cockneys, this scene takes place in the middle of one of the most violent and ideologically-charged industrial disputes of the Cold War.

Jack Lindsay was born in 1900 in Melbourne, Australia. His father was the distinguished artist Norman Lindsay, whose paintings scandalised wowserish Australia; the 1993 comedy *Sirens*, starring Sam Neill, Hugh Grant, Tara Fitzgerald and Elle Macpherson, is a portrait of the Lindsays' bohemian ménage in the Blue Mountains. After reading Classics at the University of Queensland, Lindsay moved to Sydney, and then in 1926 to London, where he established the Fanfrolico Press and the *London Aphrodite* in order to popularise his father's radical ideas about art and poetry. When the press closed in 1930 Lindsay was unable to afford the passage home. Instead he retreated to the West Country, writing and publishing poetry, fiction, biography, philosophy, translations and children's stories. He never returned to Australia.

During the Second World War, Lindsay served in the British Army in the Royal Signal Corps, before being transferred to the Ministry of Information to work as a script writer for the Army Bureau of Current Affairs. After the war, Lindsay and his second wife, the Unity Theatre actress Ann Davies, moved to Kent, and then in 1951 to Castle Hedingham in Essex. By the time he came to write *Rising Tide*,

150

Lindsay had already published more than eighty books, best-known for his historical fiction, notably the 'Prelude to Christianity' trilogy, *Rome for Sale* (1934), *Caesar is Dead* (1934) and *Last Days with Cleopatra* (1935), and a trilogy of novels about the English radical tradition — *1649* (1938), *Lost Birthright* (1939) and *Men of '48* (1948).

Lindsay joined the Communist Party in 1941, after several years of fellow-travelling. By the early 1950s, he was a senior figure in the party's cultural life, a crucial link with mainstream literary London (he was on the committee of the Wroclaw World Authors Peace Appeal *and* of London PEN). Lindsay was a long-standing and loyal member of the party's National Cultural Committee. He attended the 1948 World Congress of Intellectuals for Peace in Wroclaw, the 1949 Paris Peace Congress and the 1949 Pushkin celebrations in the Soviet Union. He visited Czechoslovakia in 1950, Poland in 1951, Romania in 1952 and 1953, and in 1954 he attended the Second Soviet Writers' Congress in Moscow. He reviewed regularly for the *Daily Worker* and was responsible for the publication in English of several writers from the 'People's Democracies'. A hostile review in the *TLS* of Lindsay's *Byzantium into Europe* (1952) concluded by calling for a purge of Communist Party members from British universities.

At the same time, Lindsay was also close to communist writers like Edgell Rickword, Randall Swingler and the young Edward Thompson, whose developing ideas about culture, national tradition and democracy represented a kind of 'Cultural Opposition' inside the party. He was on the board of Fore Publications, whose ill-fated 'Key Poets' series was denounced in the *Daily Worker* in 1950. He was also one of the founding editors of the literary magazine *Arena*, publishing European writers like Pasternak, Camus, Eluard, Tzara and Cassou in the face of severe Zhdanovite disapproval from the party headquarters on King Street.

Lindsay had already written three novels about the Second World War — *We Shall Return* (1942), *Beyond Terror* (1943), *Hello Stranger* (1945) — and three novels set in post-war Britain — *Time to Live* (1946), *The Subtle Knot* (1947) and *Betrayed Spring* (1953). *Rising Tide* was written as a kind of sequel to *Betrayed Spring*, the second of the 'British Way' series in which Lindsay tried to address 'the experiences of our people in the post-war years, combining the close study of individuals with a clear historical structure... to come close to the lives, defeats and aspirations of the people who had gone through the anti-fascist war and were now being subjected to the pressures of the Cold War.'

The title of the series clearly owed something to the Communist Party's post-war programme, *The British Road to Socialism,* adopted after much discussion in 1951. The party now envisaged the struggle for socialism as a long and strategic war of position rather than a Bolshevik uprising (several of the chapters in *Rising Tide* have Gramscian titles like 'First Skirmish', 'Manoeuvres for Position' and 'The Struggle Goes On'). But although there are overlapping narrative threads in the first three novels — the main characters of *Rising Tide* appear briefly in *Betrayed Spring* as well as in the next novel in the series, *Moment of Choice* (1955) — the series is not, strictly speaking, a *roman fleuve*. Each is a study of a specific 'ripe' historical moment — *Betrayed Spring* was about the 1946 squatters' movement, *Moment of Choice* about opposition to the war in Korea, while *Rising Tide* is set against the events of the 1949 dock strike.

In the immediate post-war years the London docks were affected by a number of serious stoppages — in 1945, 1946, 1947, 1949 and 1951. At the start of the novel the dockers are on strike again, this time over the dismissal of 'ineffectives' (men over sixty-five). Before this dispute is properly settled, the London dockers find themselves involved in a strike by the Canadian Seaman's Union. In an attempt to break the communist-led CSU, the Canadian shipowners employed a US-based company union, the Seafarer's Union International, to attack CSU picket-lines with sawn-off shotguns, axe handles and bicycle chains. Seven strikers were shot in Halifax; two were found floating in Vancouver harbour. Within a few weeks three hundred CSU members were in prison.

The dispute quickly became internationalised, with dockers in twenty-seven ports around the world refusing to unload Canadian ships. In London the Dock Board refused to employ men on other ships unless they crossed the Canadian picket lines. Fifteen thousand dockers found themselves locked-out. The Labour government, the Labour Party and the leadership of the TGW and the NASD unions appealed to the dockers to cross the CSU picket-lines. Smithfield market workers came out in sympathy. In early July the government declared a state of emergency. Six thousand troops were deployed in the port of London to unload the ships.

Rising Tide records in detail the progress of the dispute and the rising tide of trade union militancy which it released, in what might be described as a kind of experiment in documentary realism. The action takes place during just sixteen weeks, between 19th March and 23rd July 1949. Several real historical figures appear in the novel, including the London dockers' leaders Ted Dickens and Albert Timothy and the Canadian Seaman's Union leader Harry Davis. We hear of speeches made in the House of Commons by the Communist MPs Willie Gallacher and Phil Piratin; the left-wing MP John

Platts-Mills (expelled from the Labour Party the previous year) speaks in the novel at a mass meeting in Trafalgar Square. The novel includes fifteen telegrams sent by the Canadian Seaman's Union during the dispute which had not previously been published. These telegrams help to frame the story of the strike, locating the events in the red-baiting context of the Cold War and reminding readers of the violent record of union busting in north America:

> April 21. *Cuban gunboat opened fire with rifles and tommy-guns on crew Canadian Victor...* April 29. Montreal. *Hundreds of mounted police last night ambushed C.S.U. men outside St. John...* May 1. *Crew of scabs being flown over to England...* May 23. *David Joyce of S.I.U. arrested Montreal for carrying loaded firearms...* June 8. Montreal. *Third member of our Union found dead floating in bay of Los Angeles California stop.*

For all this, *Rising Tide* is primarily a love story, following the fortunes of a young docker and his wife as they struggle to make ends meet. At the beginning of the novel Jeff and Phyl are impatient to be married, but are frustrated by being unable to find anywhere to live. Eventually they find a squat in wooden hut on 'the dump' near Albert Dock:

> They went down a side-street by the Seamen's Hospital, through the thin March sunlight. Children in the roadway were kicking an india rubber ball with a hole in it, while a dog barked jealously behind a gate... They turned into Customs House Fields, which stood deserted this afternoon; then they skirted the Connaught Approach of the Albert Dock, and moved on into the open fields... the wider space of straggling grass and bush, with three hobbled horses on the left and a clump of shacks on a slightly raised level well ahead... They turned and stood scanning the giant cranes that loomed over the hidden dockland, clearly limned against the faintly luminous sky... The path became narrow and she let him lead the way between the patches of tall grass and the scratchy bushes, the heaps of coiled rusting wire and the treacherous channels. Then in a few moments they climbed up on to the raised part and she saw the gunpits plainly... Fancy living in such a dump.

Rising Tide is above all a book about London, specifically the docklands. The Bodley Head described the novel on the dust-jacket (designed by the communist artist James Boswell) as:

> a novel of London's river, of its ships and commerce, but above all of the people of dockland, the young and the old, the dockers and their families, the men and women of strength and spirit who in the past have suffered and today are perhaps more misunderstood and blamed than any other group in the nation.

Much of the novel takes place on 'the Stones', on the Custom House Fields, and in the pubs and cafés of Canning Town. Jeff drinks with some Canadian seamen in a pub off Cyprus Place. The unofficial Lockout committee holds its meetings in the White Hart in Stepney. Jeff addresses an AEU meeting in rooms near London Bridge. When he is arrested during the Lockout he spends ten days in Pentonville prison. Hackney Trades Council, Stepney Trades Council and the London Trades Council pledge their support for the dockers.

The *TLS* devoted a leading article to sneering at *Rising Tide* and the other two novels in the trilogy, disingenuously quoting Keats against Lindsay ('We hate poetry that has a palpable design upon us...'). But *Rising Tide* is not quite the programmatic novel that readers today might expect. Jeff doesn't join the Communist Party at the end of the novel (although one of his mates does). The CP characters have a habit of talking over the heads of their listeners, who are often left with a feeling of 'being strangers, humdrum nonentities quite outside the stirring world of great personal and great events'. The climax of the novel may be a set-piece mass demonstration in Trafalgar Square, but the scene concludes, not with a street fight against mounted police, but with a successful whip-round for the Canadian seamen.

Speaking at a 1953 CP conference on 'Socialist Realism and the British Cultural Tradition', Lindsay explicitly argued that Socialist Realism did not mean simply tendentious or partisan literature. 'Socialist Realism means more than just thinking of the workers as audience. It means the attempt to find an active contact with this audience in new ways, for help and for criticism... To get this give-and-take the writer must go out to the workers in new and considered ways.' In order to write *Rising Tide*, Lindsay had spent a good deal of time talking to some of the key participants in the dispute, including Ted Dickens and Albert Timothy. When the book was published in December 1953, Lindsay spoke at a public meeting at the Marx Memorial Library about the process of writing it. The importance of the novel to the Communist Party is suggested by the fact that it was reviewed twice in the *Daily Worker*, first by Patrick Goldring ('a vivid account of the dockers' struggle... a penetrating and warmly human novel of enduring value... marks the beginning of a great advance in British progressive writing') and then the following week by Reg Spalding, one of the dockers who had helped Lindsay write it ('a warm and human book... a great attempt at a real working-class novel, and it is a very enjoyable book. My wife enjoyed every word.') The Marxist critic Alick West considered the trilogy Lindsay's best work. *Rising Tide* was published in translation in Poland in 1955 and in Romania in 1960.

Lindsay was always too interested in the contradictions between and within individuals to idealise working-class life. Jeff goes on a drinking spree although he and Phyl are desperately short of money. Later he loses the last of their money at cards. When some travelling families arrive on the dump, some of the squatting families are welcoming, but others hostile. Jeff's father is an argumentative Unitarian, Phyl's father is an anti-communist *Daily Herald* reader; her brother is in borstal, and her sister is a long-suffering (and loudly complaining) martyr to her hopeless husband. Beyond their immediate families there are the gamblers, the drinkers and the good-time girls of dockland, the easily-led and the lazy, the feckless, the reckless, the overworked and the unemployed. And further still lie London, the Thames and the wide world of work and struggle:

> Above the dismantled hut next door the sky showed a dim radiant mauve. The colour-effect was startling in its subtle simplicity, with the broken hut providing a stark strong pattern of dark ruin on the soft flowing warmth of light. It's coming, he thought, it's coming. And he suddenly felt the situation unutterably strange — the lovely broken scene outside, the fragile and lovely sweetness of Phyl in the small room with him, the struggle coming tomorrow or the day after with its complex interlocking of small and large forces, the impassive and ruthless mechanisms that would seek to flatten out the resistances of the portworkers, and the unconquerable spirit of brotherhood that rose up afresh out of every defeat. We're ready, he thought, and turned to take Phyl in his arms.

At the beginning of the novel neither Jeff or Phyl are very interested in 'politics'. Their lives seem to be determined by historical forces beyond either their understanding or their control. When Jeff is locked-out he feels that she does not support him. When he comes home late from a union meeting, she accuses him of being more interested in the union than he is in her. Jeff's loyalties are divided between Phyl and the union, between his union and the government, and between the unofficial dockers' leaders and Transport House. For their communist friends, the lessons of the dispute are clear:

> 'The bosses and the Labour right wing that are the bosses' last hope,' said Hugh, 'will always go on using every element of division that class-society has created among the workers — craft-divisions, petty little variations of status and privilege, wage variations, men against women, women against men, unskilled against skilled, blackcoat against manual worker, regional and sectional jealousies or cleavages, even T.U. rivalries... Anything to keep the workers from realising their united strength. And we've got to be on our tiptoes against these efforts. Every big struggle breaks some of 'em down.'

But for Jeff and Phyl, the events have taught them something important about living together. Jeff is amazed to find that while he was in prison she has been working for the Lockout committee ('My Phyl that wouldn't say boo to a goose'). The first night together after his release, they realise that the 'crystalline balance' of their relationship has changed. 'The simple adventure into one another's privacies, physical and spiritual — a discovery and a union — had given way to something more complicated. They were now more aware of one other as individuals... One had to keep making demands on the other, or growth and full intimacy were impossible.' The novel ends with a good rhetorical flourish, connecting the personal and the political elements of the story:

> They had a feeling that they'd got to bedrock, at least they'd seen as far into things as they were likely to see for the present... He held out his hand and she took it... 'Nothing's ever going to come between us,' he said. And he felt his words as both a pledge of the deepened union between them and a warning to all the forces in the world that sought to divide and fetter the lives of men and women.

But there is an unavoidable hollowness to this passage that cannot have escaped the attention of contemporary readers. The dispute is won, but it is a small victory in a much larger historical defeat. The springtime of 1945 was betrayed by 'the failure of the Labour government to meet the challenges of vested interests and to build the new sort of society that would have expressed the emotions of the people who had voted for it in 1945... a democracy developed out of the elements of genuine anti-fascist unity built up in the war years.' By the early 1950s, the Cold War divisions about which the novel warns were still widening. Gallacher, Piratin and Platts-Mills all lost their seats in the 1950 general election. A few weeks after the end of the dispute, the Transport and General Workers Union voted to ban communists from holding office. Three of the leaders of the dispute — including Ted Dickens — were expelled from the union. In 1951 Dickens and Timothy were among seven dockers' leaders charged with 'conspiracy' following an unofficial strike in the ports of Liverpool and London. In 1956, Khrushchev revealed the extent of Stalin's crimes at the 20th Congress of the CPSU; a few months later Soviet tanks were in Budapest. A third of the membership of the British Communist Party resigned, including most of the 'cultural opposition'.

Jack Lindsay remained in the party until his death in 1990. He wrote seven more novels in the 'British Way' series — *Moment of Choice* (1955), *A Local Habitation* (1957), *Revolt of the Sons* (1960), *All on the Never-never* (1961, filmed in 1962 as *Live Now, Pay Later*),

The Way the Ball Bounces (1962), *Masks and Faces* (1963) and *Choice of Times* (1964) — slowly detailing the long arc of defeat of progressive ideas in post-War Britain. He also returned several times to London as a subject with biographical and critical studies of Blake, Dickens, Meredith, Morris, Defoe, Turner and Hogarth. When Lindsay died, he had written, translated and edited over one-hundred-and-seventy books.

Rising Tide may be as forgotten today as the events which it describes, but the novel remains a unique literary record of the years between the end of the Second World War and the beginnings of the Cold War, a fictional portrait of East End working-class life that successfully negotiated both the heroic and anti-heroic, and a compelling account of a neglected chapter in the history of London radicalism.

References and Further Reading

Noreen Branson, *History of the Communist Party of Great Britain 1941–51*, Lawrence and Wishart, 1997

Andy Croft (ed.), *A Weapon in the Struggle: the Cultural History of the Communist Party in Britain,* Pluto Press, 1998

Jack Dash, *Good Morning Brothers,* Lawrence and Wishart, 1969

Colin J Davis, *Waterfront Revolts: New York and London Dockworkers, 1946-61,* University of Illinois Press, 2003

Essays on Socialist Realism and the British Cultural Tradition, Arena Publications, 1953

Jim Fyrth (ed.), *Labour's Promised Land? Culture and Society in Labour Britain 1945–51,* Lawrence and Wishart, 1995

Jack Lindsay, *Life Rarely Tells,* Penguin, 1982

Jack Lindsay, *Meetings with Poets,* Frederick Muller, 1968

David Smith, *Socialist Propaganda in the Twentieth-Century British Novel*, Macmillan, 1978

Alick West, *The Mountain in the Sunlight,* Lawrence and Wishart, 1958

Docklands Today

Few parts of London can have changed so much in the last half-century as the dockland communities described in *Rising Tide* of Canning Town, Custom House and Beckton.

In 1949 the Victoria and Albert docks wholly dominated this part of the East End, its economy and sociology, its landscape and politics. With the expansion of the Essex container ports of Thurrock, Tilbury and Canvey

Island, both the Albert Dock and the Victoria Dock closed to commercial traffic in the 1980s. Albert Dock is now the home of the London Regatta Centre. These days Victoria Dock hosts the annual London Boat Show.

The Custom House Fields and the wasteland where Phyl and Jeff squat in *Rising Tide* were built on long ago. The Seamen's Hospital was demolished in 1993. You can still buy a drink in The White Hart in Stepney, where the unofficial Lockout committee meet in the novel, but The Ferndale on Cyprus Place where Jeff drinks with the Canadian seamen is now boarded-up. HMP Pentonville still exists; notable recent prisoners there have included Pete Doherty, Boy George and George Michael.

London City Airport is located at Albert Dock, as is the Docklands Campus of the University of East London. The ExCel Exhibition Centre is on the northern side of the Victoria Dock. Owned by the Abu Dhabi National Exhibition Company, in recent years the Centre has hosted the Motor Show, the 2009 G20 Summit, the UK arms fair as well as auditions for *Britain's Got Talent* and *The X Factor*. In 2012 it was one of the venues for the London Olympics.

It is fair to say that Phyl and Jeff would not recognise London dockland today. But they would also be disappointed to know that, sixty years later, this part of Newham should still be among the most economically deprived areas of the UK.

Andy Croft

Sam Selvon
The Lonely Londoners (1956)

BILL SCHWARZ

The Lonely Londoners, first published in 1956, opens:

> One grim winter evening, when it had a kind of unrealness about London, with a fog sleeping restlessly over the city and the lights showing in the blur as if is not London at all but some strange place on another planet, Moses Aloetta hop on a number 46 bus at the corner of Chepstow Road and Westbourne Grove to go to Waterloo to meet a fellar who was coming from Trinidad on the boat-train.

This sentence conforms to a certain mode of realism, naturalism even, in which the presence of the city is precisely located: Chepstow Road, Westbourne Grove, Waterloo Station, the number 46 bus. On the other hand, paradoxically, this is a realism intent on communicating the 'unrealness of London', a phenomenon which produces a sensation 'as if is not London at all but some strange place on another planet'.

The notion that London is in some sense 'unreal' has a long pedigree to it, not least in the imagination of high modernism. Selvon has confirmed the degree to which T.S. Eliot was an influence, and the parallels between *The Waste Land* and *The Lonely Londoners* are there for all to see, not least in the shared invocation of an 'unreal London'. However Selvon's conception of the interplay between the reality and unreality of the city is particular. It derived principally from the fact of his being a colonial migrant, part of the great Caribbean diaspora which transformed the life of metropolitan Britain in the postwar years. This was as much a sociological reality as it was a matter of aesthetic strategy: for the first generation of postwar

159

Caribbean migrants London was indeed 'unreal', barely conforming to the lessons they had learned about the imperial capital back home. From this collective experience there evolved a new way of writing about London, evident in *The Lonely Londoners*, which might be exemplified as a new form of 'diasporic' realism.

When Selvon himself arrived from Trinidad in 1950 the London he came to know resembled closely the London of his later fictional Moses Aloetta. He initially stayed in a hostel close by Earl's Court, doing menial jobs to support his writing and, when the opportunity presented itself, doing readings for the BBC's 'Caribbean Voices' programme, whose studios were located in Oxford Street. He came to be well acquainted with the Bayswater-Harrow Road area, as well as with the more bohemian BBC haunts north of Oxford Street. For all the experienced 'unreality' of London presented in *The Lonely Londoners*, the geographical London it represents is accurate in all its details. The 46 bus route, which allowed Moses to travel from Westbourne Grove to Waterloo, was indeed a route Selvon himself would have known: this was a service, in the fifties, which originated in Neasden Lane, threading its way south along Harrow Lane, before heading for Victoria and Waterloo, although (a sign of the times) with no Sunday or evening services.

Many who made the journey from the Caribbean to England welcomed the prospect of abandoning the 'unreality' of the colonial periphery for the putative 'reality' of the metropolitan centre where modern life *happened*. Galahad, in *The Lonely Londoners*, is driven by the allure of the city. 'Jesus Christ, when he say "Charing Cross", when he realise that it is he, Sir Galahad, who going there, near that place that everybody in the world know about... he feel like a new man... Galahad feel like a king living in London.' In the novel Galahad condenses the hope that the unreal self of the colonial, the split self torn between a dark skin and a white mask, might be overcome and that the West Indians might yet become truly modern, agents of their own destinies. But at the very moment he feels this promise most intensely — 'This is London, this is life oh Lord' — an everyday, banal racial encounter erupts, innocent enough to begin with, yet with the power to unhinge Galahad's sense of self. Back in the solitude of his room, in a moving soliloquy, he addresses his own blackness: 'Colour, is you that causing all this you know... Is not me, you know, is you!'

The actual England he encountered as a migrant — what Selvon called 'the actualities' — had its own kind of 'unrealness', for it didn't match at all the idealized expectations which had been incubated in the Caribbean. In shops, at work, in the street, he and a generation of West Indian migrants encountered not the abstract England of their school curriculum, nor an England derived from their reading of Dickens or Hardy, but an altogether more complex and less enchanted location, in which their role as 'natives', far from disappearing, took on new, hybrid forms: 'the land did not deceive, as the people did'.

However the magic of *The Lonely Londoners* works by presenting this specifically migrant view of London. It is the black West Indian, penniless and despised, who mutates into the authoritative anthropological investigator. It becomes the task of the novel's narrator to explain to the reader the peculiar habits of the native Londoners. Indeed, the West Indians — 'the boys' in Selvon's argot — both as migrants and transients have a privileged perspective on the city, their mobility giving them an access to the entire city customarily denied to the domesticated native. 'It have people living in London who don't know what happening in the room next to them, far more the street, or how other people living.'

Selvon has a sharp eye for the city's dispossessed, white as well as black, creating vignettes which resonate in the memory as much as the monochrome photographs of Bill Brandt or Bert Hardy, from the same period.

> A lot of the men get kill in the war and leave widow behind, and it have bags of these old geezers who does be pottering about the Harrow Road like if they lost, a look in their eye as if the war happen unexpected and they still can't realise what happen to the old Brit'n. All over London you would see them, going shopping with a basket, or taking a dog for a walk in the park, where they will sit down on the bench in winter and summer. Or you might meet them hunch-up in a bus queue, or waiting to get the fish and chips hot. On Friday or Saturday night, they go in the pub and buy a big glass of mild and bitter, and sit down by a table near the fire and stay here coasting lime till the pub close.

Or he observes, too, the men who go singing — begging — through the smart streets of the capital.

> ...now and then a window would open and somebody would throw down threepence or a tanner, and the old fellar would have to watch it good else it roll in the road and get lost. Up in that fully furnished flat where the window open... it must be have some woman that sleep late after a night at the Savoy or Dorchester, and that she was laying under the warm quilt on the Simmons mattress, and she hear the test singing... Could be that she have a nice night and she is in a good mood, or could be, after the night's sleep, she thinking about life and the sound of that voice quavering in the cold outside touch the old heart. But if she have a thought at all, it never go further than to cause the window to open and the tanner to fall down. In fact when the woman throw the tanner from the window she didn't even look down: if a man was a mile away and he was controlling a loudspeaker in the street moving up and down, the

tanner would have come the same way. Also, for the old test who singing, it ain't have no thought at all about where this tanner come from, or who throw it, man, woman or child, it ain't make no difference.

The narrator concludes:

When you come to think of it, everything in life like that...
People in the world don't know how other people does affect their lives.

London, in this vision, operates as an inhospitable, atomized environment, where human actions are little more than mechanical reflexes. This is the picaresque London made familiar by Defoe's *Moll Flanders* — Moll and Moses; Moses and Moll — in which good and bad fortune are entirely random, and where events exist beyond the control of the city's more hapless inhabitants. The endless search for food ('rations') and shelter predominates. The bodies of white women and black men are bartered indiscriminately. Moses, that 'veteran' of the city — 'Mr London' — has seen it all before. 'Take it easy', he counsels Galahad, 'London will do for you before long', advice repeated later in the novel.

Throughout the pleasures of migration, and the pleasures of the city, are almost exclusively organised through the optic of male sexual desire. There are moments when Selvon makes it clear that the objectification of black male bodies is the cause of violent retribution: no such understanding occurs in his (or in that of 'the boys') parallel conceptualisation of white women as 'pussy' or 'skins'. The deep sympathies of the novel lie with the male migrants, the lonely Londoners who against all odds make a life for themselves. As they do so, in Selvon's terms, they undermine the larger social system which conspires to substitute a life governed by human reciprocity — in which 'how... people does affect' others is recognised, known and acted upon — for one driven by a utilitarian imperative alone. Yet such a vision is compromised by the author's relentless objectification of white women, barely Londoners at all in Selvon's view of things, for it reveals the Caribbean men of his imagination to be complicit in the degradation of the city which otherwise, he suggests, they counter in their very beings.

Some two-thirds the way through the novel, darkness and dampness having become repeated motifs, the tone momentarily shifts and in breathless, lyrical and seductive prose — with no punctuation to impede its pace — Selvon celebrates the coming of summer in the city.

Oh what a time it is when summer comes to the city and all them girls throw away heavy winter coat and wearing light summer frocks so you

162

could see the legs and shapes that was hiding away from the cold blasts and you could coast a lime in the park...

The reader is drawn into this change of mood. A genuine eroticism seems to enter the tale, embracing not only the black migrants but the native English as well, dispatching the pervasive gloom of the earlier parts of the novel:

> ...everywhere you turn the English people smiling isn't it a lovely day as if the sun burn away all the tightness and strain that was in their face for the winter and on a nice day every manjack and his brother going to the park with his girl and laying down on the green grass and making love

But even in this moment of ebullience darker themes intrude, the erotic release generating violence and disaffection. The narrator indicates that with the arrival of summer 'your' first impulse — an unspecified 'you': 'the boys'? the reader? men in general? — is to barter with the prostitutes around Hyde Park Corner. A woman with whom Moses makes love nearly dies, or at least he believes that she is on the point of death; another is just coming off smack. Voyeurs cruise the park to observe the couplings between prostitutes and their clients. Black men are propositioned by whites to take part in a variety of sexual, or putatively more innocent, encounters for money. Prostitutes beat clients, clients beat prostitutes. Young black women — 'fresh blood' in the narrator's terms — join the ranks of those selling their bodies, 'but as far as spades hitting spades it ain't have nothing like that for a spade wouldn't hit a spade when it have so much other talent on parade...'. White women get off by inciting West Indian men to play the primitive. Black men beat white lovers.

Once darkness falls the entire city is propelled into an unresolved force-field of polymorphous sexual and racial energy, where the main currents of human intercourse reproduce the mechanics of everyday exploitation.

> ...all sorts of fellars from all walks of life... people wouldn't believe you when you tell them the things that happen in the city... lot of people in London who cork their ears and wouldn't listen but if they get the chance they do the same things themselves everybody look like they frustrated in the big city the sex life gone wild... all these things happen in the blazing summer under the trees in the park on the grass with daffodils and tulips in full bloom and a sky of blue oh it does really be beautiful then to hear the birds whistling and see the green leaves come back on the trees and in the night the world turn upside down and everyone hustling that is life that is London...

163

It's difficult to be sure of the degree to which the voices of the narrator and of the author are, or are not, conflated in these passages. The line separating indictment, on the one hand, and on the other, approval or acceptance (in the terms which Moses makes peculiarly his own: 'So it go, boy'), seems constantly to be on the move. Either way, these pages produce a disturbing accumulation of images. They testify, not simply to the predispositions of 'the boys', but to an entire, repressed domain of eroticism within the national landscape, conventionally concealed through the practices of English decorum. The heat of the city evening finally reveals a perverse national pathology: 'sex life gone wild'.

Galahad revels in this erotic underworld: 'oh lord Galahad say when the sweetness of summer get in him he say he would never leave the old Brit'n as long as he live...' Moses, though, is more circumspect. It is with his thoughts that the section closes. He 'sigh a long sigh like a man who live life and see nothing at all in it and who frighten as the years go by wondering what it all about.' The unrestrained erotic hedonism which summer brings appears to him essentially to be an illusion. Ultimately, the shift from winter to summer doesn't possess the power to free him from the deeper structures of migrant time, notwithstanding the hopes that spring brings with it. The seasons mark time's passing, in a repetitious cycle; but Moses imagines himself, notwithstanding the movement all about him, to be in stasis. In the words of the narrator: 'He used to see all his years in London pile up one on top of the other and he getting no place in a hurry, and the years going by, and he thought make him frighten sometimes'. Or as Moses himself tells Galahad: 'I just lay there on the bed thinking about my life, how after all these years I ain't get no place at all, I still the same way, neither forward nor backward.'

And yet Selvon was not one to be 'embarrassed' by the unreality of the societies he encountered, be it Trinidad or England, nor of their capacities for disorderliness. But he did strive to imagine societies which could be more real — more accommodating — for the dispossessed. *The Lonely Londoners*, especially, is testament to the power of the imagination — the power of the migrant imagination — to turn existing realities inside out. As the narrative proceeds, and Moses becomes more reflective, the reader can speculate that there occurs a growing convergence between the author and his principal protagonist, such that Moses emerges as the author of his own tale, undoing the 'unrealness' of what has now become his own city. By the end of the novel, standing on Chelsea Embankment, he looks down at the Thames and concludes:

...it had a greatness and a vastness in the way he was feeling tonight, like it was something solid after feeling everything else give way, and though he ain't getting no happiness out of the cogitations he still pondering, for is the first time that he ever find himself thinking like that.

Daniel was telling him how over in France all kinds of fellars writing books what turning out to be best-sellers. Taxi-drive, porter, road-sweeper — it didn't matter. One day you sweating in the factory and the next day all the newspapers have your name and photo, saying how you are a new literary giant.

He watch the tugboat on the Thames, wondering if he could ever write a book like that, what everybody would buy.

References and Further Reading

John Berger and Jean Mohr, *The Seventh Man*, Penguin, 1975

Michael Fabre, 'Sam Selvon: interviews and conversations' in Susheila Nasta (ed.), *Critical Perspectives on Sam Selvon*, Three Continents Press, 1988

Michael McKeon, *The Origins of the English Novel, 1600–1740*, Hutchinson Radius, 1988

Sam Selvon, 'Finding West Indian identity in London' (1988) in Susheila Nasta and Anna Rutherford (eds), *Tiger's Triumph. Celebrating Sam Selvon*, Dangaroo Press, 1995

Up and Down the Harrow Road

The area depicted in *The Lonely Londoners* did indeed become, as Selvon shows, a nucleus for Caribbean migrants in the post-war decades. The Notting Hill of the period consisted of once salubrious housing which had descended into streets of run-down rooming houses, in which unscrupulous and sometimes violent landlords packed in as many migrant tenants as they could manage. This was the area subject to the serious white rioting some two years after the publication of *The Lonely Londoners*, and then — a year later — the scene too, at the junction of Golbourne Road and Southam Street, of the murder of the Antiguan, Kelso Cochrane, a murder whose perpetrators never faced justice.

One immediate response to the riots of 1958 was the inauguration of Carnival in London, as a means to affirm the culture of migrant London, directly drawn from the indigenous resources of the Caribbean. In 1959 the first Carnival, held in January in the very un-Carnival environment of St. Pancras Town Hall, marked a relatively inauspicious start to what eventually became the annual summertime bank holiday event of the Notting Hill Carnival, re-imagining Sam Selvon's mean streets of *The Lonely Londoners* for a different, rather more accommodating historical age.

Since Selvon's times, many of the streets he depicts in the novel have undergone wholesale regeneration, with house prices to match. Aside from the days of Carnival itself, although many of the same streets exist, there are precious few means which can connect this section of the contemporary city to the London of Selvon's 1950s.

Yet twenty-first century migrant London, the descendant of *The Lonely Londoners*, is still visible enough in the area in which the novel was set: apparent not so much in the streets of crumbling lodging houses as in the nail parlours and hair salons which populate the Harrow Road — which is still inhabited largely by 'the people... call the working-class'. In literary terms, the transformation from Selvon's times to our own can be gauged from Zadie Smith's *White Teeth*.

Bill Schwarz

Colin MacInnes
Absolute Beginners (1959)

JERRY WHITE

And as I gazed out on the water like a mouth, a bed, a sister, I thought how, my God, I love this city, horrible though it may be, and never ever want to leave it, come what it may send me.

This is June 1958, and the anonymous teenage narrator of *Absolute Beginners* pledges his loyalty to London during a night-time taxi drive along the Embankment. London was indeed 'horrible' in that hot tense summer. And sorely would the teenager's loyalty be tried. For this was the moment of London's worst race riot, the last time when Londoners witnessed, even shared in, sustained violence against strangers just because of the colour of their skin. For a moment London seemed ready to tip in the direction of America's divided cities. With hindsight, the Notting Hill race riot would drain the sepsis of collectively-organised white racism for a decade to come at least. But when *Absolute Beginners* was written and published the cuts and bruises were stinging still. The teenager might have come through the test of right-mindedness that Notting Hill had set every Londoner, but not all his acquaintances, even his friends, had done so. And fear for the future dogs every page.

The question of race in London had become a defining issue for Colin MacInnes by the mid-1950s. The position of black newcomers in London encapsulated for him the problem of the outsider, the marginal, the misunderstood. This was not just some intellectual or moral proposition. For MacInnes himself was an outsider, he too was marginal, misunderstood. It was among black Londoners that he staked his particular claim of belonging, of sympathetic identification, of personal politics, while never really able to become more than an outsider

167

here too. In *Absolute Beginners* the fantasy of belonging — with his ex-girlfriend Suzette, or his mum and dad, or with Cool and the 'Spades' — would always just elude the teenager's grasp. There was more of himself in *Absolute Beginners*, MacInnes thought, than in any other of his books.

Certainly the main area of action was close to home, at least as the crow flies. Colin MacInnes was born at The Boltons, Brompton (South Kensington), a mile and a half or so south-east of Notting Hill, in August 1914, a couple of weeks after the outbreak of the First World War. His mother, Angela Thirkell (spoken 'Thirkle'), a popular novelist between the wars, was the grand-daughter of Sir Edward Burne-Jones, the pre-Raphaelite painter. Rudyard Kipling, whose literary achievements MacInnes rather surprisingly revered, was a great-uncle on his mother's side. With this high-Victorian artistic heritage Angela was certainly — so Bernard Kops, the Stepney playwright and friend of MacInnes, later quipped — 'one of the inner Thirkells'.

MacInnes himself though was jettisoned into some outer orbit, and it's not hard to see why. His father, James Campbell McInnes (Colin would add the 'a' in his writing years) was a Scot, a well-known lieder-singer, fatally handsome, bisexual but finally preferring men to women. MacInnes would follow his father's sexual trajectory. James and Angela divorced when the boy was just three. A year or so later Angela married again in the bewilderment of war, an Australian officer of engineers whose surname she took, and in 1919 the family emigrated to Melbourne. It didn't work out. Angela, cut-glass South Kensington, came quickly to loathe her second husband and all about him. She sailed back to London. But she left Colin and his elder brother behind at school in Australia. When he was seventeen he followed his mother 'home'.

MacInnes proved more than just a Londoner by accident of birth. He loved the place — just as his teenager did — and he lived all over it. He stayed at first with relatives at Pembroke Gardens, Earls Court, from 1931; in Finborough Road, Brompton, from 1936, 'in a sinister old slum where the ground-floor tenant was a cordial prostitute'; in another 'slum in Camden Town' from 1938 while studying at the Euston Road School of Drawing and Painting. After war service, from 1946, he rented a floor at Regent's Park Terrace where, while working for the BBC, he turned decisively to men for sex and to drink for oblivion. He embraced black men most hungrily of all. From the mid-1950s, as befitted his commitment to bohemia, he lived out of a suitcase at an indeterminable list of one-room addresses in Soho, Spitalfields, Pimlico, Marylebone, and just 'nfa' — no fixed abode. And from anywhere and everywhere he would 'go on marathon walks through the streets of London.'

It's no surprise then that London figures boldly in MacInnes's fiction and in his journalism. Indeed he wrote the text for an especially fine instance of a genre that has become particularly London's own, an intimate visual travelogue where the illustrator (Gustave Doré, Joseph Pennell, Evelyn Hofer, John Allin) plays equal, sometimes dominant, partner to the Londonist (Blanchard Jerrold, Justin McCarthy, V.S. Pritchett, Arnold Wesker). MacInnes's *London, City of Any Dream* (1962) is one of the most successful, accompanied (it is that way round, I think) by the grainy colour photographs of Erwin Fieger. But MacInnes is rightly remembered most of all for his great London trilogy: *City of Spades* (1957), *Absolute Beginners* (1959), *Mr Love and Justice* (1960). Their canonic status was recognised when they were republished collectively as *Visions of London*, with an introduction by Francis Wyndham, in 1969.

Of the three, *City of Spades* is most evidently MacInnes's exploration of the lives of black newcomers in London. He then sought to move on, and it's clear that he had very different intentions in *Absolute Beginners*. The 'teenager' phenomenon had struck him forcibly from around 1956. In the pages of *Twentieth Century* and *Encounter* in particular, MacInnes was one of the first weighty journalists to take teenagers seriously — their idols, their music, their fashions, above all their spending power and new-won independence as job opportunities for the young opened up in the post-war economy as never before. In the 1950s, London was still leading the charge in the teenage revolution. Tommy Steele ('The Pied Piper of Bermondsey' as MacInnes, a respectful and enthusiastic admirer, called him) was in the van.

The independent world of the new teenager was the ostensible theme of *Absolute Beginners*. It is independence from all the baggage of the old adult war-worn world — financial, political, cultural, spiritual — and MacInnes wholeheartedly applauds it. His identification with the teenage 'thing' is, he would have us believe, entire. Embarrassingly so at times, especially when he invents for the teenager a hip lingo of his own to distinguish 'the teenage ball' from the world of 'the tax-payers', the 'elderly sordids', even the 'short-pant sperms and chicklets' who were merely 'teenagers in bud'. Despite the linguistic innovations, this proves to be a teenager who left school at fifteen but can't bear to put a 'whom' out of place. Whatever he did, MacInnes could never quite leave the inner Thirkells behind him.

But if a celebration of the 1950s teenager is the primary objective of *Absolute Beginners*, race is always close to the surface and in the

169

final quarter of the book takes over completely. Race will prove the test by which teenagers, and indeed the adult world, will be judged and some of both will be found lacking. By the end we know there are good teenagers and bad. In *Absolute Beginners* the Teddy Boys are as bad as they get.

As good as they get, though, is the teenager himself, a fantasy MacInnes as he would like to have been, freed from The Boltons legacy. The teenager is nearly nineteen, and so approaching his last teenage year. He works as a photographer, a prescient classless icon especially of the decade to come. He is freelance, working for himself a necessary component in MacInnes's vision of teenage independence. And because business is hand-to-mouth he is entwined in the scrounge-flush cycle which MacInnes himself knew well. As he can't be too fussy about where the next fiver comes from, the teenager will photograph anything, and anyone doing anything, as long as it's for cash or an uncrossed cheque. Fashion, portraiture and pornographic poses are all grist to his Rolleiflex. His camera and his Vespa — a gift from a South American diplomat whose manly contortions he captures on film — are his only possessions of value. Like his creator, the teenager can live from a suitcase, even if strapped at the back of his scooter.

This is 1958, so the teenager is a Blitz Baby, born in an air raid or so his mother tells him. And the fractures of war — just as for MacInnes in an earlier conflict — have left baneful wounds. The teenager's mother is too good-looking and well-endowed for her own good. She dotes on Cypriots and 'Malts' with hot-blooded appetites, and cavalierly cuckolds the teenager's meek dad in his own home. His dad he loves, his mum he hates — and there's much of the real Colin here too. He has a step-brother, Vernon or Vern — the teenager calls him Jules — who is the specky fruit of one of their mother's flings. But the teenager and Vern don't get on and their mutual antipathy sways always on the edge of a full-out scrap. When the teenager goes home to use the darkroom he keeps there, it's really to keep an eye on his lonely ailing father — whose main preoccupation is collecting materials for a history of Pimlico which inevitably he'll never finish. One knows the feeling.

The teenager tries to keep an eye on Suzette too. She is his former girlfriend, a shop-girl with a model's looks, moulded from her rich-mix Scotch-English-Gibraltarian-Jewish heritage. Suzette has abandoned the teenager for black men — she is 'a Spade-lover', 'Spade-crazy'. Even so, Suzette ends up marrying Henley, a well-heeled fashion-designer, for his money. Henley is pallid and unequivocally gay so this will be a platonic union, and it all falls apart before the novel is over.

170

So, too, for different reasons as we shall see, does the teenager's friendship with Wiz or the Wizard, wise and calculating and cold-hearted beyond his teenage years. He is the teenager's 'blood-brother', but there's bad blood here, for Wiz has a hair-trigger temper to go with his 'razor-edge face' — 'give my hate to little Suze' is one parting-shot to the teenager. Wiz is a wheeler-dealer, a fixer or broker, who brings buyers and sellers together in the murky metropolitan sub-economy. Pursuing the commission-agent's course to a logical conclusion Wiz ends up a ponce, a figure of some significance in MacInnes's London iconography. Frankie Love in his next novel would be just such an 'other man'.

Suzette and Wiz are fellow teenagers. So is Mr Cool, a mixed-race London-born fellow lodger of the teenager's. So is the Hoplite, outrageously queer. And so is ghastly Ed the Ted, who grunts in savage cockney — no whoms here — which has MacInnes following in great-uncle Ruddy's footsteps. Ed is representative of the larger Ted community which will batten like carrion on the troubles in Notting Hill.

Yet although this is a teenage novel, adults get something more than a look-in. Most are either sadly beaten down or shiftily on the make. The acceptable face of adulthood is provided by Mannie and Miriam Katz. Mannie is a writer (like his original, Bernard Kops) and it is the Katzes' warm-hearted intellectually-inquiring Jewishness that MacInnes celebrates here. Though he loves London, the teenager tells us, if all the Jews were to pack up for Israel or America then he'd leave too. He even claims (like Suzette) to have some Jewish blood himself — at least, 'I know I'm circumcised'. *Absolute Beginners*, we might note here, is dedicated to Alfred Maron who was MacInnes's Jewish landlord in Hanbury Street, Spitalfields, around the time of writing and publishing the book.

The Katzes live in the Borough, not the East End, and inner south London figures as one among several significant locations in the novel. They occupy 'a fine old reconditioned derelict', probably in one of the Georgian terraces lining the Borough Road. Ed the Ted, who hails like the teenager from Pimlico, has also 'emigrated' south of the river, 'down to Bermondsey, to join a gang', and it's right that south London, east and west of the Elephant, was true Teddy Boy territory at the time MacInnes wrote. Smarter London gets a look in — Belgravia, for instance, where the teenager does a photo-shoot, a part of 'picturesque Great Britain' with 'the flower-boxes, and the awnings over doors, and the front walls painted different shades of cream.' So does the *News-of-the-World* London of Soho basement jazz and jive clubs. And so does picture-book London — the teenager has a nocturnal paddle in the

Serpentine, disturbs a furtive couple in the Hyde Park bushes, samples with his father the riverside delights down to Cookham, and indulges himself in taxi-rides along the Embankment at night, as we've seen. It's delightful to note how such a journey could be inspirational and life-affirming even in 1958.

There are then two London districts with overriding significance. The teenager has come out of Pimlico. That's where his mum and dad and Vern remain and where the teenager returns from time to time. By 1958 Pimlico had long been an equivocal déclassé district. It had never fulfilled its South-Belgravian aspirations. By the time MacInnes first discovered it (in the 1930s) and lived there (in the 1940s) it had lost caste for two generations. It was seedy, shabby-genteel at best, outright slummy at worst, with a transient marginal population that lived on second-hand dealing, the proceeds of petty theft, and the sex trade, liveliest towards Victoria station. The teenager's mum is not quite a Pimlico whore, but nearly. She runs a sort of boarding-house for Mediterranean men with perma-stubble and offers sexual services on the side — for kicks as much as cash it seems. Dad, resigned to his lot as an essentially kept man who is kept in the dark, is far from a ponce, but his presence makes the house respectable. And although his 'ancestral home' is firmly along flyblown Pimlico lines, the teenager shows us that Pimlico itself is changing, and for the better. 'Down by the river' are 'the big new high blocks of glass-built flats' at Churchill Gardens, a happy instance of post-war municipal housing, 'like an X-ray of a stack of buildings with their skins peeled off'. Nearby is a 'kiddipark of Disneyland items erected by the borough council' for 'the juveniles'. And up in Victoria there is the Empire air-terminal, in the process of extension as MacInnes was writing, where airport coaches began the journey to exotic locations.

This kind of modern world, though, had not yet reached the teenager's present home district, 'my manor in the area of w.10 and 11'. His part of this large area the teenager calls Napoli. The name marks it out as at once lawless in the context of metropolitan authority but living to its own rules. Napoli has 'got left behind by the Welfare era *and* the Property-owning whatsit' and is 'nothing more than a stagnating slum. It's dying, this bit of London, and that's the most important thing to remember about what goes on there.'

Now topography here is not helped by MacInnes's inability, though a seasoned traveller, to tell east from west. But what he describes as Napoli is North Kensington and Notting Hill west of Ladbroke Grove. And at the heart of it lies Notting Dale — its boundaries indeterminate on the ground — in the western part of this district off 'long, lean' Latimer Road. Out of it, close to Latimer Road tube and running east 'like horrible tits dangling from a lean old sow', range 'what I think must really be the sinisterest highways in our city, well, just listen to their names': Blechynden Street, Silchester Road, Walmer Road, Bramley Road and Testerton Street, and numerous others he doesn't trouble to list. Here the houses are 'old Victorian lower-middle tumble-down'. They 'live on like shells' and 'there's only one thing to do with them', which is 'to pull them down till not a one's left standing up.' Yet nearby, on the edge of Napoli, to the south and east near Ladbroke Grove, a different story is just beginning to be told. It's another aspect of change in modern London but not one the teenager likes because here 'are one or two sections that are positively posh: not *fashionable*, mind you, but quite graded', even though, just 'cheek by thing', 'you're back in the slum area again'.

It's in the slum Notting Dale Napoli that the teenager has his room in a house with others who would not be living there 'if you could live anywhere else'. Yet, not quite. It is 'so cheap' and naturally draws the very poor. But the great attraction for the teenager and his fellow lodgers is that 'you're *free* there!' His fellow lodgers are consequently from almost every metropolitan out-group known to the 1950s reading public, and some perhaps not known at all: Hoplite the homosexual; Big Jill, the lesbian ponce; Mr Cool, the mixed-race Londoner who doesn't fit in, forced to make a lonely and harsh way in the world. He has a white half-brother who doesn't like Cool much, and likes his few white friends even less. And it's in these tensions of race and allegiance that the teenager and the other *Absolute Beginners* find their toughest trial in that August and September of 1958.

There was no more fitting place for a race riot — indeed, a riot of any kind — than Notting Dale. Fifty years before it had been called by George R. Sims and others London's hell on earth. There were years then when half of all the babies born there would be dead of hunger, disease and neglect before their first birthday. Perhaps the worst slums in London had been in the Bangor Street area, cleared in the early 1950s for public housing. And nearby, at 10 Rillington Place off St. Mark's Road, John Reginald Halliday Christie had murdered seven women and an infant over a ten-year period ending in 1953.

It was into this desperately poor and sordid district of London that a few hundred blacks had migrated from the late-1940s on. They found themselves in competition with their poor white neighbours: first, for housing, and second, for sex. The housing struggle had just been made fiercer than ever by the 1957 Rent Act, which weakened the rights of tenure of longstanding working-class tenants, all of whom were white of course, in favour of high-rented furnished accommodation and owner-occupation. Peter Rachman, whose name has entered

173

the language, sharpened his claws as a landlord in North Kensington in these years. Many of his tenants were black. And the explosive combination of black men and white women readily provoked sexual envy among white men with low self-esteem. Some said it was the efforts of outraged neighbours to punish a black man with two young white girl-friends that first set Notting Hill alight.

There had been trouble between blacks and whites in Nottingham, and isolated assaults on black men in the streets of west London through that summer of 1958. Gangs of Teddy Boys smashed up cafés used by West Indians and attacked a house in Shepherd's Bush. In the early morning of 24th August, a Sunday, nine white youths went 'nigger-hunting' in a car. Aged 17 to 20, mainly from Notting Dale and the White City Estate, they were armed with a knife, chair-legs, a car starting-handle, and 'iron bars torn from street railings', the traditional weapon of the London tough. They assaulted five black men in separate incidents in Shepherd's Bush and Notting Hill; three West Indians were seriously hurt. That same night there was prolonged rioting, involving whites against West Indians, in Nottingham. A week later, North Kensington went the same way.

The 'Notting Hill Riots' began around midnight on Saturday 30th August. Crowds estimated at 400 strong attacked houses occupied by West Indians in Bramley Road, Blechynden Street, Lancaster Road and Silchester Road in the north of Notting Dale where, of all the clusters of West Indians in North Kensington, fewest lived. Windows were broken and at least one house was set on fire by a petrol bomb. Weapons included milk bottles, favoured for throwing, choppers, iron bars and knives. On Monday and Tuesday, 1st and 2nd September, petrol bombs were thrown in an attack on a house in Blenheim Crescent, Notting Hill, and windows were smashed in Oxford Gardens. Thousands of people were said by police to be roaming the streets of North Kensington and there was trouble in the Harrow Road, Paddington. Violence continued in the north of Notting Dale and North Kensington and to a lesser extent in parts of Shepherd's Bush, Paddington and Marylebone, until 5th September when the riots petered out. The streets were tense and conspicuously policed for some time after. Some 140 people, blacks among them, were arrested.

These bare bones are pretty faithfully fleshed out by MacInnes's teenager. MacInnes followed the press reports avidly, especially those in the *Manchester Guardian*. Some factual incidents, like the attack on Seymour Manning who fled a mob to find sanctuary in a Latimer Road greengrocer's, appear in the novel with little embellishment. MacInnes's account in *Absolute Beginners* was singled out by the first sociological analysis of the riots a couple of years later as 'realistic'

174

and 'derived from a great deal of personal observation'. There are many telling details that stick in the mind, not least 'the battered little delivery vans... usually dark blue, and with the back doors tied on with wire, or one door off', in which the Teds and their allies sped from one 'nigger-hunting' foray to another.

But what exercises MacInnes here is how his characters will respond to the nightmare going on around them. It is a test of their very humanity. Here everyone has to take sides. There could be no mere spectators now. If you weren't with the blacks, then you were against them.

Who can the teenager rely on? Who will take the right side? The Katzes will, of course. Outsiders by birth, they'll stand up and fight beside the underdog. But some of the teenager's middle-class clients and acquaintances are more difficult to engage. Observers by nature or profession they keep their distance, physically and morally, and fail the Notting Hill test. One urges the teenager 'to get some snaps' of the troubles for an exhibition they'd been planning together. One more turns up to film the violence for a newsreel and has an interest in seeing people hurt each other. Another urges the teenager to take care of himself. But the ex-Deb-of-Last-Year, out sight-seeing in a 'cream vintage Bentley' with a 'bunch of Hooray Henries', turns up trumps. She and the Henries see in the Teds and their supporters 'nothing but a lot of bloody scum'. That's what the teenager wants to hear. For MacInnes and the teenager, Notting Hill is a race struggle where the lowest-class slum-dwellers are the enemy's stormtroopers. To that extent it's a class struggle too, and The Boltons' Kiplingesque endowment proves comfortingly right-minded in what becomes for MacInnes a battle between two Kensingtons, North and South, and between two Englands, old (before the blacks) and new.

Questions of allegiance were yet more complicated among the teenagers in that Napoli tenement house. Hoplite, for instance, is too much of an outsider to come inside with the teenager even on this most vital of all questions. He has always fancied the teenager, and to see him bruised and battle-scarred is just a turn-on, not a call to arms. Besides, he doesn't really care for the blacks and so fails the teenager from the outset: 'Really, darling, I know you love them, but they're so rough.' On the other hand, Hoplite is such 'a tit' that this is more forgivable eccentricity than true malevolence.

Big Jill, none more outsider than she, proves more staunch in her live-and-let-live libertarianism. She has nothing to say against the blacks, is if anything in favour, but finds more ignorance than evil in those who feed the nation's paranoia with their anti-immigration rhetoric. Even so, she acts with the teenager, offering tea and sympathy and the free use of her phone to tell the outside world of the terrible doings in Napoli. Cool, of course, shoulders arms with the blacks, and is 'the only Spade in Napoli who's thought of us', the white tribesmen who side with justice and against their own kind. Even better, his half-brother, forced to choose whose side he's on, stands four-square with Cool in the street battles: their mother becomes a fire-bomb victim near Oxford Gardens as the troubles move east into Notting Hill proper.

Most of all, it is Suzette who disinterestedly and wholeheartedly commits to the blacks, just like the teenager. He stumbles across her in a basement club where 'the boys' are under siege from a crowd with petrol and milk bottles at the ready. Suzette has left Henley and been in Napoli a week to fight with her friends. In the mêlée she and the teenager flee to his room and make love. It's their first time. And in their clumsy half-spoken way they move towards some kind of commitment to one another. Just what kind we'll never know.

By this time, and in the opposite direction, the Wiz has shown the teenager his true colours. And while with Suzette the riots mark a coming together, with Wiz they provoke a terminal fracture.

They meet by accident in the Notting Dale streets and come across one of the KBW (Keep Britain White) street-meetings where fascists — Jeffrey Hamm and his British League of Ex-Servicemen and Women or Victor Burgess's Union for British Freedom — stoke the flames and the fury. It's night, and in 'the yellow-coloured glare' of the street lamps the faces in the attentive crowd were 'a kind of unwashed violet grey'. To the teenager's horror, Wiz refuses to condemn the fanatical speaker and eventually, 'his little body... all clenched', he throws out a salute and cries 'Keep England white!' The teenager wreaks immediate and violent revenge, hitting Wiz in the face 'with all my life behind it'. With one look back, he flees the crowd.

At the end of the riots, as adrenalin and fear and anger seep away, the teenager is left empty and exhausted. He feels shame and revulsion too: 'I'd fallen right out of love with England. And even with London...' His first thought is escape. He takes an air-terminal coach to the airport but through confusion doesn't board a plane. And it seems likely that, in fact, he'll stay to help build a London where black newcomers can feel truly welcome.

Which is what, in his own way, MacInnes did himself. His attachment to the hustler margins of West Indian and African migration hardened. There he found comfort in an anarchic blend of hard drinking, drugs, casual exploitative sex and hand-to-mouth freelance writing. At the end of 1965, in a move which must have given some anarchist friends a fright, he began to propagandise for Michael de

Freitas (Michael X) and his English brand of Black Power. But MacInnes remained too much of an outsider ever to enter a real movement, let alone something as sham and corrupt as Michael X had on offer. He drifted away, though not without appearing as a character witness for the Mangrove Nine (prosecuted for charges including conspiracy to incite a riot in a case which put the focus on police racism) in 1970. A year or so later and he would begin to loosen his London ties and establish a home in the house of a woman friend at Hythe on the Kent coast. He died there, of cancer of the oesophagus, in April 1976, aged 61.

MacInnes's London writings are his most important legacy. Among some superb essays, headed by *London, City of Any Dream* (1962), his London trilogy of 1957–60 has become the iconic portrayal of the metropolis at a defining moment in its modern history: at the point where it was about to remake itself as a multicultural world city.

References and Further Reading

Colin MacInnes, *City of Spades*, Macgibbon and Kee, 1957

Colin MacInnes, *Absolute Beginners*, Macgibbon and Kee, 1959

Colin MacInnes, *Mr Love and Justice*, Macgibbon and Kee, 1960

Colin MacInnes, *England, Half English*, Macgibbon and Kee, 1961

Colin MacInnes, *London, City of Any Dream*, Thames and Hudson, 1962

Tony Gould, *Inside Outsider: The Life and Times of Colin MacInnes*, Chatto and Windus, 1983

George R. Sims, *Off the Track in London*, Jarrolds, 1911

Ruth Glass, *Newcomers: The West Indians in London*, Allen and Unwin, 1960

Pearl Jephcott, *A Troubled Area: Notes on Notting Hill*, Faber, 1964

Napoli Revisited

What sort of London and what sort of Londoner would MacInnes have found in Napoli now?

Well, it's been all change, and mostly for the better. Change for the worse has been in the road system. The Westway bisects North Kensington east-west above Lancaster Road. And the West Cross Route now cordons off the western boundary of Notting Dale. It has also obliterated the Notting Dale part of 'long, lean' Latimer Road, so that the street down which Seymour Manning fled for his life is no more. Similarly, the streets that MacInnes wanted pulled down have all gone, or very nearly. Blechynden

Golborne Road W10

Street and Silchester Road must have been cleared shortly after he wrote, replaced by a five-storey council block, Bramley House. Testerton Street is now Testerton Walk, absorbed into the Lancaster West estate, brutalist brown-brick high-density low-rise, built in the 1970s, with raised walkways that mimic in dwarf form the flyovers nearby and with a gaunt tower block in the middle. Henry Dickens Court to the south, pretty new when MacInnes wrote, its blocks named cosily after Henry's father's characters (Copperfield, Barkiss, Marley, Carton and others), has worn astonishingly well. All this public housing looks presentable, some of it spick and span.

We should be grateful for it. Council housing is the reason why this part of Notting Hill remains a diverse area in terms of class. The remaining Victorian housing nearby is astonishingly manicured and solidly haut-bourgeois. One wonders what Blechynden Street and the rest would have become had their fate been left to the market. There would surely have been no room for Notting Dalers in this yuppy paradise. We have a hint of this in the tiny remnants of MacInnes's Notting Dale that have survived. In Bramley Road, at the St. Ann's Road end and opposite the junction with Whitchurch Road, a rundown terrace of half-a-dozen double- and single-fronted tene-ment houses is a faint echo of fifty years ago. With this difference: one, 'unmodernised', was on the market in June 2012 at £890,000.

The other main difference, of course, is in the complexion of the Londoner. Notting Dale is no longer merely the resort of the rough cockney, the wayward provincial and the boys from the Windies. They've all been greatly leavened by people from every country under the sun. Of all the changes, this would perhaps have surprised MacInnes most. And satisfied him most, too.

Jerry White

Lynne Reid Banks
The L-Shaped Room (1960)

CATHI UNSWORTH

irst published in 1960, Lynne Reid Banks' *The L-Shaped Room* is set in a London on the cusp of radical social change. Six years after the end of rationing and three years before The Beatles' first number one, the book opens on 'a greyish sort of day' in 'one of those gone-to-seed houses in Fulham', painted in shades of coffee stain, soot-smeared paintwork and the yellowish tint of creeping smog. From the first sentence, Banks vividly evokes transient, post-war, pre-Swinging West London through the medium of a cut-and-shunt boarding house with its prostitutes in the basement, chipped sinks and flickering landing lights, endless, wearisome stairs and beady-eyed landlady, Doris.

The feelings of dread and dislocation stirred by the initial observations of the book's narrator, twenty-seven-year-old Jane Graham, are heightened by the mentions of these working girls and the memory of Doris's gaze resting on her waistband as she shows her the crudely partitioned room of the title. Jane is in a position that no unattached career girl would want to find herself in as the Sixties began. Seven years before abortion was made legal and a year before the Pill first arrived in Britain, she is one month pregnant.

This is what has brought her to the unfamiliar neighbourhood, in search of the sort of place where 'nobody asks questions' as Doris pointedly puts it. Having secured the tenancy of the room, Jane wanders through streets of slumped, shabby houses that seem to reflect straight back the suspicion with which she regards them through the deadeye gaze of their curtain-less windows. On learning her news, the newsagent in whose shop she found the ad for the room

181

treats Jane to a crash-course in local manners — including his opinion of her new landlady.

'Don't you go paying your rent on the dot, miss,' he advises. 'You keep the old cow waiting, like she does me.' This sour old boy regards the 'chippies' in the basement as more honourable than 'that old faggot' Doris, with her cavalier attitude to the settlement of bills and disregard for current popular opinion on race relations. His speech is littered with references to 'bobos' who 'have got to be kept in their place', the casual deployment of which gives as tangible a feel for the attitudes of the time as the descriptive evocation of the place.

Taking pity on Jane's obviously reduced circumstances he finally finds a little heart, directing her to his friend Frank's café for a decent cuppa. 'Pity they don't divide cafés off into saloon and public, if you ask me. People like to be with their own sort. Not as how you'd find many of your sort around here...'

Over a comforting cup of coffee, Jane reflects on her predicament, and a life that has similarities with the author's own. Born in London in 1929, Lynne Reid Banks was evacuated to Canada during the Second World War, returning as a teenager in 1945 to train and then work as an actress. Jane's recollections of pre-Equity survival in rep, living off tinned spaghetti in dreary northern towns, ring with the authenticity of autobiography.

Jane's spell as an actress came to a sorry end, which she revisits with a sense of shame, and she ended up working in a café similar to Frank's in Yorkshire, turning the farce of her career into a kitchen sink drama in order to avoid telling her widowed father the truth. When Jane returned to London, she took up a PR job in a West End hotel. Reid Banks herself turned instead to television journalism, becoming one of ITN's first female news reporters. She started tapping out this novel between shifts when she worked there. Throughout *The L-Shaped Room*, there is a brutally honest sense of self-examination in the character of Jane and her relationships with those closest to her.

For Jane now faces a familiar situation. It is her father she is running away from, a distant, awkward man, who, like most English males of his generation, has survived the Depression and two World Wars without ever expressing his feelings. The combination of confessing her plight to him and the situation surrounding her own birth invoke emotions in Jane too terrible to bear.

What do you want of me father? *I thought fiercely.* What have you ever wanted? Not this anyway. Not a scandal, not a bastard grandchild.

> This won't go far to make up for my shortcomings, like not being a son and like killing my mother by getting born.

She has already visited the sort of Harley Street doctor that could make her problem go away for the sum of sixty guineas; an experience that left Jane determined to keep the baby instead. Her father's reaction to the news — and her own regret at the way she broke it to him — in his civil service office, in the middle of the day — have brought her to this juncture.

The room of Jane's self-enforced confinement has been created from one much larger by the simple expediency of a partition wall. Crammed inside are a gas stove; a wash-basin doubling up as a sink; a table scarred with cigarette burns; a camp bed covered in a wartime afghan (a multi-coloured knitted blanket); a three-legged chest of drawers, a lumpy armchair and a mantelpiece adorned with two plaster Alsatians, under which resides a tiny gas fire. The Alsatians fill Jane with horror; the afghan affords her solace.

But there is more consolation than Jane had imagined to be found in the community of fellow social outcasts she discovers within Doris's domain.

The first one she meets is a slight, dark-haired young man who looks like a 'fledgling blackbird'. Hollow eyed and scruffily attired, acerbic and self-depreciating in equal measure, hiding his Jewishness behind his non-de-plume, Toby Coleman is the literary outsider in this world, a would-be Angry Young Man who can't quite finish his first draft. Over the course of her months of tenancy, Jane and Toby will fall in love and then be ripped apart by the revelation of her pregnancy.

Residing on the other side of the flimsy hardwood partition to Jane is West Indian jazz guitarist John, a huge, hulk of a man with a surprisingly delicate demeanour. Jane's first sighting of John, his black face pressed against the window of their dividing wall, terrifies her and forces her to dissemble her own prejudices. John and Toby help Jane turn her grim little abode into somewhere worth living — most memorably, when John gets rid of Jane's bedbugs with a piece of softened soap, provoking a comical confrontation with Doris. But it is John's bitter reaction to Jane and Toby's affair that helps doom their relationship before it has really begun.

The tarts in the basement offer Jane a window on another forbidden world. When she makes a tentative visit downstairs, in an attempt to measure her own fall from grace against those that sell sex professionally, she finds that her older namesake Jane is not so hard-bitten as she had imagined. Both this Jane, and her Hungarian room-mate Sonia, have fallen into this way of life more by accident than design. The former takes on the resigned demeanour of a hard-pressed social worker:

> 'Now you're going to ask me if I hate all men. Well I don't. You can't hate what you don't respect. I'm sorry for them — I don't suppose you believe that, but it's true... You probably think my life's some kind of tragedy, but I'll tell you — one of the hardest parts of it's keeping a straight face.'

Then there is Mavis, the curious spinster on the ground floor, with her room full of knick-knacks and a viperous cat. A Cockney ex-wardrobe mistress, Mavis is always listening into conversations on the hallway telephone. When she overhears Jane talking to a doctor's receptionist, Mavis creeps up the stairs to offer her another way out of her predicament — some special pills to be downed with gin. Jane doesn't take Mavis' 'remedy' but instead gorges herself on curry, thinking that she is miscarrying when she subsequently suffers violent indigestion. After Jane recovers, Mavis cannot understand why her prescription has failed — but still cheerfully runs up baby clothes for the chastened mother-to-be.

With such a beautifully rendered cast and tender exploration of societal taboo, it is little wonder that Reid Banks' book was attractive to a film industry fired up by the work of Toby's real life contemporaries. After John Braine's *Room at the Top* and John Osbourne's *Look Back in Anger* had successfully transferred to the screen in 1959, the journalist Daniel Farson coined the term 'Angry Young Men' to encompass contemporary literary social realism, and it's how Jane refers to Toby in the book. These films kickstarted a cinematic new wave: Karel Reisz's adaptation of Alan Sillitoe's *Saturday Night and Sunday Morning* was a smash in 1960, closely followed by Tony Richardson's production of *Angry Young Woman* Shelagh Delany's *A Taste of Honey* in 1961. *The L-Shaped Room* would follow them onto the big screen in 1962, under the direction of the multi-talented Bryan Forbes.

In a recent interview with this book's co-editor, Andrew Whitehead, Reid Banks does not look back with fondness on Forbes' movie. 'Not that the characters were less interesting in the film, perhaps even more — he laid it on with a thicker trowel — but I felt them so real in my imagination that I didn't like them being altered,' she says.

While Reisz and Richardson worked closely with the authors of their source material, Forbes wrote his own adaptation of *The L-Shaped Room* in which several of the central characters — most notably, Jane's father — are done away with. By casting the French actress Leslie Caron in the title role, Jane herself is necessarily altered, going by the screen surname of Fosset and not having the career that the book's Jane does. Although Forbes cleverly picks up the ideas that float around Jane's head in Frank's café and gives his film version a job there instead. Meanwhile, Toby becomes a Yorkshireman — an echo, perhaps, of an Angry Young Stan Barstow or Keith Waterhouse — played by Tom Bell, an actor who nonetheless embodies the moody ambivalence of the book's character.

There are a couple of masterstrokes to Forbes' vision. He relocates Doris' boarding house from Fulham to Ladbroke Grove, which works better as a location in which class and race divides are shifting. Fulham is important in London's black history — the Jamaican anti-slavery campaigner Marcus Garvey lived at 53 Talgarth Road from 1935 until his death in 1940, and has a nearby park named after him. It was a place of cheap lodgings — The Rolling Stones' mouldy digs at 102 Edith Grove, where they survived the freezing 1962 winter by staying in bed all day, being a legendary example. But, the district where the book is set, around North End Road market, was predominantly white working-class.

Ladbroke Grove, however, was precisely where you would have found a West Indian jazzer, an angst-ridden writer and a couple of toms competing for limited space under the same roof. Memorably described by Colin MacInnes as 'our little Napoli' in *Absolute Beginners* (1959), Ladbroke Grove was a world apart from the rest of London, where the most noticeable flux in the social mix took place. Hard to imagine now, in the post-*Notting Hill* world, but its towering stucco terraces, communal parks and gardens were, post-World War II, riven with bombsites; the soot-blackened houses carved up by mainly upper-class landlords into slums in which they exploited successive waves of immigrants.

Incomers first started arriving to the area from Jamaica, Trinidad and Tobago in 1948, when, seeking to boost its post-war workforce, the British government encouraged Commonwealth citizens to settle in 'the Mother country'. However, the *Windrush* generation, named for the ship that brought them into Tilbury Docks, had a very cold welcome, finding the attitudes espoused by Jane's newsagent to be fairly entrenched. Years of resentment boiled over in the race riots of 1958, which climaxed in the streets of Ladbroke Grove.

Until the Street Offences Act came into force the year after, these same streets were also lined with working girls. In 1959, the Royal Borough of Kensington, as it was then, had the biggest population of prostitutes in all of London. Taking advantage of them were the osteopath Stephen Ward, who first introduced Christine Keeler to high society; and the serial killer Jack the Stripper, who murdered eight girls with links to the Profumo scandal between 1959–65, in one of London's most disquieting unsolved crimes.

Interestingly, Reid Banks tells Whitehead that the room that originally inspired her to write the story was actually located in Chepstow Villas, W11, but that her decision to set the book in Fulham was based on one miserable night she spent in a boarding house there after running away from home. Chepstow Villas was slap bang in the middle of the territory of Peter Rachman, the landlord and consort of Keeler whose name is now synonymous with slum dwellings, but who was one of the very few that would allow black tenants in his properties. Original Angry Young Men writers Colin Wilson and Alexander Trocchi resided at number 24. Forbes' location is close by — 'Brockash Road' is actually St. Luke's Road, across the other side of Westbourne Park Road.

Relocating to the Grove also allowed Forbes to set the pivotal scene where Jane falls in love with Toby at John's jazz club from the West End to the sort of shebeen described in Trinidadian writer Samuel Selvon's *The Lonely Londoners* (1956) and MacInnes' *City of Spades* (1957). A place where all the residents of Doris's house, and many more like it besides, come together to forget themselves over potent rum punches, delirious music and dancing. In real life, there was a jazz club on Westbourne Grove, opposite St. Luke's Road on the corner of Powis Mews.

John, played by the American Brock Stevens, here plays trumpet rather than guitar. Although most of John's scenes in the book remain intact — including the bedbug incident — there is one further major alteration.

As heavily hinted at by his fondness for needlework and cookery, John in the book turns out to be gay. In the film, it is Mavis, played to tear-jerking perfection by veteran actress Cicely Courinedge, who hides a lavender secret. Altered from a costumier to a retired actress, her East End roots pansticked with Received Pronunciation, Courinedge's Mavis is a more sympathetic, melancholy character than the original. Her Christmas Day rendition of 'Take Me Back to Dear Old Blighty' would later be appropriated by The Smiths — those Eighties plumbers of the kitchen sink — on the opening of their *The Queen Is Dead* LP.

What is most poignantly missing from the film is the relationship between Jane and her father and how it is resolved, with the help of his elder sister Addy. The generation gulf between the baby boomers and their parents is another pertinent topic that Reid Banks flushes from the shadows. Like the day trip the Teenager in *Absolute Beginners* takes with his father to Cookham that turns into a voyage of mutual recognition, Jane and her father's gradual awareness of each other's fundamental humanity is the most moving aspect of all in a book shot through with compassion.

Whatever the author's reservations, though, Forbes' sensitive adaptation and the luminous central figure of Leslie Caron as Jane as a tribute to the strength of Reid Banks' often beautiful but never sentimental writing. *The L-Shaped Room* lingers far longer in the memory than later explorations of similar themes, such as Margaret Drabble's 1965 *The Millstone* (adapted by her for the screen as *A Touch of Love* in 1969) or even Peter Collinson's enjoyable 1968 film of Nell Dunn's riotous 1963 novel *Up The Junction*. Perhaps because it forever captures that black-and-white, bomb-hit and gaslit world, whose compromised inhabitants nonetheless dared to dream.

References and Further Reading

Max Décharné, *King's Road*, Weidenfeld & Nicolson, 2005
Nell Dunn, *Up The Junction*, MacGibbon & Kee, 1963
Anthony Frewin, *London Blues*, No Exit Press, 1997
Stewart Home, *Tainted Love*, Virgin Books, 2005
Colin MacInnes, *City of Spades*, MacGibbon & Kee, 1957
Colin MacInnes, *Absolute Beginners*, MacGibbon & Kee, 1959
Brian McConnell, *Found Naked and Dead*, New English Library, 1975
Anthony Richardson, *Nick of Notting Hill*, Harrap, 1965
Mim Scala, *Diary of a Teddy Boy*, Sitric Books, 2000
Samuel Selvon, *The Lonely Londoners*, Wingate, 1956
Tom Vague, *Getting it Straight in Notting Hill Gate*, Vague Publishing, 2009
Colin Wilson, *The Angry Years: A Literary Chronicle*, Robson, 2007

Searching for the Young Soul Rebels

You can still furnish your bedsit and feed yourself from North End Road market, on any day of the week. Established in 1887, some stallholders are the descendants of the original costermongers — but the newsagent would be horrified at the multitude of different nationalities that have joined them since: Egyptian, Moroccan, Turkish, Filipino and Caribbean, to name but a few. Doris blazed a trail — the residents of this part of Fulham are now truly multicultural.

That said, the area in which the market resides, between Lillie Road and Walham Grove Road, near Fulham Broadway tube, still has echoes of the

Munster Road SW6

grotty old place. Pound shops, pawnbrokers, dubious fast food outlets and off-licences abound — and while some of the windows may be made of UPVC these days, they retain their sinister regard. You might yet find an L-shaped room around the intersection with Lillie Road (which, charmingly, also has a junction with Munster Road). With its sagging masonry and second-hand furniture shops, this area seems to be loitering with intent.

The cinematic *L-Shaped Room* was on the top floor of 4 St. Luke's Road W11, adjoining St. Luke's Mews, now one of the most well-maintained properties on the street. If Doris could have held on until the film *Notting Hill* came out in 1999, she would have been a very rich old landlady.

Frank's café, on the corner of Westbourne Park Road and Powis Terrace, is now The Mutz Nutz, a dressing-up outlet for dogs. Nothing could illustrate just how much the area has changed than the arrival of this, and its sister Dog Deli and Spa, on Powis Gardens. The Travel Bookshop in Blenheim Crescent, on which Hugh Grant's shop was modelled in *Notting Hill*, did not escape the fate to which so many local businesses have succumbed, being forced out by the increase in rents since Richard Curtis's film became popular with American investment bankers. Toby would have a lot to get angry about if he was still around — not least the fact he could no longer afford to slum it in Ladbroke Grove.

Cathi Unsworth

Alexander Baron
The Lowlife (1963)

KEN WORPOLE

Alexander Baron was born in 1917 to Jewish parents who had separately grown up in Bethnal Green and Spitalfields prior to marriage and setting up home in Hackney. The new family started with one room in Abersham Road, then two rooms in Sandringham Road, before settling in a small terraced house in Foulden Road, Stoke Newington, the setting for what became one of his most accomplished novels, *The Lowlife*. His father, Barnet Bernstein, was a fur cutter, a 'very prim and correct chap', and his mother a former factory worker in the docks.

The young Joseph Alec Bernstein, as he was then called, attended Shacklewell Lane Primary School, which was then considered 'rough', though he later described his years there as 'the happiest time of my life.' At the age of eleven he won a Junior County Scholarship to attend Hackney Downs Grammar School (also known as The Grocers' Company's School), subsequently made famous as the place where the young Harold Pinter was first encouraged to write. In 1954 Pinter adopted the stage name of David Baron, the surname possibly adopted from that of his by now already famous namesake — who had anglicised his name from Bernstein to Baron soon after the war. Baron's first novel, *From the City, From the Plough*, a fictionalised account of the D-Day landings, published in 1948, went on to sell over a quarter-of-a-million copies and made him famous: a fame with which he was never comfortable and went out of his way to avoid.

Prior to the war Baron had been politically active on the left, frequently in clandestine ways given the political temperature of the times. In 1983 I interviewed him for a book I was writing, *Dockers and*

Detectives, which addressed several themes which then preoccupied me: the literature of the East End, and the popular literature of the Second World War. Baron's fiction covered both. The interview was memorable because of the modesty and honesty with which Baron talked about his life, his politics, and his literary career. A number of his best novels have now been re-issued.

The more I return to the novels, the more heartfelt and anguished I realise them to be, whether writing of the horrors of war, of anti-semitism, or of the collapse of the political ideals which led a generation, including a disproportionate number of British Jews, to attach themselves to the communist cause. Nevertheless, there was most certainly happiness in his early life, and a genuine love of the streets in which he grew up and played, and the book which best conveys Baron's affection for this part of Stoke Newington and its wider Hackney environs is undoubtedly *The Lowlife*.

First published in 1963 it is a mordantly picaresque novel of contemporary local life and colour, yet a carefully interwoven back-story hints at Baron's need to address the fate of the Jews in the Holocaust, only then being fully realised for the enormity it was. Critic Susie Thomas is surely right — acknowledging and following in the wake of the work of Holocaust historians — that post-war euphoria and national reconstruction programmes in Europe had, for several decades after the war, prevented a full realisation of the nature of the 'Final Solution' planned and enacted by Hitler.

It wasn't until the trial of Adolf Eichmann in 1961 that the true horror of what had been a vast programme of racial genocide dawned on the world. Until the early 1960s, there had been a considerable degree of historical repression, or inability to find a way of describing, let alone analysing, what even then seemed unimaginable. *The Lowlife* comes at this subject tentatively, but with great — and disturbing — effect. Initially regarded as a comic novel, full of wide-boy *schtick*, today its bleaker themes now seem the more enduring.

When I interviewed Baron I had asked him how his own Jewish background had influenced his fiction. Initially, he said, he had declined the opportunity to put the Jewish experience, either of London's East End or of the war, in his writings. There were two reasons for this. Firstly, he 'always had a personal rebellion against the idea of a separate Jewish identity. My father and both my grand-fathers were freethinkers and so am I. I'm an atheist. I never wanted to live within this defensive world called the Jewish community.' Secondly, he saw his respectable, free-thinking Hackney childhood as being geographically and culturally well beyond the classic Jewish East End, even though both parents had once belonged there. After the first two volumes of what we might now regard as his war trilogy — *From the City, From the Plough* (1948), *There's No Home* (1950) and *The Human Kind* (1953) — he began to change his mind on this. 'I had to write a Jewish novel,' he told me. 'I had to get something off my chest.' *With Hope, Farewell* (1952) is replete with Jewish themes and anxieties, though in *The Lowlife* these preoccupations are integrated into a more fully realised and exemplary piece of fiction.

At the novel's heart is its narrator, Harryboy Boas, a sometime Hoffman presser, gambler, reader of 19th century French novels, and one of a dying breed of *luftmenschen*, the elderly Jewish gamblers and street philosophers, who once filled the pavements of Whitechapel, Mare Street and Stoke Newington of a summer's evening to put the world to rights, exchange news of casual work in the rag trade, and discuss the form of the evening's dog-racing at Harringay, Clapton or Walthamstow. We might be encouraged to believe that these men led charmed lives, without responsibility, but Harryboy's story cuts to the bone: he is an economic refusenik but not a moral one.

While the novel opens in celebratory style, as an evocation of a childhood home and street life that he adored, it soon reaches into the darker corners of human experience and history. It may well be that Baron, like many intuitive writers, did not know where this novel was going to take him when he started. 'It's actually set in Foulden Road, Stoke Newington — Foulden Road in its heyday,' he told me. As a child he had grown up and lived with his parents at No 6, though in the novel the street is re-named Ingram's Terrace, and is initially evoked as a multi-racial arcadia. It was in Foulden Road that Baron learned to tell stories. 'In the street when I was a small kid, I used to tell stories. I wasn't very good in a punch-up. Story-telling gave me status. I could sit down on the kerb, with the others all around me, and tell them a story.'

After the war, when the demobbed would-be writer returned to live at his parents' home in Foulden Road, the street was beginning to change. 'The black people who came were so gorgeous and respectable,' he recounted. 'The sight of them all going up to the Baptist chapel on a Sunday morning, the wives wearing these big Ascot hats and the dads polished, the boys in Eton suits, was marvellous. I've always had a great love for Foulden Road. I've sometimes said to my wife, "If I ever became a really successful writer, I'd buy that house in Foulden Road", my mum and dad's house. I would have made it my working place, to go to every morning — instead of working at home. Or I would have arranged for some nurses to live in it.'

However, soon after the novel's opening the cracks are beginning to show. Into the three-storey house where Harryboy rents a room from his depressed and fearful Jewish landlord, Mr Siskin, arrive new tenants: Mr and Mrs Deaner and their young son Gregory. The Deaners argue all the time over money and parental responsibilities, and the young boy quickly gravitates towards Harryboy's room where he finds a more sympathetic, avuncular interest. Harryboy's strength is his generosity towards others. His weakness, apart from reckless gambling, is the desire to present himself to the world as a bon-viveur and wealthy boulevardier. This happy-go-lucky persona quickly results in him lending money to the Deaners — money he doesn't have. Soon he is in trouble with his sister and her husband — as well as a group of gangsters — as he hits the racetracks and the card games, borrowing money and losing it in a series of dramatic scenes. With nowhere left to run to, he has to fight his way out of an encounter with a Buick-load of 'heavies' sent to punish him for failing to pay his debts. The novel concludes with what remained of his family loyalties in tatters, while his one great moral gesture — the decision to donate an eye to save the sight of the Deaners' son badly impaired in a fire-work accident — is no longer required.

It is this complex overlay of storylines — humorous and tragic — which works to give the novel a lasting resonance, and it is today the work which for Baron is best known. It has been enthusiastically adopted by *aficionados* of the London novel as one of most successful evocations of the post-war city in a period of rapid cultural change, as one group of immigrants is displaced by another. In fictional terms it could be regarded as an update of the well-established tenement or lodging house novel, of which Richard Whiteing's *No. 5 John Street* (1899), Norman Collins' *London Belongs to Me* (1945), Patrick Hamilton's *The Slaves of Solitude* (1947) and Lynne Reid Banks' *The L-Shaped Room* (1960) are amongst the most well-known and influential examples. The rooming house conveniently provides the novelist with a ready-made set of characters, each with their story to tell, and has been one of the staple genres of the London novel.

Yet though *The Lowlife* initially adopts this formula — and Baron always saw the novel as an exploration of social morality, best imagined and elaborated in the more confined settings of the conscript army, the political party, the lodging house or the street — it soon develops a quite distinctive plot-line of its own. This is principally achieved by having the story narrated in Harryboy's world-weary, laconic voice, enlivened as it often is by Yiddisher borrowings. Here men are *schnorrers*, *schmocks*, *meshuggahs* or decent *mensch*. Tone of voice is vital to Baron, and he was particularly struck by the similarities between Yiddish and East End styles of speech and inflection. 'I don't know if you've noticed it in East End life,' he told me, 'the humour, the ironic expression which is as much East End as it is Jewish. To me... there was a symbiosis between young Jews and the young Anglo-Saxons. You couldn't tell one from the other. They spoke the same language. East End boys, if they had dark hair, you couldn't tell from Yiddishers. Cultures mingle. These characters radiate the will to live.' He later said that when he joined the army he was surprised — pleasantly — to find that a lot of gentile East End recruits knew more Yiddish words than he did, which they had picked up in the street market or at the dog track.

Other story lines weave through the novel, reinforcing the overall mood of disillusionment (compared with the post-war optimism of *Rosie Hogarth*, for example, published in 1951, though not evident in *With Hope, Farewell*). We are provided with a harrowing portrait of Harryboy as a gambler and as a self-destroyer: a person who ultimately eschews all human relationships in preference to the adrenalin of chance and fortune. 'The gambler is the one who goes with no peace, no release, till he has annihilated himself,' Harryboy says to himself at the end of yet another evening of losing everything. It is 'something like death'. Baron had often come across such men: 'I've known that gambling streak in the Jews. I have come across, in the army among other places, some of these chaps. One or two of the old school Jewish gangsters as well.' Gambling of course represents a classic form of existential despair — life is absurd, arbitrary, and meaningless, so why not live for the moment and forget tomorrow. After all, tomorrow never comes. Harryboy is also haunted by the miserable deaths of both of his parents: his mother in a flying bomb conflagration which reduced the street to a 'crater full of garbage', and his father of gangrene in the London Hospital, alone.

The arrival of the Deaners and the attentive devotion of young Gregory, also stirs memories within Harryboy of an affair he had once had in Paris, with a young Jewish restaurant cashier, Nicole, ending with the outbreak of war and his return to join the army in England. Some months later he received a note telling him she was pregnant. Soon after, we are led to assume that she and the child disappeared into the death camps. Even the sight of young children is enough to evoke in Harryboy's mind the most desperate of thoughts.

I only have to see a nursery school teacher leading her procession of toddlers to the park, and at once I imagine a procession of little innocents, endless, endless, being herded with every possibly cruelty to their deaths. If I walk into the Deaners' living-room and see a pair of Gregory's shoes in the corner, I think of the mountain of children's shoes, the shoes of dead children, found in one of the camps, sixty feet high.

Harryboy's never-to-be-seen child could have been, almost certainly was, one of those children. We are, by now, a long way from the playful multi-racial street portrayed in the novel's opening scenes.

Another key *mise-en-scène* in the novel is the expensive and ornately furnished home of Harryboy's sister, Debbie, and her book-maker husband, Gus, in Finchley, where from time to time Harryboy is invited to eat (with an obligatory lecture on his need to reform his life and settle down), or to which he is compelled to visit when in desperate financial straits. Initially the reader feels that Debbie and Gus have been set up to satirise those Jews who have left behind the slums and terraced streets of Stepney and Hackney to acquire respectability in the northern suburbs. But in the course of the novel we come to appreciate that they really do care for Harryboy, even though time and time again he betrays their trust (while relieving them of considerable amounts of stake money to be gambled away).

Debbie is convincing and the exchanges between her and Harryboy contain all the pain and anxiety of troubled sibling relationships. She was once the protective older sister 'who ran with a gang of rough boys and protected me', which she still does, though with ever-decreasing success. The other women in the novel are less sympathetic, notably Evelyn Deaner, the nagging, ambitious and explicitly racist wife of Vic, and Marcia, a Soho call girl whom Harryboy frequents when he has the money. The money-scraping lives of Vic and Evelyn ring true. Vic earns a pittance as a trainee accountant who spends his evening studying for his exams, while Evelyn cannot wait to move to a more respectable area. Meanwhile, sharing a house with a black family is for her the ultimate humiliation. The exchanges between the couple, with endless arguments over money, childcare responsibilities, and other domestic matters, possesses genuine dramatic tension. Yet when portrayed on her own, Evelyn's character is mostly unflattering, though Baron does provide a personal background to her demeaning sense of lost opportunities — a recurrent Baron theme — and when her son Gregory is badly injured, she rises to the occasion.

Marcia is even more of a problem. A wealthy married woman who seeks financial independence from her devoted husband, she operates as a high class prostitute with her own maid in a central London apartment, building up a financial empire through property speculation (including the use of hired thugs to harass tenants), while happily accompanying Harryboy to smart Brighton hotels and restaurants, ostensibly out of the goodness of her heart. There is a scene between Marcia and her husband when the latter arrives in a restaurant — where Harryboy is entertaining Marcia to a splendid meal — to plead with her to return to him. It is ferocious in its portrayal of public sexual humiliation. Sexual desire and its frustration is a continuing undercurrent in the novels of this period, and on such matters Baron was forthright and ahead of his time. In the various clothing factories where Harryboy works when needing the money, casual sexual encounters are an everyday affair, sometimes degrading, sometimes satisfyingly pleasurable, as they are in other Baron novels, including, unsurprisingly, the war trilogy.

Unusually for a classic 'London novel' there are no pub scenes. In the period of which Baron was writing, even bohemian or quasi-criminal Jewish life found its social milieu in the gambling joint, the dog track, the restaurant, the dance-hall or the night club rather than the public house. Food was especially important as a form of luxury and conviviality. Debbie's meals for Harryboy are fully described, as are Harryboy's expensive restaurant meals with Marcia. A common love of food as a metaphor for a love of life is made explicit when Harryboy shares a chicken cooked and served by his black fellow tenants, Milly and Joe. They ask him why Evelyn dislikes them so much, and he replies that it is because 'We got too much life. We are not liked because we have too much life in us... the way we eat, that way we live. You and me, Joe, we mop the plate dry. We suck the last gob of marrow. We lick our fingers. From our fathers and grandfathers we know hunger, and we value food. In our blood we know an axe can fall on us at any second. So we live. We live.' Yet those who take life as it comes are in a minority, for when Joe further asks how he and Milly can become accepted by the other residents, Harryboy simply replies, 'You're living in the house of the dead. I don't know what to advise you.'

This contrast between the sensual delight in food shared by Jews and black people and the miserable evening meals eaten by the Deaners evokes the place of ritual in family life which recurs in Baron's fiction, even though he had largely disavowed his Jewish beliefs. Living for the day, not heedlessly or irresponsibly, but because the future is uncertain, is a one of the underlying reasons for domestic ritual and the enjoyment of the pleasures of food, family, companionship and sexual fulfilment. However, because of his gambling mania, Harryboy carries this living for the moment to a dangerous and ultimately self-destructive degree. He is a man with a past, a present, but no future. What makes his predicament even more intolerable is that very much like a character in a Kafka story, he carries a burden of continuous guilt: 'So the inside of my head, not for the first time, turned into a courtroom.'

With the advantage of hindsight, we can now appreciate *The Lowlife*, not just as a piece of urban comedy, which it is, but also as a season in hell, leavened by Harryboy's gallows humour and self-deprecating wit. He is one of London fiction's most memorable characters, and we can only wish him well.

References and Further Reading

Titles by Alexander Baron: all editions given are the most recently published:

The Lowlife, with an introduction by Iain Sinclair, Black Spring Press, 2010

King Dido, with an introduction by Ken Worpole, Five Leaves, 2009

Rosie Hogarth, with an introduction by Andrew Whitehead, Five Leaves, 2010

With Hope, Farewell, Corgi Books, 1962

From the City, From the Plough, with an introduction by Sean Longden, Black Spring Press, 2010

There's No Home, with an afterword by John L.Williams, Sort Of Books, 2011

The Human Kind, with a foreword by Sean Longden, Black Spring Press, 2011

Iain Sinclair, *Hackney, That Rose-Red Empire: A Confidential Report*, Hamish Hamilton, 2010

Susie Thomas, 'Alexander Baron's *The Lowlife* (1963): Remembering the Holocaust in Hackney', *Literary London Journal* online, September 2011

Gil Toffell, 'Cinema-going from Below: The Jewish film audience in interwar Britain', in *Participations*, November 2011

Ken Worpole, *Dockers and Detectives*, Five Leaves, 2008

Foulden Road Today

Foulden Road today is much as it was when Alexander Baron lived there from the 1920s onwards, though many of the houses have been returned to single family homes after decades of multi-occupation. The Foulden Arms at the eastern end of the road closed in the early 1980s and was converted into flats, like many street-corner pubs in this part of London. The road was lucky to survive several nights of bombing during the Blitz, which badly affected Stoke Newington. On 13th October 1940, a parachute-mine landed on the tenement buildings in Coronation Avenue, no more than one-hundred-and-fifty yards from Foulden Road, killing over a hundred people, many of them Jewish, in one of the worst civilian incidents of the war, and this terrible event is alluded to in Baron's novel, *With Hope, Farewell*. In *The Lowlife*, Harryboy's mother is obliterated in a similar disaster.

At the 'top end' of Foulden Road, where it joins Stoke Newington Road, there were two small mews terraces, formerly stables, which would have been converted into sweat-shops in Baron's time, and a large drinking trough for horses stood near this junction until the 1970s. Baron's family lived almost next door to these mews, and home and work were often near to each other in the 'rag trade' which flourished in this area. Close by was the monumental Simpson's clothing factory at 92–100 Stoke Newington Road, built in 1929 and at its busiest employing over 3,000 people producing 11,000 garments per day. Harryboy almost certainly would have done a few shifts there as a Hoffman Presser. The company closed the building in 1981, since when it has functioned as a storage depot, with a Turkish community centre occupying the front part of the building.

The main parade of shops at the top of Foulden Road largely consists of Turkish cafés, restaurants, wedding shops, florists and supermarkets, all serving the Turkish, Anatolian and Kurdish communities resident in this district. Within a hundred yards of No. 6 Foulden Road, on Stoke Newington Road, was the Apollo Cinema. Opened in 1915 it contained over a thousand seats and was designed in a twin-domed Moorish style. A photograph taken of the cinema in 1928 shows it — very unusually — featuring a Yiddish film, 'Souls in Exile', made in 1926 by Maurice Schwartz. This film had a few showings in London and Manchester, and that it was shown in Stoke Newington attests to the large Jewish population in the area at that time.

The Apollo ended its life as The Astra in the early 1980s, specialising in Kung-Fu films. It is now an ornately decorated mosque. Next door to it is the Stoke Newington Baptist Church, which is where Harryboy would have observed and admired the smartly dressed West Indian population attending service on Sunday. Another hundred yards down Walford Road, by the Baptist Church, you come to the Walford Road Synagogue, still in use, its coloured glazed windows permanently protected by metal grilles, giving it something of a fortified appearance, evidence of the sporadic incidents of anti-semitism which occurred in this area for most of the twentieth century. Such attacks on Jewish properties feature in the plot lines of many of Baron's novels, most notably in *With Hope, Farewell*, which concludes with a mildly hopeful gesture of solidarity, when Mark is joined at his local synagogue by two Cockney trade unionist railway workers who have come to help him defend it against another arson attack.

Ken Worpole

Hanif Kureishi
The Buddha of Suburbia (1990)

SUSIE THOMAS

My name is Karim Amir, and I am an Englishman born and bred, almost. I am often considered to be a funny kind of Englishman, a new breed as it were, having emerged from two old histories. But I don't care — Englishman I am (though not proud of it), from the South London suburbs and going somewhere.

In the opening paragraph of Hanif Kureishi's *The Buddha of Suburbia,* the seventeen-year-old narrator feels compelled to announce his nationality three times. At first, Karim is semi-apologetic (he's almost English) but by the third declaration he is defiantly not proud of it. No other English novel begins this way. It is set in the 1970s, when the fact that Karim has an English mother and an Indian father means that he is constantly asked where he is from, as if his very existence required some kind of explanation. He is not English enough (too brown) for some, nor Indian enough (he's never been there) for others.

In 1990 there were hardly any English novels about growing up as a mixed race child so *The Buddha of Suburbia* and Kureishi's first film with Stephen Frears, *My Beautiful Laundrette* (1985), were important interventions in the debate about what it means to be British in the wake of post-war immigration. A lot of critical attention has quite rightly been paid to this. Now, in large part because of Kureishi's work, multiculturalism is mainstream. So this is a particularly good moment to look back at a less discussed but equally significant aspect of *The Buddha of Suburbia*: its treatment of class and the links between class and place.

London's unglamorous suburbs have attracted much less literary attention than the city proper, and it is rare for a novel to flaunt its suburban origins in the title. Kureishi, like Karim, was born in Bromley in 1954. His father, who came from an aristocratic Indian background, was employed by the Pakistani embassy in London; while his white English mother, who comes from a local Bromley family, worked in a shop. The young Kureishi moved to west London to study philosophy at King's College and had his first plays performed at the Royal Court theatre in Sloane Square. He has lived on the same page of the A-Z all his adult life and, with the exception of the Bradford setting of his film *My Son the Fanatic,* all his films and novels have been inspired by the city. *The Buddha of Suburbia* zigzags north and south of the river, from periphery to core of the city, as Karim tries to find himself: no locality turns out to be quite what either he, or the reader, expects.

The opening paragraph announces not only that Karim has emerged 'from two old histories' but also that he is from the 'South London suburbs and going somewhere'. The journey from a boy's bedroom in Bromley to 'the centre of this old city' charts his struggle to 'locate' himself as 'a new breed of Englishman' but Karim is also navigating his way around the class system. Each locality in the novel is precisely depicted in terms of class markers: Karim is desperate to escape suburban stagnation but sceptical of pretentious social climbing, hierarchies and authoritarianism.

The Buddha of Suburbia is divided into two parts: In the Suburbs and In the City. It seems at first as if the novel is straightforwardly linear. Karim progresses from the margins to the centre and from the suburban lower middle-class (with a future as a clerk or car mechanic) to the growing metropolitan middle-class (working in the theatre, media or academia). Moreover, at least superficially, the novel seems to uphold the conventional opposition between 'suburbia' and the 'city': Bromley epitomises philistinism while London is the cultural capital.

The suburbs, which give the book part of its title, are 'a leaving place' while the city is 'bottomless in its temptations'. On the eve of his departure from Bromley, at the end of part one, Karim fantasises about London and what he will do there. Although it is only ten miles away, it is another world entirely:

There was a sound that London had (...) There were kids dressed in velvet cloaks who lived free lives; there were thousands of black people everywhere, so I wouldn't feel exposed; there were bookshops with racks of magazines printed without capital letters or the bourgeois disturbance of full stops; there were shops selling all the records you could desire; there were parties where boys and girls you didn't know took you upstairs and fucked you; there were all the drugs you could use. You see, I didn't ask much of life; this was the extent of my longing.

The city represents freedom and anonymity: more, 1970s London is breathlessly anticipated as a countercultural cornucopia. It is the absolute antithesis of suburbia most significantly, perhaps, in terms of racism. Moving to London means an end to the painful sense of exposure which Karim suffers in the mainly white suburbs and a new safety in numbers. Unlike many coming-to-London novels, the city isn't a disappointment: 'So this was London at last, and nothing gave me more pleasure than strolling around my new possession all day'. But within the novel's basic framework of suburban dullness and bigotry versus metropolitan, multicultural playground, there is considerably more complexity.

Kureishi's suburbs are frequently weirder and madder than we might expect. Partly because it is set against the background of suburban uniformity, the transformation of Karim's father, Haroon, from civil servant and commuter into yoga teacher and Eastern mystic, takes on a surreal quality. As he sneaks out of his respectable semi-detached, wearing a red and gold waistcoat and pyjamas concealed beneath his overcoat, he announces proudly: '"They are looking forward to me all over Orpington"', delighted for the first time to be listened to with respect.

The south London suburbs are portrayed as anything but a homogeneous mass of semis. On the contrary, Karim calibrates the social status and gradations of culture in each neighbourhood meticulously. His family inhabits a respectable lower middle-class area, which his step-mother, Eva calls 'the higher depths'. Setting off from the cul-de-sac which is Victoria Road, Karim and his friends Jamila and Helen walk to the pub:

> Past turdy parks, past the Victorian school with outside toilets, past the numerous bomb sites which were our true playgrounds and sexual schools, and past the neat gardens and scores of front rooms containing familiar strangers and televisions shining like dying lights.

Bromley combines degraded public spaces with a philistine display of private status.

There is nothing in Bromley to make Karim want to stay even though he has no clear idea how he is going to get out. His first step on the road to London is Beckenham, which is upper-class by Victoria Road standards. When they arrive at Eva's house, Karim, sounding like a budding estate agent, notes that it had 'a little drive and a garage and a car. Their place stood on its own in a tree-lined road just off Beckenham High Street. It also had bay windows, an attic, a green-house, three bedrooms and central heating'. It's not (only) the display of money that impresses Karim, rather he's seduced by the combination of sensuality and intellectualism. But, despite the bidet and the bamboo scrolls, the talk of 'music and books, of names like Dvorak, Krishnamurti and Eclectic', Beckenham typifies only a pretentious simulation of culture.

Beckenham represents a premonition of what is on offer in the city and proof that there's more to the suburbs than DIY and conformity. According to Karim it may be populated by advertising executives at best but suburbia has also been the incubator of genuine musical talent. Bromley produced Peter Frampton, Billy Idol and Siouxsie Sioux, while David Bowie, Bromley's most famous son after H.G. Wells, is worshipped by the kids in *The Buddha*. The novel nods in approval of suburban English pop when Karim persuades his father to stop for a pint at the Three Tuns in Beckenham, where Bowie's career began. It's full of boys wearing 'cataracts of velvet and satin, and bright colours; some were in bedspreads and curtains'.

Biding his time until he can get to London, Karim sizes up Chislehurst, the venue for Haroon's second guru gig: 'The houses (...) had greenhouses, grand oaks and sprinklers on the lawn; men came in to do the garden'. But this is a detour which gets him no nearer to London than Beckenham. Closer geographically to the centre but way down the class ladder is Penge, where Karim's best friend Jamila lives with her parents Anwar and Princess Jeeta above a grotty corner shop called Paradise Stores:

> The area (...) was closer to London than our suburbs, and far poorer. It was full of neo-fascist groups, thugs who had their own pubs and clubs and shops. On Saturdays they'd be out in the High Street selling their newspapers and pamphlets. They also operated outside the schools and colleges and football grounds, like Millwall and Crystal Palace. At night they roamed the streets, beating Asians and shoving shit and burning rags through their letter-boxes.

As the pigs' heads fly through the shop window and Jamila's father is racially harassed in the street, her family live with a fear of violence that Karim does not have to deal with on a daily basis in Bromley. South London is a shit-hole of poverty and racism; the streets are more dangerous than in the suburbs and domestic life is equally miserable.

A major strand of the plot concerns Anwar's attempt to force his daughter to marry Changez, freshly imported from India for the purpose. Karim is at first baffled by his uncle's hunger strike and his father's guru gigs until he realizes that they represent belated attempts to 'resist the English' who have never fully accepted them. Jamila agrees to the marriage in order to protect her mother from Anwar's violence but refuses to sleep with Changez. In one of the novel's many comic reversals Changez at first tries to whack Jamila into submission but discovers that she is 'not whackable'; he falls in love with his wife without vacillation and is the only character in the novel to love someone more than he loves himself.

Guided by his step-mother, Eva, Karim eventually gets to smart, central London. The initial setting is West Kensington: nearest tube, Baron's Court. The author describes the area as caught between 'expensive Kensington, where rich ladies shopped' and Earls Court. Typically, it's the latter that attracts Karim's attention, an area full of 'small hotels smelling of spunk and disinfectant, Australian travel agents, all-night shops run by dwarfish Bengalis, leather bars with fat moustached queens exchanging secret signals outside, and roaming strangers with no money and searching eyes'.

Although West Kensington is made up of 'rows of peeling stucco houses broken up into bed-sits' what matters to Karim is that it is on the cultural map:

> Unlike the suburbs, where no-one of note — except H.G. Wells — had lived, here you couldn't get away from VIPs. Gandhi himself once had a room in West Kensington, and the notorious landlord Rachman kept a flat for the young Mandy Rice-Davies in the next street; Christine Keeler came for tea. IRA bombers stayed in tiny rooms and met in Hammersmith pubs, singing 'Arms for the IRA' at closing time. Mesrine had had a room by the tube station.

What more could you ask from your neighbourhood? Just as Karim assesses suburbanites according to their driveway, greenhouse, and the contents of their bathroom and bookshelves, so he values Londoners in relation to their 'cultural capital' and their post code.

He is thrilled to be offered a job in a radical theatre company in Chelsea, where he meets the beautiful, upper-class Eleanor. He is drawn like a magnet to her flat in Ladbroke Grove:

> An area that was slowly being reconstituted by the rich, but where Rasta dope dealers still hung around outside the pubs; inside, they chopped up the hash on the table with their knives. There were also many punks around now (...) And there were the kids who were researchers and editors and the like: they'd been at Oxford together and they swooped up to wine bars in bright little red and blue Italian cars, afraid they would be broken into by black kids, but too politically polite to acknowledge this.

Eleanor's set, 'with their combination of class, culture and money,' represent the 'apogee' of Karim's 'social rise', a 'cocktail' that intoxicates Karim's soul.

Karim wants to be accepted and approved of by London's bohemian aristocracy, and he is ecstatic to be invited to St. John's Wood: 'Sensational, I thought (...) We'd changed at Piccadilly and were heading north-west, to Brainyville, London, a place as remote to me as Marseilles. What reason had I to go to St. John's Wood before?' But Brainyville turns out not to be quite the cultural jackpot that Karim had anticipated. Instead of discussing Caryl Churchill's dramaturgy, he is sexually exploited by Marlene and 'virtually ruptured' by Pyke. Moreover his dream of clever people, artistic fame and hedonism in London is undermined by an awareness of how phoney the rich can be, even the really cultured rich. Although he is initially impressed and excited, he soon comes to see Eleanor's crowd as 'the kiss of death': 'I saw how much was enervated and useless in them. What passion or desire or hunger did they have as they lounged in their London living rooms?'

When the bohemian elite trample all over Karim's dream of London, he is not sure where to go next. Part of him simply wants to crawl home and lick his wounds but he doesn't know where home is anymore.

At various crucial moments in the novel, the forward march of progress from the suburbs to the city is interrupted by a sudden swerve towards the swamp of south London. The 'shit people have to deal with' in Brixton and Peckham is sharply juxtaposed with the comfort and complacency of Notting Hill. Jamila's activist commune in Peckham doesn't just supply a negative contrast: the commune is a radical space; an alternative to both suburban conformity and metropolitan radical posing. Changez finds contentment looking after Jamila's baby by another man while she makes documentaries with her girlfriend. Karim mocks the 'posters advertising demonstrations against South Africa and Rhodesia' which grace the walls of the communal kitchen, but he also takes their values seriously: 'As we sat there they talked about how to construct this equitable society. I said nothing, for fear of appearing stupid; but I knew we had to have it.'

The fact that the novel is divided into two parts might suggest that there are only two terms up for grabs. But there is a third value and locality: neither suburbs nor city but urban south London; Jamila's subversive in-between space. Jamila is clearly the political heroine of the novel:

I couldn't help seeing that there was in her a great depth of will, of delight in the world, and much energy for love. Her feminism, the sense

206

of self and fight in engendered, (...) the things she had made herself know, and all the understanding this gave, seemed to illuminate her tonight as she went forward, an Indian woman, to live a useful life in white England.

An anti-racist march that she organises is the most important event in the book — even though Karim misses it. If his story is not simply a postcolonial snob's progress this is largely because of Jamila in South London. It's no wonder, then, that with his lucrative but trashy role in a soap opera at the end of the novel, Karim both celebrates his journey to the centre and knows everything is still a mess.

The Buddha of Suburbia was going to be called *The Streets of My Heart;* a title which emphasises the fact that the novel is, on one level, a sentimental education as Karim struggles to 'learn what the heart is'. The first title also suggests that this is an urban novel in which the streets, instead of being a place of danger as so often in London literature, are the site of erotic possibility. In some ways, *The Streets of My Heart* might seem to reflect the contents of the novel more accurately. After all, only the first part of the novel is actually set in the suburbs; and Karim's father, the eponymous Buddha, fades from view for much of the second part. Despite this, the title *The Buddha of Suburbia*, is not only more memorable but also emphasises the heterogeneity of the novel's suburbs, which are not all steely conformity and twitching net curtains. 'Was I conceived like this,' Karim wonders, 'in the suburban night air, to the wailing of Christian curses from the mouth of a renegade Muslim masquerading as a Buddhist?' Surprisingly, it is on a suburban garden bench — not in the city — that the novel embodies the virtues of cultural hybridity. The novel's re-envisioning of the suburbs as a locus for the birth of multiculturalism is Kureishi's most prescient intervention in the debate about Englishness.

References and Further Reading

Bradley Buchanan, *Hanif Kureishi,* Palgrave Macmillan, 2007

Susan Alice Fischer, 'Embracing Uncertainty: Hanif Kureishi's *Buddha of Suburbia* and *The Black Album*', in Nicola Allen and David Simmons (eds) *Reassessing the Contemporary Canon: From Joseph Conrad to Zadie Smith*, Rodopi, 2011

Bart Moore-Gilbert, *Hanif Kureishi,* Manchester University Press, 2001

Ruvani Ranasinha, *Hanif Kureishi,* Northcote House, 2002

Sukhdev Sandhu, 'Pop Goes the Centre' in *London Calling: How Black and Asian Writers Imagined a City,* Harper Collins, 2003

Nahem Yousaf, *Hanif Kureishi's The Buddha of Suburbia,* Continuum, 2002

Down on My Knees in Suburbia

Walking around Bromley today, the architecture does not seem to have changed dramatically in the years since *The Buddha of Suburbia* was published. The area feels more spruced up than in the pages of the novel; the bomb sites are long gone and the parks are well kept. The defining difference between Bromley in the 1970s and now has less to do with bricks and mortar than racism.

'Down on my knees in suburbia/Down on myself in every way' — Bowie's haunting soundtrack plays in the film adaptation of Kureishi's novel, made for the BBC in 1993, as Karim (played by Naveen Andrews) whizzes along the streets of Beckenham, Chislehurst and Penge on his bicycle. Bromley could be seen as a crucible for the sometimes bloody revolution in attitudes to Englishness that has been wrought in the suburbs. England's post-war history of immigration is often referred to in the binary terms of ethnically diverse city and monocultural countryside; very little attention is paid to the suburbs, where most people live.

In a key early scene in the suburbs, Karim visits Helen, a girl from his school, and is brutally dismissed by her father as a nigger, wog and little coon, before being set on by a Great Dane. Typically, Karim tries to laugh off the humiliation by saying the dog was in love with him: its quick movements against his arse told him so. But later in the novel he admits that the racist insults made by Hairy Back (as he dubs Helen's father) made him 'nauseous with anger and humiliation'. There is no whining about being spat on at school in *The Buddha* and the routine racism in the suburbs is contemptuously shrugged off for the most part. Nonetheless, when Karim returns to Bromley, his sense of oppression is palpable. The first person he sees is Hairy Back: 'How could he stand there so innocently when he'd abused me? (...) I knew it did me good to be reminded how much I loathed the suburbs, and that I had to continue my journey into London and a new life, ensuring I got away from people and streets like this.'

In his landmark essay, 'The Rainbow Sign' (1986), Kureishi pulled off the comic mask in order to describe his childhood in Bromley with his white English mother and his Pakistani father: 'From the start I tried to deny my Pakistani self. I was ashamed. It was a curse and I wanted to be rid of it. I wanted to be like everyone else. I read with understanding a story in a newspaper about a black boy who, when he noticed that burnt skin turned white, jumped into a bath of boiling water.' This shame and denial were compounded by the absence of any vocabulary with which to resist the suburban culture of demeaning subordination and stigmatisation. Nothing was said: nobody in the family seemed to talk about what happened to them outside the house when they came home.

Recently I had lunch at an Indian restaurant in Bromley with Kureishi's estranged sister, Yasmin, and his mother who still lives in the semi-detached house in a quiet cul-de-sac which was the fictional model for Karim's home. His sister said that as a teenager she loathed going out in Bromley and was glad to have got away to boarding school. His mother still seemed pained and incredulous at the very idea of colour prejudice and insisted that she knew nothing about the racist abuse until she read about it in her son's books, when it came as a great shock. If she had known he was being spat on at school, she said, she would have complained. The mother's ignorance seemed to exasperate her daughter, either because she didn't believe her mother hadn't known or because she felt Mrs Kureishi should have known.

When I asked Yasmin about her father she seemed to think that his charisma allowed him 'to transcend racism'. Although the one thing that all the family seem to agree on is that Shanoo Kureishi loved his home in the suburbs, Yasmin's belief that he was untouched by racism seemed to mirror her mother's wishful thinking. Yasmin said that she had known about what happened to her brother alright because 'he took it out' on her. As I walked back to the house, away from her daughter's watchful gaze, Mrs Kureishi said that when her son was about five years old he had come home upset and asking why he had been called a nigger. I wondered what she had said and she replied sadly that she just hadn't known how to respond. As a teenager in his bedroom in Bromley, Kureishi began his first novel, 'Run Hard Black Man': he had to find his own answers through writing.

Growing up in Bromley today would certainly be very different from forty years ago when the novel was set. Crucially, the area is now casually multi-cultural and groups of school kids — black, white, Asian — chat in the park during the lunch hour. Doubtless it has the usual contemporary problems but a mixed race boy today would not stand out painfully, as Karim does in the novel. It is not as if racist violence is a thing of the past but at the very least no one has to suffer in silence. Through its wit and honesty, its sweetness and brutality, *The Buddha of Suburbia* made speaking about the essential questions of class, sex and racism that much more possible.

Susie Thomas

Neil Bartlett
Ready to Catch Him Should He Fall
(1990)

GREGORY WOODS

In the first half of Neil Bartlett's novel about gay men *Ready to Catch Him Should He Fall*, London is not named. Nor are any of its streets, squares, parks and other locations. But, come to think of it, the people are not named either. For the purposes of this narrative, anonymity is a condition of existence. Each character is given a designation that is both individually distinctive and archetypally representative: O, Boy, Madame, Father... Nameless they may be — and this, of course, locks in with the history of the closet — but each is no less recognisable for that. For gay people, as for many others, the anonymity of city life may be its main attraction rather than a cause of alienation or loneliness.

Bartlett's London is a gay London (but not the only gay London), mainly experienced nocturnally. Anonymity and marginality give these gay men a spectral presence behind the scenes of the city. London itself, although eventually recognisable in a few of its details, seems to be more a state of mind than a city of brick and stone. As if uncannily conjured up as the setting for an allegorical masque, it is shimmering and insubstantial, a city shaped by a specifically gay act of the imagination. There are no heterosexuals here, except as looming stereotypes of otherness.

As is already suggested by its title, *Ready to Catch Him Should He Fall* adopts a heightened rhetoric that sensitizes every detail, to the extent that the whole urban environment — topographical, architectural, social — seems to participate in the novel's central emotional events. Bartlett has derived this technique more, I think, from

211

Dickens than from his great hero, Oscar Wilde. But, for better or worse, his emotional palette is more limited than Dickens'. Even mundane events are raised — if that is the right word — to operatic levels of intensity from which the narrative never rests. Everything is extraordinary, everything beautiful, everything tragic. This is a rich diet — too rich for some — but not gratuitously so. It suits the book's strong sense of a life made meaningful by the ceremonials of everyday life. For me, it also carries more recent echoes of Maureen Duffy's remarkable novel *The Microcosm* (1966), mainly set in a lesbian bar in London, with parallel narrative strands that put gender-bending into a context going back to the eighteenth century.

Like its main characters, *Ready to Catch Him*'s main location is given a generic name, The Bar. This establishment, run by Madame (perhaps based on Mme Lysiane in Jean Genet's novel *Querelle de Brest*), sits in its street anonymously, with no sign at its door, no lights, not even a street number. For special occasions it is sometimes temporarily renamed — The Lily Pond, The Jewel Box, The Gigolo, The Hustler, The Tea Room, The Oasis, The Hole, Grave Charges, The You Know You Like It — but its door is never marked and, by the time of narration, it has either closed or moved elsewhere. Although it has a regular clientele, deeply involved in each other's nocturnal lives and unfailingly loyal to Madame, whom they all treat as a ruling matriarch (and who subsequently asks to be called Mother), The Bar's permanence is ephemeral. There is a shared understanding that, by some obscure rule of collective consciousness governing such places, any gay bar may close down without notice, or a trend or rumour may suddenly lose it its clientele as they move on to some other establishment. Like Duffy's lesbian bar, it hosts a microcosm of gay life.

There are times when The Bar is dressed up, for a special occasion, as 'Amsterdam or Paris or something like somebody's idea of America for the evening', or at other times as a past era in the life of 'our own dear city'. Not until more than half-way through the book do we start to get named locations that finally identify this as London. A storm takes place. (This is, apparently, the notorious night of 15th–16th October 1987, when, after the BBC weather forecaster Michael Fish reassured his viewers that there was not going to be 'a hurricane' overnight, a massive storm did devastate the south of England.) The novel's account of this night brings out a sudden flurry of names: the Strand, Trafalgar Square, Ludgate, Aldwych, Park Lane... In particular, various monuments and statues are invoked, and the city itself is named at last: 'on churches, tombstones, banks and derelict theatres, all the angels of London wept'. In a subsequent account of people and objects injured in the storm, the Charing Cross Road and the

National Gallery are named. But then we lose sight of the West End again and go back to the real city in which people actually live.

The hostility of the city, which Bartlett is constantly emphasising, is somewhat neutralised by the effects of sub-cultural solidarity. The Bar provides not only a refuge from the outside world but a small social world in its own right, as well as an extended family for those who have left their biological families behind in the provinces and those whose families have rejected them. This is what had come to be known as the 'gay community', built not so much on a shared minority sexual interest as on the social politics of marginality. What The Bar's clientele have in common is their shared oppression. Although the novel's events take place at the height of the AIDS epidemic, Bartlett hardly dwells on that at all. It is enough to know that Mother keeps a stock of free condoms on the bar.

The novel outlines the development of a love affair between an older and a younger man, O and Boy, a story foretold and hoped for by the gossips in The Bar before its two protagonists are even aware of each other's existence. When they do come together, the aptness of their existence as a couple is viewed by the others with a sense of fated inevitability. Mother formally announces their engagement and gives them financial help in setting up their first home together. In due course, she performs the rites of their marriage. For a while, they live as a nuclear family, looking after the child-like Father, who may or may not be Boy's actual father, until his death.

Much of this narrative takes place indoors, in either The Bar or one of a couple of council flats. At the beginning of the novel, Boy lives in a flat 'on the twentieth floor of a council block right close by the river on the east side of the city'. By day, he has a wonderful view of 'the great and glittering river', and by night 'the great towers of the financial district to the west'. With a guide book open in front of him, he identifies the various landmarks he has visited on foot (he is living a hand-to-mouth existence on Social Security) and he has learned the names of 'all the streets where the distant, anonymous towers of the banks and finance companies' stand. These are unspecified references to the Square Mile, that great rats' nest of state-sponsored embezzlers, rather than to the later One Canada Square (Canary Wharf), which was still being erected at the time the novel was being written. Not until his third novel, *Skin Lane* (2007), would Bartlett look at the Square Mile in full, realist detail, conjuring up an atmosphere both spooky and sinister.

Despite the virtual fog of its deliberate vagueness about urban detail, Bartlett's novel subscribes to a theme that is also crucial to much of his other work, both literary and theatrical (he is better known as a director and performer than as a novelist), that gayness as we live it today has a cultural history that links us closely with our sub-cultural past. Bartlett has a particular interest in the late nineteenth century, but when he was writing *Ready to Catch Him* others had been researching London's 'gay' past with very revealing effects. In his pioneering work on London's eighteenth-century 'molly houses', Rictor Norton had reported that 'there were actually more gay clubs and pubs in the heart of London in the early 1720s than there were in the 1950s'.

Bartlett begins his wonderful book on Oscar Wilde, *Who Was That Man?* (his first book, 1988), with a monologue by a modern gay Londoner, himself. He speaks of having moved to the city in his early twenties ('I don't think anybody's life changes as fast as a gay man's when he moves to a big city') and of a tendency to connect his own life there with those of previous generations of man-loving men:

> I'd be walking up the Strand, dressed to kill, and then I'd find myself looking up from the street to all the nineteenth-century façades above me, and fantasize that all the buildings of the West End had seen other men before me living a life after dark, that somehow the streets had a memory. What if I rounded the corner of Villiers Street at midnight, and suddenly found myself walking by gaslight, and the man looking over his shoulder at me as he passed had the same moustache, but different clothes, the well-cut black and white evening dress of the summer of 1891– would we recognise each other? Would I smile at him too, knowing that we were going to the same place, looking for the same thing?

I assume Bartlett's midnight walk down Villiers Street towards the Embankment is going to lead him not all the way down to the river but to Heaven, the famous gay nightclub under the railway arches behind Charing Cross Station. That he should imagine a man of Oscar Wilde's time 'going to the same place' is characteristic of Bartlett's disregard for literal accuracy when making a large number of radically revealing comparisons between the two periods. Regardless of their differences, Bartlett's London is Wilde's London.

In Wilde's only novel, *The Picture of Dorian Gray* (1890), Dorian has to step outside the glamour of his life as a wealthy, upper-class aesthete to indulge in his most unrespectable vices. Although he takes some of his wealth and all of his personal glamour with him when he crosses the city from West to East, it is among the outlaws and immigrants of the docklands that he purchases his nocturnal pleasures, both sexual and narcotic. In the classless brothels and opium dens of the East End, his beautiful body pays him its meagre dividends while his portrait ages and decays up in the attic of his exquisite house in the West. Aesthetes though they are, and unemployed, the characters in *Ready to Catch Him* are not the idle rich of Wilde's novel. Yet their lives are no less cultured, elegant and glamorous than those of Lord Henry Wotton, Basil Hallward and Dorian Gray. In Bartlett's fiction, as in his theatrical work, glamour is not the fixed essence so many people make it out to be. It is a construction, a performance, a state of mind. All it requires is not money but imagination — and, of course, a dressing-up box. And glamour knows no gender.

Concentrating on the nocturnal sub-culture and on the kind of men who identify themselves as belonging to it, Bartlett's novel notably ignores various key urban locations that feature in other important gay novels. Prominent among these are public lavatories, where men-who-have-sex-with-other-men (as opposed to men who identify as gay) are wont to access the sheer convenience of sex-without-conversation with men-without- sexual-identity. These are spaces of the deepest ambiguity, dedicated to the lowliest of physical functions yet conducive to thoughtfulness; places of enrapturement and entrapment; coldly functional yet romantic; designed for solitary shame yet apt to enable the most unexpected connections; boring and exciting, disgusting and delightful... (I could go on doing this indefinitely.) For some, they are places of regrettable necessity; for others, as exotic as any palace of Harun al-Raschid's, promising all manner of sensual pleasures. Angus Wilson took a radically different approach when he located the central moral event of his first novel, *Hemlock and After* (1953), at the entrance to the gents' public lavatories in Leicester Square. It is here that the conscience of the book's central character, Bernard Sands, is tested and found wanting. An exemplar of and standard bearer for liberal humanism, Bernard, himself homosexual, witnesses the arrest of another man for importuning. In contrast with another witness, Bernard feels no impulse to try and save this youth. Instead, seeing the terror in the arrested man's eyes, he feels a surge of 'violent excitement'. This, as Wilson's unrestrained narrator puts it, leaves Bernard Sands on the side of 'the wielders of the knout and the rubber truncheon'.

The London of Alan Hollinghurst's *The Swimming-Pool Library* (1988) is divided into distinct sectors of activity, interconnected by the tube network, travelling on which the novel's narrator and central character Will Beckwith experiences as having a consistent erotic charge. Blessed with as many excuses for complacency as Dorian Gray — beautiful, clever, rich, privileged — Will smugly shuttles between his flat in Holland Park and a gentleman's club on Great Russell Street in Bloomsbury, the swimming pool and changing rooms of the latter being his principal source of young men to have sex with; but he is shocked out of his self-indulgent routines by two key events, one in a public lavatory in Kensington Gardens, the other in a generic council estate of tower blocks in the East End. In the former, he rescues a peer of the realm, Lord Nantwich, by giving him the kiss of life when the old man suffers a heart attack; and in the waste land of the latter he is queer-bashed by a bunch of skinheads.

For all its social attractions, the whole of Bartlett's London is a potentially dangerous place for gay men. Throughout the narrative, they are being subjected to homophobic attacks. There are at least six knife attacks, one arson attack on a gay couple's home, one attack by fists alone, one hard smack intensified by spittle and laughter, metal bars applied to the legs, and innumerable verbal assaults. (In some respects, the portrayal of this gay London under constant threat of random but predictable attack reminds me of Sarah Waters' portrayal of the Blitz-torn city in her 2006 novel about lesbian lives in 1940s London, *The Night Watch*.) Finally, inevitably, in a year when two gay men have already been killed, O and Boy are themselves attacked while making their way on foot towards The Bar, O walking in a protective attitude to Boy, 'ready to catch him should he fall'. Five men surround them and start to ridicule them; but when one reaches out as if to touch Boy's hair, O scares them off by shouting at them, giving a good impression of not being afraid. Although not physically injured, it is clear that O and Boy are hurt nonetheless. The trauma arises from the mere threat of violence in a context of frequent attacks on others. Context is all.

Ready to Catch Him emerged from a repellent period in British social history, when the vindictive instincts of Tory back-benchers and tabloid journalists had combined forces with the contingent tragedy of the AIDS epidemic to try to reverse the limited gains gay men and lesbians had achieved in the 1970s. Much of the society seemed unreconciled even to the Sexual Offences Act 1967, which had partially decriminalised male homosexual acts in England and Wales, let alone to the more visible freedoms demanded by gay liberationists in the subsequent decades. As Bartlett's narrator says, 'you have to remember how strange the times were. Dangerous, looking back... You have to remember that we lived in a city in which, according to the latest figures' (whereupon he cites what appears to be a genuine survey from then), 63% of Londoners 'did not think that people like us should exist', 72% 'did not think that we should be allowed to express affection in public', 82% 'did not think that the names of men like us [...] should be read out at school assemblies', and so forth. He adds, 'You, of course, living in a rather different time or in different countries, will find all this hard to credit now.'

Bartlett portrays this as a city waiting to be handed back to its people. Those who have misappropriated it are not named, but at the

216

time the novel was published Margaret Thatcher was still in power after more than a decade, and Section 28 of the Local Government Act 1988 was inhibiting public discussion of homosexuality despite a desperate need for such discussion in the face of the AIDS epidemic and the hostility it had aroused. Section 28 stipulated that a local authority might not 'intentionally promote homosexuality' or 'promote the teaching in any maintained school the acceptability of homosexuality as a pretended family relationship'. Hence the topicality of Bartlett's representations of constructed and performed family rituals. Although not blood relatives, the characters in his book nominate each other as family members and, even without literally delving into the dressing-up box, do a better job of looking after each other's interests than the 'real' families they came from.

In the closing pages of the book, Bartlett imagines a future night of celebration and liberation: 'I wish that Boy could look out from their fifth floor balcony and see something like that.' He thinks of other cities: 'let it be the night Franco died... let it be Riga, let it be Budapest, let it be Berlin... let it be the night they changed the law and we danced all night'. The gay men of 1990 were still waiting for their 1989. Until then, their London would remain a twilight world, always out of focus and always out of sync. Reading this book now, we do indeed live in 'a rather different time'. The gay male age of consent was reduced in 1994 and equalised with the straight one in 2001; Section 28 was repealed in 2003; and the offences of 'buggery' and 'gross indecency' (of which Oscar Wilde had been convicted in 1895) were abolished at last in 2004.

References and Further Reading

Neil Bartlett, *Skin Lane,* Serpent's Tail, 2007

Neil Bartlett, *Who Was That Man? A Present for Mr Oscar Wilde,* Penguin, 1993

Maureen Duffy, *The Microcosm,* Virago, 1989

Alan Hollinghurst, *The Swimming-Pool Library,* Vintage, 1998

Matt Houlbrook, *Queer London: Perils and Pleasures in the Sexual Metropolis, 1918–1957,* University of Chicago Press, 2005

Rictor Norton, *Mother Clap's Molly House: The Gay Subculture in England, 1700–1830,* GMP, 1992

Sarah Waters, *The Night Watch,* Virago, 2006

Oscar Wilde, *The Picture of Dorian Gray,* OUP, 2006

Angus Wilson, *Hemlock and After,* Faber, 2008

Gregory Woods, 'Queer London in Literature', *Changing English,* December 2007

The Bar

The last place in which you could find a bar like The Bar is Old Compton Street in Soho, the main drag of central London's 'gay village'. Although it has a long history as a place of resort for sexual dissidents, and therefore as a neighbourhood to be reviled by resentful homophobes (the gay pub the Admiral Duncan was nail-bombed by one such on 30th April 1999), Old Compton Street has become a kind of showplace for liberal tolerance, much frequented by sightseers and visitors to the city, both provincial and foreign. It is to the ordinary gay population of London as Oxford Street is to ordinary shoppers in Streatham or Hackney.

A recent discussion thread on Facebook, initiated in February 2012 by the writer Rupert Smith, called up memories of the London gay scene of the 1980s. Beginning with central venues like the Salisbury on St. Martin's Lane — a pub so venerable as to have appeared on film in both Basil Deardon's *Victim* (1961) and Ron Peck and Paul Hallam's *Nighthawks* (1979), yet remembered for its consistently anti-gay staff and as having eventually barred its gay customers and gone straight — the discussion soon blossomed out to the Coleherne and Boltons in Earls Court, Benjy's in Mile End, the Fallen Angel in Islington, Silk's in Shepherd's Bush, the Quebec in Chelsea, the King William IV in Hampstead, the Calabash in Kensington, the Royal Oak in Hammersmith; south of the river, the Vauxhall Tavern in Vauxhall. And, although the discussion was about men's bars, honourable mention went also to the Gateways Club, the fabled lesbian bar that, before it closed in 1985, gained the distinction of appearing in both Duffy's *The Microcosm* and Robert Aldrich's film *The Killing of Sister George* (1968).

Of these clubs and pubs, some would be known for a leather crowd, others for drag, others for rent boys; and as fashions come and go, so would different crowds, drugs and music. Men would be led to them by hearsay, but also by the London guide pages of newspapers like *Gay News* (1972–1983) and the freebie *Capital Gay* (1981–1995). Some of the above and many comparable places still exist, dotted around London's towns and villages, still varied in style, still apt to change at short notice, and still subject to the whims of collective taste. They are now more likely to have a mixed clientele (gay and straight) than in the 1980s; and, instead of searching for them in the gay press, one finds them now via online guides and general social networks like Facebook or specifically gay ones like Grindr. Bars as protective and enclosed as The Bar have, I think, vanished into history.

Gregory Woods

218

Zadie Smith
White Teeth (2000)

LISA GEE

Written when its author was twenty-one and published, in 2000, when she was twenty-four, Zadie Smith's debut novel was an instant critical and popular success. Commentators and readers alike were beguiled by the novel's exuberance, intelligence and superb prose as well as the way the author captured the spirit of the age. Young, brilliant, beautiful and mixed race, Smith was the perfect image for an optimistic London at the start of a new millennium. The Y2K bug hadn't caused ATMs to implode as the twentieth century ticked into the twenty-first, Britain was between wars, the Chancellor was predicting an end to boom-bust cycles and stock markets around the world hit all-time highs as the dot.com bubble continued to expand. London was prosperous: a place where people from a variety of backgrounds could mix it up and make it. Londoners might not have been queuing for the Millennium Experience, but we weren't yet disillusioned with Tony Blair's government, its rhetoric of social inclusion and the black hole between its principles and its practice. *White Teeth* is audacious, ambitious, and optimistic: absolutely the right book for its time.

The novel received only one dissenting review: this appeared in a small literary magazine called *Butterfly* and described the book as 'the literary equivalent of a hyperactive, ginger-haired tap-dancing 10-year-old'. That review was written by Smith herself.

Centring on an unlikely friendship between white, working-class Archie Jones and Bengali immigrant Samad Iqbal, *White Teeth* opens with Archie attempting suicide early in the morning on New Year's Day, 1975. He's gassing himself, in his car, outside a halal butcher's shop on Cricklewood Broadway. The owner — Mo Hussain-Ishmael — is not happy, because Archie is parked in his delivery area and he's

219

expecting a large consignment of meat any minute.

Mo's explanation to Archie about why he can't kill himself *there* sets the tone for all that follows: 'We're not licensed for suicides around here. This place halal. Kosher, understand? If you're going to die round here, my friend, I'm afraid you've got to be thoroughly bled first.' It's zippy, irreverent, and, most significantly, mashes up cultures and religions, the sacred and secular in unexpected ways.

Gifted a second try at life by this unlikely saviour, Archie (aged forty-seven) fetches up at the fag-end of a nearby hippy New Year's Eve party, where he meets nineteen-year-old Clara: tall, black, escaping from a tangled combination of dark basement flat in Lambeth, a Jehovah's Witness mother and romantic disappointment. They marry within weeks and move to a 'heavily mortgaged, two-storey house in Willesden Green': the area where Zadie Smith grew up and learned to tap dance at Adele's Dance School. Clara reflects that it's 'not the promised land — but... nicer than anywhere she had ever been'.

While Archie is kind, long-suffering and passive to the extent that he can only make significant decisions by flipping a coin, his friend Samad, a Bangladeshi Muslim with one arm rendered useless by friendly fire ('A bastard Sikh,' he tells Archie, early in their acquaintance. 'As we stood in a trench his gun went off and shot me through the wrist'), is pompous and boastful. Obsessed with his proud Bengali origins and particularly his great grandfather Mangal Pande, who fired the first bullet in the Indian Mutiny/Rebellion of 1857, Samad works as a waiter in a restaurant owned and run by a younger, less intelligent relative in Whitechapel and lives nearby. He's married, via the traditional arranged route, to the much younger Alsana: a complex and realistic mix of traditional values, modern attitudes, bad language and a fierce left hook. Samad, who had been hoping for an easy, biddable wife, is disappointed in this, as in much else.

After a year in which Alsana has been bent over an old Singer sewing machine, fashioning PVC into clothes for a Soho sex shop — 'many were the nights Alsana would hold up a piece of clothing she had just made, following the pattern she was given, and wonder what on earth it was' — she and Samad also move to Willesden Green. Alsana, like Clara, judges the area to be 'nice' and, importantly, safer than Whitechapel. Not because people are more liberal, less racist than in East London but because 'there was just not enough of any one thing to gang up against any other thing and send it running to the cellars while windows were smashed'.

Samad and Archie's wives soon fall pregnant, Alsana with twin boys, Magid and Millat, Clara with a girl, Irie. Alsana and Clara, tentatively at first, become friends and then spend increasing amounts of time together, going to the cinema until they get too pregnant and then meeting Alsana's lesbian, tell-it-like-it-is 'Niece-of-Shame' Neena for lunch in Kilburn Park (aka Kilburn Grange).

It's during one of these get-togethers that recent history bursts into the present. As, in her opinion, men have caused most — if not all — the trouble in the world, Neena isn't impressed that Alsana is pregnant with boys. Feeling responsible for jolting her and Clara out of their false consciousness, she says if it was her, she would consider abortion. Alsana is shocked to the point of choking on her lunch, Clara finds Neena's comment hysterically funny. Sol Jozefowicz, the elderly former park keeper still policing the park despite his job having 'long since having been swept away in council cuts', comes over to check if they're all right. Alsana, explaining what's happened and, complaining about Clara's response, asks:

> "The murder of innocents — is this funny?"
> "Not in my experience, Mrs Iqbal, no", says Sol Jozefowicz ... It strikes all three women — the way history will, embarrassingly, without warning, like a blush — what the ex-park keeper's experience might have been.

The difficulties with history, together with the devotion to tradition — something the book's narrator fingers as even more corrosive, more dangerous than religion — intrude throughout *White Teeth* like the 1950s council blocks that occupy bomb holes in Harlesden's Edwardian terraces. The past, and people's relationship with it, is, one way or another, always a problem: 'immigrants', we are told, 'cannot escape their history any more than you yourself can lose your shadow'. And, 'In Archie's experience anything with a long memory holds a grievance.'

But then, despite the fizzing optimism of the book's tone — and it's the way the story's told, rather than the story *per se* that sets the upbeat tone — the future ain't easy either. Every prediction made, or followed, by the book's protagonists, every attempt at influencing the outcome of events — major or minor — turns out wrong. The twin impossibilities of controlling and foreseeing the future and escaping the past thread through the novel like cyclists avoiding traffic. And while, on the one hand, this powerlessness is frustrating for the characters who've made or followed a prediction, or acted in ways intended to produce specific, desired results, on the other, it's rather reassuring. No one individual or group has the capability to either predict or control anyone else's future.

During the BBC Radio 4 'Book Club' devoted to *White Teeth*, Zadie Smith described Willesden Green as an 'extremely successful' example of how people of different ethnicities and beliefs can live, work and study together. She spoke about how kids of every race would walk to school (she attended Hampstead School in Cricklewood), grow together and go to each other's parties. In the novel, the Iqbal and Jones children do much the same thing. They go to the same schools and hang out together in a similar time and place. Like Irie Jones, lots of the kids have first names from one country or culture and last names from another. This isn't always because their parents were born into two different cultures: some people's mums simply give them a name they liked from someone else's.

Having transposed her own experience into the novel, Smith later described this melting pot vision as naïve. She was, she felt, right to show that people don't give up their own gods easily, wrong in assuming that living cheek by jowl with each other would inevitably overcome fundamentalism and parochialism. It doesn't in real life, even in a place as happily mixed as Willesden Green. But, to be fair, it doesn't in *White Teeth*, either.

Clara's mother, Hortense, clings on to her faith even after the end of the world fails to materialise on the date the Jehovah's Witness leaders predicted (again). Meanwhile, at primary school governors' meetings, Samad embarrasses Alsana by campaigning for the Harvest Festival to be struck from the school calendar. In his opinion, the nine Muslim festivals are squeezed out by the thirty-seven Christian ones. If, Samad suggests, they dispensed with the ones that aren't properly Christian — like the pagan Harvest Festival — there would be time to celebrate the proper Muslim ones.

'Where in the bible does it say, *For thou must steal foodstuffs from thy parents' cupboards and bring them into school assembly, and thou shalt force thy mother to bake a loaf of bread in the shape of a fish?* These are pagan ideals! Tell me, where does it say, *Thou shalt take a box of frozen fishfingers to an aged crone who lives in Wembley?*'

That typically irreverent mix of symbolic fish and everyday fishfingers grounds the novel more firmly in London than Smith's light-touch descriptions and name checking of the novel's main locations: Willesden Green; Cricklewood; Kilburn; Finchley Road; Harlesden Jubilee Clock; its occasional forays into Lambeth and central London and its trips to the local parks – Gladstone Park, Kilburn Grange Park, Queen's Park and Roundwood Park (these parks with their cafés and playgrounds are important community hubs). In fact — especially once the focus of action shifts to the younger generation — place itself is something taken largely for granted. Only Alsana truly appreciates its significance. Conversely, born into a temperate climate and living on land that tends to remain stable under their feet, 'the English have a basic inability to conceive of disaster'. This statement is illustrated, neatly, a few pages on, with weatherman Michael Fish's infamously wrong 15th October 1987 there-won't-be-a-hurricane-tonight prediction.

Alsana is brooding about place because Samad, disturbed by the way his sons are influenced by their environment, has, without consulting her, sent Magid — the better behaved, brighter twin — off to Bangladesh. There, he believes, at least one of his sons (he couldn't afford to send both of them) will receive a proper traditional upbringing and return the man Samad wants him to become. And yet Samad finds not being in control harder to live with than any other character. He can't cope with being unable to control his own desires, his wife or his sons, their choices and their futures.

Sense of place and people's relationships to it are, inevitably, different in an environment that is – under normal circumstances — structurally safe. And, though it's an obvious point to make, *White Teeth* makes clear how, through the twins' separation, it's also inextricably bound up with people's relationships with each other. If human beings can be compared to plants, most of us are more akin to those with aerial roots than we are to trees. Our roots grow laterally into family and friends, through time and space into cultures, traditions and religions as well as (or sometimes instead of) down into the earth.

Sense of place and people's relationships to it vary across Smith's novels, too. In her second, *The Autograph Man*, one of the themes is the power and value of names. So, although we get to visit the Royal Albert Hall at the outset, many of the London locations in this later novel are, as Adam Mars-Jones points out in his review of the book in *The Observer*, deliberately anonymised. Places are alluded to or described rather than named, and the novel's main protagonist, Alex-Li Tandem, lives in a fictitious northern London suburb called Mountjoy. Smith's third novel, *On Beauty*, returns us to Willesden Green, Cricklewood and the surrounding area, but this time viewed through the eyes of young American visitors, rather than natives. For one — Zora — everywhere apart from Hampstead is 'crappy'. Meanwhile, her brother Jerome romanticises the area, finding it wonderfully mixed compared to 'back home'.

Alsana is, predictably, furious with Samad. She calibrates her revenge precisely to hit the exact frequency that will drive her husband to distraction and refuses, from that moment, to answer any of his questions directly. Meanwhile, as if to compensate for his relative safety, Millat's behavior becomes increasingly risky. He gets into fistfights, drinks, smokes cigarettes and marijuana. He enjoys unprotected, promiscuous sex with a string of willing white, middle-class girls to whom his combination of good looks and self-destructive behaviour prove irresistibly attractive. He immerses himself in all the glorious, easily accessible sins London has to offer, before converting to a fundamentalist brand of Islam. His father torments himself with the thought that he's sent the wrong son to Bangladesh.

Samad finds refuge in his evenings with Archie at O'Connell's Pool House on the Finchley Road. Run by Abdul-Mickey (to teach them humility, all the boys in his family are called Abdul with an English name appended for practical purposes), O'Connell's is 'neither Irish nor a pool house'. It's a greasy spoon-style caff-cum-gambling den, sans pork products, where you can either play for money, or, if it's against your religion, just play. It's the book's most stable environment: a place of regulars, all men, who can be relied upon, year in, year out, to do the same things and behave in the same way.

When the novel reaches 1990, a family who'd appeared as bit-part players in Smith's Harvest Festival scene supporting Samad's motion, shift centre-stage. Living just a couple of roads away from the Iqbals and Joneses, the Chalfens are more Hampstead than Willesden. Celeb gardening matriarch Joyce (who will, later, discover how little human beings are like plants), her husband, the ultra-rational Jewish scientist Marcus and their four sons: Joshua (a contemporary of Irie, Magid and Millat), Benjamin, Jack and Oscar are — with the exception of the deliciously contrary six-year-old Oscar, who is, at one point, observed by Irie 'creating an ouroboros from a big pink elephant by stuffing the trunk into its own rear end' — *White Teeth*'s least successful characters. This is for two reasons. Firstly, unlike the other protagonists, the Chalfens are caricatures. They are two dimensional, chattering-class smugsters; self-congratulatory in the extreme and lacking in awareness to a comic, but unrealistic, extent. Secondly, as Irie notes, scanning the thing on the wall in Marcus's study, they have a family tree that stretches way back: 'Dates of birth and death were concrete'. The Chalfens, in contrast to Irie's mixed-up antecedents, 'actually *knew* who they were in 1675'.

Whilst this could be true of Joyce's family, Marcus's ancestors were, we've just been informed, Polish/German immigrants; original name Chalfenovsky. It's highly unlikely that Marcus would have been able to trace his lineage back further than the few generations his family had been in England or Germany.

Irie falls in love with the Chalfens, their confidence, free-flowing conversation, apparent openness (they are all in perpetual therapy). She misreads their self-satisfaction for a general air of fulfillment:

a blatant contrast with her home environment. Zadie Smith has said that she hated the process of writing Irie but later came to think that her character displays some of the novel's most natural writing.

It's true. Whereas the Chalfens are transparent caricature and Millat and Magid are, for conceptual neatness, shoehorned into bad/a bit dim and good/highly intelligent roles, Irie is free to grow up, do okay and fuck up like any normal urban teenager. She endures some fairly standard teenage female self-inflicted miseries: unrequited love; a bad hairdressing experience; the inability to see her own beauty; underestimating her own intelligence, but gets through her mistakes and sometimes learns something from them. She's alternately tongue-tied and mouthy. En route to the novel's somewhat unsatisfactory and contrived conclusion, she has a superb outburst on the packed number 98 bus she's riding from Willesden Lane to Trafalgar Square with her parents, Samad, Alsana and Neena. She shouts at the rest of her party to "shut up the lot of you", then delivers an extended, high-volume monologue about how lovely and quiet other families are.

Smith is, she's said, unsure where her debut novel's title sprang from. Her mother, a psychiatrist, has suggested it's a subconscious reference to the joke about how you spot black people in the dark. The joke appears in a darkened form in *White Teeth*, when Irie, together with Magid and Millat — in defiance of Samad — take their Harvest Festival fare to elderly Mr Hamilton in Kensal Rise. This harmless, elderly gent turns down all their Harvest offerings because they're too hard. His teeth aren't up to anything that hasn't first been pulverized. But he still invites the children to stay for tea. He reminds them how important their teeth are, before offering them more sugar and describing how, when he was fighting in the Congo, "the only way I could identify the nigger was by the whiteness of his teeth... They died because of it, you see?... Biscuit?"

References and Further Reading

The Londonist on *White Teeth* locations:

http://londonist.com/2010/09/london_literary_locations_white_tee.php?show-page=1#gallery-1

Wikipedia on Willesden: http://en.wikipedia.org/wiki/Willesden

Rose Rouse's Harlesden blog: http://roserouse.wordpress.com/

Adam Mars-Jones reviews *The Autograph Man:* http://www.guardian.co.uk/books/2002/sep/08/fiction.zadiesmith

Adele's Dance School: http://www.adelesdanceschool.com/

White Teeth, Green Spaces

The main locations for *White Teeth* aren't at the top of most London tourists' must-see list. But to experience the novel's Willesden-Harlesden-Kilburn settings it's worth spending a sunny Sunday touring the parks its characters frequent. All four will be crammed with people of all ages, from a variety of cultures, speaking any number of languages. There will be ball games, frisbees, shrieking children speeding round on/falling off bikes and scooters, earnest joggers with headphones and water bottles, gossiping parents pushing babies in buggies and older people relaxing on park benches, eating ice cream, watching.

If you live round here, it's nigh-on impossible to make your way through any one of them without bumping into someone you know, being enticed into an impromptu African drumming or Zumba session and/or striking up a conversation with a complete stranger and their surprisingly friendly dog. The parks vary slightly in character as do their demographics: the thirty acre Queen's Park, as Alsana notes, is the poshest of the bunch. It's also your best bet if you're into celebrity spotting. Its café sells Harlesden-made DiSotto's ice cream — as, naturally, does the Roundwood Park one. Queen's Park also has tennis courts, a putting range, petanque pitch, a bandstand and a children's playground with a paddling pool and a humungous sandpit that's almost invariably full of toddlers.

Gladstone Park, situated between Willesden and Dollis Hill and named after the Victorian Prime Minister who used to hang out there when it was private property, is the biggest of the four, has the most suburban vibe and also the steepest hill. It features tennis courts, a walled garden, and a delightfully peaceful and secluded café. This contrasts markedly with the Queen's Park and Roundwood Parks caffs, both of which are usually packed with children expressing their urgent need for chips at high volume. The annual Gladstonbury Festival isn't quite as much like Glastonbury Festival as its name might imply.

Kilburn Grange Park is on the eastern side of Kilburn High Road, almost directly opposite the fabulous Tricycle Theatre, with its unimaginably comfortable cinema. At eight acres, it's the smallest of the parks, but has a lovely rose garden, loads of benches — so even when it's heaving, you can be lucky enough to find somewhere to sit — tennis courts and a floodlit games area with changing rooms. It also has a fabulous adventure playground and activity centre that opened in May 2010 and formed the prototype for another twenty playgrounds across the capital city. No café, but there are loads just outside on the High Road.

Roundwood Park, which connects Harlesden and Willesden, is the least sports-oriented of the bunch, although it does boast a well-used football/basketball pitch and a beautifully-maintained bowling green that's protected by a wall of the perfect length and height to walk along if you're between two and five years old. It has a colourful, if undemanding, children's playground and a small aviary, the inhabitants of which are rather overshadowed by the noisy green parakeets who've recently settled in the trees, where they argue with magpies and crows. The park's café was the centre of a recent scandal, involving its former proprietor, the charismatic, community-oriented and utterly charming Countess Mariaska Romanov (born Robert Duxbury). At the time of writing, she is serving a four-and-a-half-year jail sentence for defrauding the local authority of £197,000 over a dozen years partly by claiming to be her own twin sister. A number of local residents felt her contributions to the community outweighed her misdemeanours.

Lisa Gee

Chris Petit
The Hard Shoulder (2001)

VALENTINE CUNNINGHAM

C hris Petit is a hard-eyed documentarist of the city in film and in fiction, the recorder especially of modern London. His credits include being a great ally and aesthetic associate of Iain Sinclair, the CEO of contemporary London writing and film-making. Petit is especially drawn to violent city low life, the doings of urban bad-men — criminals politically motivated, as in his novel of the Northern Irish Troubles *The Psalm Killer*, but mainly criminals who are criminals out of mere and sheer wickedness, of evil even. The result is seriously good urban thrillers, fiction-noir of the hardest-boiled kind. And *The Hard Shoulder*, Petit's Kilburn-noir effort, is at least as good as his Will Self-ish Soho novel *Robinson*, his Belfast novel *The Psalm Killer*, and his New York horror-comic cop-fic *Back from the Dead*.

Petit's fictional territory is what Iain Sinclair has labelled the 'psychogeographical badlands'; in the case of *The Hard Shoulder*, Kilburn and its environs and hinterlands. It's as if Sinclair's favourite East End, Jewish criminal, Kray Brothers' London has been shifted northwards and westwards to Irish (Catholic) criminal NW6. This Kilburn is the loving habitat of O'Grady, one-time local hard-man, just out of prison where he's done ten or so years' time for being the getaway driver in a botched hold-up job. This ex-con is soon being cruelly pressured by a creepily know-all gangster chum Shaughnessy and his broken-kneed alcoholic sidekick Tel to put the squeeze on godfather Ronnie, now living a lush life on the Costa del Crime, partly on O'Grady's share of the loot from the messed-up raid. O'Grady is most reluctant to get back into the old ways. He prefers serving the breakfast at his pious sister Molly's 'hotel', going to the pictures with the sexually eager housemaid Kathleen, and visiting his old mum in a Home in Willesden. He's emotionally screwed up, crippled in fact, by guilt over the little girl he ran over and killed in the getaway car, and about his own lost daughter Lily from his broken marriage, same age as the little girl he knocked down. But he's inexorably sucked into replaying the old violent games, which involve hunting down Lily and her rough-and-ready rock musician boyfriend in their flash pad in posh Totteridge, and a black-comic attempt by the bad-boy trio O'Grady, Shaughnessy and Tel to kidnap Lee, Ronnie's rich little brat of a daughter, out at Ronnie's mansion near Lambourne End in hopes of extorting the ill-gotten that's owed, money O'Grady has promised to Lily.

Violence and violent death impinge menacingly from the start of the novel and home in on O'Grady with terrifyingly needy accuracy. In Ronnie's pay, Shaughnessy obtains — with the help of a pair of Upper Holloway heavy-plant hirers connected to the IRA — a mouthy young Northern Irish hit-man called Brendan to bump off O'Grady, but the 'thick' Mick misfires, managing only to wound his target. Disgusted, Shaughnessy offs Brendan (a 'clot'), and has a go at O'Grady himself, but fails ludicrously, even though assisted by the jumpy Tel armed with a big knife. He opens fire at his own mirror image in Molly's bedroom, from which O'Grady is happily absent. It turns out that Shaughnessy has a bad heart and he kicks the bucket in Ronnie's crappy Essex seaside bungalow to which the kidnappers have resorted as a miserable safe-house. Ronnie is arrested as he lands at some private airfield, the cops beating O'Grady to the man who might have the money. O'Grady robs an Asian post office for lamentably small pickings, which he hands over to the rather surprised Lily. He dies at the end, it would seem, at the wheel of Ronnie's Merc, the gunshot wound in his side finally doing him in, fantasizing the while about fun for Lee and getting to Florida, where sister Molly is moving to run a motel. It all makes for a blackly comic low-tech krimi, which wryly milks the fabled bad luck of the Irish to most attractive effect.

You can feel what's coming right from the opening page. How repro Grahamegreenish (to use Auden's label) can you get?

> O'Grady, a big man once, stood in the empty carriage of the silver train as it moved faster through the long tunnel from St. John's Wood into daylight at Finchley Road. He wore an overcoat but looked like a man that rarely did, and the battered holdall at his feet was far from full. He stood awkwardly, waiting for the doors to close, blinking at the light after so long underground.
>
> After West Hampstead the train travelled a ridge. Slate sky bled the colour from the view. To the left he could see the tower of the

Kilburn State cinema, like a small finger of Manhattan stuck into the London skyline. O'Grady felt his stomach contract and thought of riding on, but he got out at Kilburn, pausing to watch the train move away down the long, straight track. He couldn't remember if the carriages had always been silver.

He took the stairs down to the street. He was still unfamiliar with the process of everything and whatever he did felt like it was at the wrong speed, even handing in his ticket to the unmanned booth. Outside, the two railway bridges, cutting the road at an angle just above the station entrance and booming whenever a train passed over, were his first familiar landmark. To his left Shoot Up Hill ran up towards Cricklewood. To think he had once aspired to Cricklewood. O'Grady turned right.

The Kilburn High Road had been a ditch when he left, and still was from what he could see. He wondered if Morans, where he'd had his first job, was still there. It was, the same...

Further down on the other side was the Black Lion. He had favoured the Black Lion after being barred from the Roman Way for brawling.

Petit is superior at grab-you openings. This one is as impelling as any of Graham Greene's inductions into modern threats — as it might be *Brighton Rock*, Greene's thirties novel about gang-warfare in Brighton. Petit looks over his shoulder knowingly at Greene's sort of Ealing Comedy, Best of the Brits version of the hard-boiled thriller, as much as to the great American Chandler-esque tradition it's also referencing. Precedent literature calls. That ridge the train travels after West Hampstead is surely meant to grapple your readerly attention like the bump in the Manhattan street in the opening of Martin Amis's great novel of urban corruption *Money* (1984), which reaches out to catch the hero's cab like a 'grapple-ridge'. And of course there's a business called Morans: we assume they're members of the clan that Moran the longsuffering narrator of Samuel Beckett's *Molloy* belonged to. In literary terms this is very street-wise; which is apt, one might think, to this highly street-wise — in every sense — fiction.

Wise, especially, about streets. With our Rip Van Winkle ex-con we're plunged straight away into the territory that will be devotedly mapped: the cartography of Kilburn — Finchley Road, Shoot Up Hill, Kilburn High Road. Those roads will spread out and around into the suburbs and Essex, but Kilburn's the epicentre of the novel's mapping — Petit's version of what Iain Sinclair has in *Lights Out for the Territory* called the 'alternative cartographies of the city' (phrase from a Chris Jenks essay on 'The History and Practice of the Flâneur'). Sinclair heralded such doing in a catalogue of alternative London cartographers in *Lights Out*, a sort of canon of commendable rescuers of London 'dead ground' — J.G. Ballard, Michael Moorcock, Angela

Carter, Peter Ackroyd, Alexander Baron, Emmanuel Litvinoff, Bernard Kops, Stewart Home. Petit, a recurrent presence in *Lights Out*, is of course in the list — meeting a 'fetch' of Robin Cook (ie Derek Raymond) as he 'minicabs between Soho and the suburbs'.

The generous alternative cartographics of *The Hard Shoulder* are done in a kind of detailed *A-Z* guide to unglamorous London. This is revelatory, documentary, realistic text as an *A-Z*. We're driven with O'Grady and Shaughnessy 'over the Harrow Road and across the top of North Kensington... down North Pole Road... turn left at the junction of Scrubs Lane... [then] right into Du Cane Road', en route to see Ronnie's mate John in Wormwood Scrubs prison.

> They crossed three of the roads that O'Grady had always thought of as the great divides, the Kilburn High Road, the Finchley Road, then, via the back-streets of Chalk Farm and Kentish Town, the Holloway Road, always to his mind the most sullen of the lot. He... recalled going as a child with his mother to the Jones Brothers department store and her telling him they were on the edge of the land of the darkies, and the frequent threat of punishment of being sent there to live with them.
>
> Once they were in the Seven Sisters Road most of the shops became open-fronted stores with vegetables on display. In Kilburn a greengrocer was a rarity...
>
> Shaughnessy made him turn left up Hornsey Road, which was clogged with traffic. They inched past the baths, with a big painted sign of a diving woman in a bathing suit...
>
> Further up the road was a big police station. Shaughnessy kept nervously clearing his throat, and O'Grady wondered if he was wanted or had form...

There's a lot of driving around in Shaughnessy's rotting Datsun, much of it as O'Grady makes his parodically slow car-chases in pursuit of his lost women and elusive loot. O'Grady does some walking, but not a lot; he's a twentieth-century parodic upgrade of the Baudelarian flâneur, who embraces the urbs and suburbs mainly by courtesy of a decaying internal combustion engine. Round and round he and we go, motorized, but slowly, getting farcically to know the 'dead ground' of Sinclair's list — modern, even super-modern non-places, as they've been called (in Marc Augé's *Non-Places: Introduction to an Anthropology of Supermodernity*, about living in the 'non-space' of supermarkets, airports, hotels, motorways; or in John Burnside's novel about Corby, *Living Nowhere*): the banal England of the North Circular, of Wembley, of Harlesden, and such. Places where not a lot happens to glamorize them out of tedious flatness. Where even the bloodletting is pale stuff. Characteristically, at the South Mimms service station the planned exchange of Lee for Ronnie's cash fails to

232

happen. 'Wembley struck O'Grady as one of those places that were too far from the centre to count and not far enough out to have any point of their own'. He 'wasn't even sure where they were. Kingsbury or Queensbury, maybe even Canons Park. It no longer felt like the suburbs, more like the suburbs of the suburbs. He managed to locate a municipal car park near a shopping centre with toilets that turned out to be locked'. They finally catch up with Lily and her rock-musician on the Staples corner flyover of the North Circular after cruising haphazardly along the Barnet by-pass, and head for Harlesden. 'What the fuck's in Harlesden for the likes of them?' 'He followed the Mercedes to a turning off Old Oak Lane, close to the railway sidings, not far from the prison where they had been earlier that day'.

Their destination 'looked like an industrial shed stuck on a trading estate'. A place for a rave, which is one of the many new things which have come along while O'Grady was inside. 'Thousands cram into them and they all take a happy pill and jig up and down to loud music. Sounds like hell to me', Shaughnessy informs. O'Grady doesn't dissent. The old London awfulnesses he was used to have certainly had their upgrades, but their modernizings are never less than concerning to our Rip Van Winkle as he ticks them off on his return, like Lazarus, from the tomb of prison. The big dance hall where he'd spent his disappointing Saturdays chasing Irish girls, optimistic condoms in his top-pocket but never used because the girls were well-coached in mortal sin, is now an even more discomfiting place for oldies' dance-classes. Byrne's newsagent is Byrne's only in name now; disconcertingly, an Indian runs it ('"Where's old man Byrne?" "I'm Byrne now", said the man brightly').

What Petit is putting on the map is what Sinclair relished in the writing and films of Petit lookalike Patrick Keiller as 'the under-described quarters of the city'. Petit is rescuing neglected Kilburn and its hinterland for fiction, inventing it for new aesthetic consideration, as Dickens invented London's East End, Mrs Gaskell invented 1840's Manchester and Alan Sillitoe 1950's Nottingham. Petit keenly maps out the telling urban stuff, the revelatory streets and their furniture, the local pubs (always known as locals) and their local inhabitants, and the buildings which are the large signifiers of local meaning. These local truths of the locale are the penetralia of understandings utterly beyond the scope of the outsider, elusive to the keenest-eyed visiting anthropological observer and documentarist, and especially to the novelist as slummer. This is psychogeography as inside story. That Kilburn State Cinema which the narrative notices on the opening page, with its unmissable tower (modelled on the Empire

State Building), the once nationally famous Gaumont picture palace of the Kilburn High Road, opened in December 1937 with an astounding 4,000-plus seats: O'Grady's been in there, and he goes inside its now reduced modern state later in the novel with Kathleen to see *Silverado*, a newly released Western of 1985.

This is insider trading, courtesy of Petit's minute local knowledge and experience, and we are repeatedly inducted into it. We're let into the Black Lion, for instance, first port of call for the released O'Grady, and for us. 'It was soon after opening and the place was empty apart from a couple of biddies in a corner chasing bottles of stout with what looked like sweet sherry... the barman was a surly lad more interested in his paper than pouring Guinness. O'Grady asked for a Jameson's too, to give him something extra to do.' Come Sunday lunchtime O'Grady's in there again, sipping the Jameson's, putting money in the IRA collecting tin, bearing with Shaughnessy's boasts about a pal who's got a crate of Jameson's 'for a very fair price, considering'. O'Grady haunts pubs, essential to him in every way. In one on York Way he taps an old chum the barmaid Carole for information about his wife's whereabouts and enthuses about the satisfactions of the local. 'She fixed a vodka from one of the bottles hanging upside-down behind the bar. Those bottles and their optic measures summed up for O'Grady what was most satisfying about a pub: the promise and choice, the endless permutations and rituals to the straightforward objective of getting plastered.' These trips inside these ordinary proletarian spaces are a reminder of what Sillitoe did in *Saturday Night and Sunday Morning*.

This is dull reality made arresting through Petit's confident deictic, pointing-out practice: the shared knowability of London which Dickens made his own. It's the kind of close-up pointing out of *realia* which takes place, for example, when in *Oliver Twist* Rose Maylie and Mr Brownlow meet the fallen woman Nancy on the stairs on the Surrey side of London Bridge, and are spied on by Noah Claypole — 'just below the end of the second' flight of stairs, 'going down', where 'the stone wall on the left terminates in an ornamental pilaster facing towards the Thames. At this point the lower steps widen: so that a person turning that angle of the wall, is necessarily unseen by any others on the stairs who chance to be above him, if only a step'. This is the verity of the photograph. You could go and check it out for yourself. Just so, *The Hard Shoulder* keeps pointing to touchable, knowable places. Look *there*, come *here*, it says; follow O'Grady to *this* place — *that* rave shed in Harlesden, it might be, 'off Old Oak Lane, close to the railway sidings, not far from the prison where they had been that day'. Locations located and locatable, utterly knowable in the confident epistemology of this narrated city, possessed by those unwavering definite articles and demonstratives. *The* railway sidings, *the* prison, *that* day. O'Grady knows which, where and when; like his author. Petit has been there, and takes you the reader there, and you could indeed go there to see for yourself. Which is a fine realistic assumption and practice: the realistic Dickensian prose mode the English novel was initiated into by Daniel Defoe (that Londoner who founded the English novel in masterly mappings of his home city). An utterly assured pointing prose, showing us this, that and the other, as they are: 'one of the bottles hanging upside-down behind the bar. *Those* bottles and *their* optic measures... *the* promise and choice, *the* endless permutations and rituals to *the* straightforward objective of getting plastered'. This is unflustered, lucid prose which knows what's what and where, keeps registering how things are and how they're done. (The prose George Orwell did his best to work with.) And particularly revelatory about being, about selfhood, in this London of the novel's mid-eighties setting, especially as they're affected by money and class-consciousness and how they get expressed in bricks and mortar, bigger and better barns (as the Good Book has it), slicker motors, changings of place.

Much of the novel is about social and economic aspiration and upgrading, as signified by moving house, the acquisition of property, moves into better streets, better parts of town, leafier suburbs. O'Grady's sister Molly is buying up houses. His ex-wife Maggie has up-shifted to Stanmore, along Honeypot Lane — a modern development, 'executive style' cul-de-sac, houses widely spaced, place as 'empty as a dream', out by the 'big American-style supermarket' with 'its own road and shrubbery' and the feeling 'of driving into some private estate that let you take things out'. Crooked Ronnie is building bigger and better in city-edge footballer territory. This is loadsamoney Thatcher's Britain (she's almost local, MP for Finchley, 'just up the road', as O'Grady's mum knows). It's the dubious new prosperity-time enjoyed and exemplified most of all by Lily's nasty rock-band boyfriend and Ronnie the villain who's made his money by crime.

Petit knows the territory and how to convincingly chorograph — as well as choreograph — its bristling blend of the ethical, economic, social and political. *Chorography*, the writing of urban settlements, which has run continuously as a main fictional business alongside biography, 'written lives', ever since Henry Fielding offered them in *Joseph Andrews* (1742) as rival models for his new mode, the novel in English. Petit is wonderfully cunning, slyly laconic even, in his managing of his biographies and chorographies. O'Grady's story, his past and his present, are eked out in a canny, slowly built-up, hint-full narrative. It's full of lovely, ordinary, banal Londoner lingo, so revealingly outspoken, but like the novel giving away just enough, never too much at a time. This is the narrating of urban and suburban spaces and spacings which speaks eloquently not just in and about those spaces but in the astute gaps between them. Petit's style exemplifies his fondness for the film-maker Wim Wender's narratological recipe: 'The story should unfold in the spaces between the characters'. Petit is such a good manager of his diverse materials and their presentation. In *Lights Out for the Territory* Sinclair lauded Petit's novel *Robinson* for its 'ex-film director's grasp of essentials' — the essentials of urban truth-telling. And that's the essential truth about Petit's truth-tellings: his sure grasp of the essentials of a certain place and its people, its economics, history and ethics and, not least, his grasp of the generic needs of a (London) noir thriller.

References and Further Reading

Chris Petit, *Robinson*, Jonathan Cape, 1993

Chris Petit, *The Psalm Killer*, Macmillan, 1996

Chris Petit, *Back from the Dead*, Macmillan, 1999

Chris Petit, *The Hard Shoulder*, Granta, 2001

Marc Augé, *Non-Places: Introduction to an Anthropology of Supermodernity*, Verso, 1995

John Burnside, *Living Nowhere*, Jonathan Cape, 2002

Iain Sinclair, *Lights Out for the Territory*, Granta, 1997

Kilburn High Road

Following Irish O'Grady's 1985 footsteps along Kilburn High Road is quite easy. Much has changed, even in the few years since the novel's 1980s, but the main landmarks and ports of call, as it were the bone-structure of the place, are still intact enough to be recognisable. This is the A5 out of London, a log-jam of traffic slewing up and down a perceptible slope. It rises more sharply at the top end leftwards out of the Jubilee Line station, up Shooter's Hill to Cricklewood (posher once, O'Grady tells us, though not really posher now). O'Grady turned right out of the station, wondering whether Morans, where he'd had his first job, would still be there. It was; and still is; on the right, just a little way down. M.P. Moran & Sons Ltd, a Builders' and Timber Merchant, selling tools and plumbing stuff, with large bathroom showrooms. It's the last of the Road's big stores. Its one-time big companions, B.B. Evans, Woolworths, the British Home Stores, have all, alas, gone. Shopping here is not what it once was.

Once the road was a spectacular shopping drag, a 'ditch', as O'Grady puts it, walled in by great fetchingly square five-storey blocks, many with ornamental eaves, all loops and arabesques and machicolations, housing three hundred or so shops. Solid, bourgeois and petit-bourgeois citadels of purchases they were — the big departments, smart grocers, wet-fish shops, coffee and tea emporia, several Sainsbury's, Lyons teashops (Foyles began in Kilburn) — interspersed with ornate banks, grand pubs, cinemas, the big dance-hall (one-time cinema) which O'Grady remembers from his youth. Kilburn High Road was renowned for the domes which crowded its skyline. M.P. Moran's two domes survive, as does Lloyds Bank's, and the old dance hall's. The pubs mainly survive as well: the Sir Colin Campbell (named for the hero of Lucknow); the Greene King ('Licensed 1486, rebuilt 1900' it proclaims); the Black Lion, in which much of the novel's drinking takes place ('Rebuilt 1898'), a listed building which entirely merits its place on Camra's Historic Interiors Inventory; and many more. 1898 and 1900 sing out proudly on those pubs. This settlement was clearly entering its heyday then. The many side roads are crammed with substantial late-Victorian, Edwardian houses.

But how the shops have changed. Now they're dominantly bazaars of ultra-contemporary need — Botox parlours, Sports Direct, Vodafone, Laser Hair Removers — neighboured by the pitiless flagships of urban economic decline, grim tokens of a citizenry hanging in there, but only just — pawnbrokers, cheapo household goods marts, Poundland, Everything £10 or Less shops, instant money sharks — Pay Day Loans brazenly offers money at APR 319.1%. Long ranks of brightly plasticated ground-floor desperation prop up floor after floor of dingy-looking apartment windows and offices of need — so many solicitors, specialists in immigration problems — or just gloomily empty floors. And if those immigration advisors are outward signs of population change, even more so are the numerous Halal butchers and grocers, a Halal restaurant, and the boxes of exotic veg spilling onto the pavement, all manned, as is the way, by men — middle-easterners and easterners of all sorts, Bengalis, Arabs, Turks, Lebanese. The Road's Safeways supermarket, which O'Grady favours for his food needs, sticks out now as a rather alien supplier.

Plainly the Irish Kilburn of O'Grady's and Chris Petit's acquaintance ('County Kilburn' as the area was once known), is legible now rather as a kind of palimpsestic trace. The Road does have, to be sure, a couple of Paddy Power bookies. The Sir Colin Campbell offers Traditional Irish Music Nights. The huge, upturned galleon, Roman Catholic Church of the Sacred Heart in the side Quex Road (O'Grady's sister's church, where O'Grady hangs out to meet old chums), still functions. The Irish Centre Housing Association is putting up a huge apartment block opposite. But the Church does seem rather big in funerals, and the St. Eugene de Mazoned Primary School next door in Mazoned Road is open nowadays to all religious comers. 'Irish Times Sold Here' the metal signs outside a newsagent announce, but they are getting a bit rusty. You can still eat Irish Salt Beef on this road, but that's at Woody's (Lebanese?) Grill, where every other dish is very unIrish indeed. So though it's not quite a case of everything being, as the Yeats poem has it, 'changed utterly', it is a close-run thing.

The big Deco-ish building that was the Road's dance hall is still intact, but it glooms mysteriously, shut up, apparently occupied, but as and by who knows what. And the Road's most prominent architectural citizen, the onetime Gaumont State Cinema, is now a branch of the Ruach Inspirational Church of God of Brixton. A form of Christianity very far indeed from the Quex Road Romans. The State was the largest cinema in Europe, a wondrous Art Deco palace, with a vast four-manual Wurlitzer organ which had, notoriously, a grand piano somehow attached. The cinema's tower, the tallest edifice in this road of tall buildings, boastfully echoed New York's Empire State building, whence the cinema's name: 'STATE', the tower proclaimed on three sides in huge letters which lit up at night. The grand opening on 20 December 1937 was broadcast nationally on the wireless by the BBC (Gracie Fields sang, harmonica genius Larry Adler played, as did the BBC's resident Henry Hall dance band). The State was one of London's main popular-music venues. Louis Armstrong, Stephane Grappelli, the Rolling Stones, the Beatles all performed there. Eventually the vast auditorium gave way to a small cinema — O'Grady takes a woman to see a film in it. Now the building resounds only to the Ruach Ministries' pentecostal rhythms, and that just once a week, on Sundays at 12.30. They're not too put off, one hopes, by the building's pavement-level rash, the Beauty Laser Hair Clinic, US Nail Art, Cancer Charity Shop and Hair and Beauty Salon which cluster where once the film posters went, under the crumbling white Deco tiles and the rusting empty flag-pole holders. The great STATE letters are still in place, but they light up no longer.

Here, as on every hand in the Road is manifest cultural shift, even reduction, if not absolute decline and fall (piquantly, Evelyn Waugh, author of *Decline and Fall*, once lived in Kilburn). But it's a pervasive declivity that's greatly alleviated, unexpectedly, amazingly even, by the neighbour that arrived too late to get onto O'Grady's radar, the wonderful Tricycle Theatre and Cinema — in the adapted and built-on old Foresters Friendly Society building, over the road from the Sir Colin Campbell. The Tricycle's a brilliant community Arts hub, specialising not just in great superior drama and film but in radical docu-dramas, re-enactments of the Iraq War Inquiry, and such. It's said that on the Tricycle's occasional Irish music/film/drama nights the small auditorium is emotionally packed with Kilburn's residual native Irish. And daily at the Tricycle, and not just on Irish nights, a kind of beauty, even, to quote Yeats again, a terrible beauty, is born again: cheeringly defiant in the face of the Road's so many occasions for gloom about change and loss.

Valentine Cunningham

238

Iain Banks
Dear Air (2002)

Courttia Newland

It is often said that London is a many-faceted jewel, ever changing, no two sides the same. The city explored in Iain Banks's *Dead Air* is one of unmistakable debauchery, a world of media moguls and PR women, gangsters and their wives, drug takers and DJs, the seething depiction of night owls and their sins. Banks's not entirely pleasant journey is a whistle-stop tour around bright lights and inevitable dark spots. It's a London most would have seen through a bus, car, or black cab window, yet very few would have experienced first-hand.

The city as a manifestation of its inhabitants' more negative aspects, most importantly Banks's protagonist, shock jock Ken Nott, often means that London is awarded a bit-player's role in Bank's narrative, a fleetingly viewed cast member. There is very little rest or respite for Banks's people. They are career driven, destined to work and play hard for as long as they are able, which echoes many contemporary Londoners' view of themselves and the place they live. Characters are busy answering phones, taking meetings, socialising with work mates and friends, are constantly on the move. They largely represent the drones of the media hive, both brighter and higher in the hierarchy than worker bees, knowing distinctly that there is no possibility of ever becoming royalty. It's difficult to tell if they are satisfied with this existence or whether they yearn for more. Nott seems content to amble through life as a largely self-serving personality, and is certainly not in search of any epiphany when we first meet him, high above London's streets. Following this lengthy prelude, the only chapter of relative tranquillity, we hopscotch from neighbourhood to neighbourhood, action to reaction, each location providing a fast paced, bird's eye view of the capital and its hedonistic citizens. In Nott's own words, the rapid pace of his story resembles:

> One of these... Record-breaking domino-falling displays... A whole toppling, fanning, branching cascade of tiny events, which happen so fast and so together they become one big event...

From the opening chapter, which takes place at a wedding reception for an Asian friend of Nott's and his English wife, contemporary multicultural London is placed centre stage. Yet quickly, we see this is the domain of the haves, rather than have-nots. The reception is set on the roof of a New York-style loft apartment in the East End: 'One big space, full of minimalism, but very expensive and artfully arranged minimalism'. After a conversation with his girlfriend, record label PR, Jo, Nott tells us breakfast was 'orange juice and a couple of lines of coke each'. A gleaming yellow Porsche is parked below, a far cry from the London of the under-privileged. Banks allows the reader a brief critique of his characters and their environment when Nott decides to supplement his liquid breakfast: 'I hoisted the apple from the glass and took a bite. It looked shiny and great but tasted of nothing much.'

The chapter ends with the admittedly drunken wedding party, led by Ken and his amorous friend Amy, throwing items from the roof; first small fruits, but later old hi-fi systems, radios, bottles and a broken TV. It takes a teenage girl to tell them that throwing away perfectly good food and household items might be wrong, but that doesn't stop them pitching over a few more bottles of Cava. When the phones begin to ring, the party begins to lose its vigour, and people begin to realise something is wrong. The date is September 11th, 2001. It is a momentous point of change, even if the true repercussions are not immediately apparent.

It's interesting to note that Banks was once famed for writing novels that explore the '80s zeitgeist. *Complicity*, published in 1993, concerned the city under Thatcherism and was told through the eyes of a morally righteous serial killer. In *Dead Air*, first published in 2002, the conflicted narrator who lives wrongly while extolling a rigid moral code has returned, and there is an almost morbid attempt to capture London's frivolity: when the city is still bathed in the notion that the Tories had been kept at bay, if not banished; when commerce flowed and economic downturn was nothing more than a sombre cloud on the horizon. This is an unsympathetic London, full of cruel people who live the high life and cast bold judgement on the world, none more so than Ken Nott, who has no qualms about spouting righteous indignation on his radio show, (via topics ranging from 9/11, religious radicalism, the ridiculous names of pop artists) and then spending the night in a Soho bar, taking copious drugs, and sleeping with many women, including his best friend's ex-wife. In turning this mostly underground, unseen depiction of London to face the light, a city of excessive spending, drinking, eating, drug-taking and copulating, one has the feeling that Banks may be trying to articulate the nature of the times, and his frustration with those times, as much as a latent frustration with himself (much has been made in reviews of the similarity between Banks and Nott).

What I'm suggesting is not that the author has made an attempt to give voice to London and its environs through verisimilitude — there is very little evocation of place in the novel; areas are name-checked, but not described in any great detail. Scenes take place in these well-known areas, and rapidly move on. Rather, the city becomes a distorted carnival mirror, emotionlessly reflecting the lives of a lead character who lives for the moment, and whose intellectual arguments speak of a man in heated debate with himself, and his own principles.

The first person narrative stays close on Nott's shoulder, and we remain by his side for the entire novel. This makes a compelling — if claustrophobic — read, especially when he is the subject of so much outside disdain. It sometimes feels as though one is walking a crowded London street at fast pace, constantly shoved by people. The river is traversed back and forth by taxi, Land Rover, bike and white van; but if the vehicles and places are diverse, the mood and people generally remain of a similar type. Nott lives on a houseboat, but it's moored in Chelsea Wharf. He drinks in a 'basic Central London pub', but the Soho clientele are advertising creatives, theatre types, music people, film people, who feel better about themselves because they mix with a smattering of workmen, off-duty drug dealers and the homeless. There are mid-summer river cruises and glittering Limehouse penthouses, raves in disused Beckenham cinemas, drunken camaraderie in elegant three-storey Highgate abodes. Yet through it all, Nott seems dedicated to embedding himself in the underworld of London nights. Even when the novel begins, he is already having a dangerous affair with the wife of a prominent crime boss. One of his two best friends is a club DJ with underworld connections. Nott's world is one of secret liaisons, meetings with dangerous men to acquire dangerous objects, a high life with inevitable consequences.

It's this push and pull motion between Nott's ideas and how he lives that can be taken as an indicator of how Banks himself feels about modern life, exemplified via the city of London. In concentrating his attention on an unsympathetic protagonist, who behaves unspeakably throughout most of the book, while continually drawing attention to the more negative traits in humankind, Banks immerses us in the mind of someone whose rants, on-air and off, are so all-consuming he rarely questions his own life. There is the blind rush from one locale to the next, the lack of any real friendships, the lack of pride in his chosen career, flagged up at the beginning of the book, in the chapter that follows the food-dropping incident. Nott is casually aware that there is something wrong in his life. There is a weariness of resignation that comes across as flippant, but turns out to be more desperate, more strident, than originally guessed. Read that way, *Dead Air* presents a cynical, one-sided view of the capital, but a London that exists, in part, all the same.

Midway through the novel, Nott has a rare heart-to-heart with Jo as they stroll along Bond Street. Jo begins by questioning Nott's work (she is not the only one to do so), and this quickly leads to her summarising his life. She reminds him that he hates most of what he does and what he's involved in, citing that he doesn't listen to Capital Live!, and doesn't like the commercial music he plays, his fellow DJs, or the ads. When she provides a list of Nott's pet hates, he's made to realise that in fact, he doesn't like much of what the world has to offer. When she asks him if there's anything he does respect he provides a long, mostly insubstantial list, before finally saying: 'This city'. His reasoning is as random as his constant rants (a shop window of antique fish slices), which Jo easily counters by detailing Nott's own conflicting views, but again, there is a feeling of nostalgia, an attempt to journey beyond the frivolous. London is turned slowly before the reader's eyes, bright side to dull, each glimpsed for another, flimsy moment before we move on.

Banks famously said that *Dead Air* took six weeks to write, and it may be this frenetic energy, the constant feel of movement even though we're unsure to what end, that fuels the book and gives it a constant 'nervous' tinge. Nott, true to his occupation, talks non-stop, babbling about anything and everything to anyone, debating the most mundane but pervasive subjects of modern living — CCTV, Black London slang — to the most compelling. In one particular episode, after a nasty on-air attack on Islam which leads to numerous complaints, Nott is forced by his station manager to conduct a TV interview with a Holocaust denier. Unbeknown to anyone, he concocts a plan to wait until the cameras are rolling, jump out of his chair and punch the interviewee square in the face. Afterwards, when Nott has followed through on his plan and he's asked why he resorted to violence, he denies the whole thing. The point is somewhat irrelevant, but this basic action speaks volumes about Nott's moral compass, which tends to swing wildly throughout the novel, a man with the right ideas but the wrong methods, a man most people seem to like despite themselves, even while balanced on the verge of loathing, even when they are offering him their grudging respect.

The cast of friends, co-workers and lovers that orbit Nott seem locked into hapless trajectories. Phil, his long suffering Capital Live! producer, is dazzled enough by Nott's rock star lifestyle just to tag along and trade on-air witticisms, but for the most part, steers clear of his rag-tag social life. He tolerates his presenter's more extreme characteristics with the weary air of a man who has seen his type before, and is comfortable in his role as the ever-faithful sidekick. Jo, Nott's PR girlfriend, flits in and out of his life and barely seems to register most of the time, even though he's momentarily devastated when she eventually leaves him for one of her more debauched rock star clients. Her character serves to characterise the fickle nature of London's media tribe; fashionable, ambitious, sexy and independent, free-spirited. When they break up, a fairly one-sided exchange that takes place in the bowels of the London Aquarium, a 'bluey-green wash of underwater luminescence', Jo is embarrassed, yet casual. She expects she wasn't the only one cheating, which causes Nott to storm off in a rage, even though it's true. Craig, his only Scottish friend, whom Nott has been close to since adolescence, meets for drink and smoking sessions borne of a tenuously kept tradition, more for the purposes of ritual than solidarity. As things progress, Craig subtly probes Nott's choice of career, his attitude to women, eventually his loyalty to him and their friendship. Nott's illicit affair with Craig's wife is finally revealed when Craig and Emma decide to resume their relationship. His actions and lifestyle are severely called into question for the first time, by someone who not only views Nott's behaviour as distasteful, but actually means something to him. His world is rocked. When their friendship ends, Nott is devastated, and the rapid domino culmination of events begins to roar to an ear-splitting conclusion, as Nott responds the only way he knows how, submerged in alcohol and self-pity.

Only club DJ Ed, and Nott's beautiful mistress Ceel (Celia), are equally single-minded in their admiration, despite everything he does to betray their trust, and all they do in return. Ed is a quite obvious attempt at representing the normalcy of contemporary multicultural London, compared to past fictions, where the presence of people of colour is almost taboo. For the most part Banks does a good job at dramatizing the type of conversations that could take place between a Scot and a man of Caribbean heritage, if the artistic licence of complete honesty was in play. There are times when the dialogue grates, but this is more to do with Banks's unfamiliarity with London language than any race issues. As his closest London friend and in lots of ways Nott's foil, unlike Craig, Ed's moral compass shifts in much the same way: he operates by underworld ethics yet abhors the reputation of Celia's husband, John Merrial; he loves his mother and sister, yet has no qualms sleeping with Jo behind Nott's back. Interestingly enough, when Nott learns of his indiscretion, Ed is routinely forgiven.

As the most intriguing of Banks's cast of characters, Celia Merrial is an almost mythical figure, sexually liberated and spiritually aware. When they first meet, Celia tells a fantastical story of her own death, recounting when she was struck by lightning on her island of heritage, Martinique, while watching a storm on a high cliff. She believes that the world went in two directions from that point onwards — that one half of her lived, and the other was killed, either by the bolt itself, or by plunging down onto the rocks below. On one side, from shoulder to hip, she has markings on her skin, as if a henna tattoo:

> 'That is from when I half-died,' she said matter-of-factly.
> 'What?'
> 'From the lightning, Kenneth.'
> '*Lightning?*'
> 'Yes, lightning.'
> 'Lightning as in thunder and — ?'
> 'Yes.'

This is an interesting use of character, which perhaps speaks of chance and Banks's belief in alternate possibilities, both for the characters and the capital. While again, Celia represents in part the diverse peopling of the city — and after a long, continuing battle, how ordinary that has become — she is very much Ed's polar opposite, both rich and cultured, married to the mob but entirely divorced from its actions, an ex-model who travelled the world and was moneyed long before she met her gangster husband. She offers Nott a fairy-tale ride, leading him first to the lofty climes of the Dorchester and the Connaught; then, at the novel's end, down into the rotten underbelly of an underground car park when her husband suspects their affair; before finally, in the last moments of the book, providing Nott with the chance of a fresh start, the possibility of remaking himself anew. But before that, in those grim moments of the underground car park, when Nott has been tied up and punched and has soiled himself in fear, he suddenly believes Celia's story, and soon afterwards, embraces a major epiphany;

> Maybe I deserve what might happen here. I know I'm not a particularly good person; I've lied and cheated and it's no consolation that little of

it was illegal... So maybe I'd have no real cause to complain if I'm made to suffer

In the end, Nott is reprieved due to luck more than design and Merrial's suspicion is cast elsewhere, towards an entirely fictional lover. He is released into the world with a renewed sense of himself, and slowly, carefully over time, Nott and Celia begin to enjoy the normal, everyday relationship they have always dreamed of. Although this is an uncharacteristically optimistic tone for Banks, and indeed for the novel, there is a clear attempt at trying to flood his shadowed tale with light, in trying to allow some escape for us, his readers, and for London, the city loved by protagonist and author alike. When, in the penultimate chapter, Nott admits to Celia that he loves her, she is characteristically wise and profound. "Where love is concerned," she told me, "you must be a behaviourist." This, more than anything, seems to encapsulate Banks's meditation on London, Londoners and our relation to each other, and in turn the world. It's an admirable stance, definitely one worth reading; but perhaps more importantly, one worth fighting for.

References and Further Reading

Iain Banks, *Walking on Glass*, 1985
Iain Banks, *Complicity*, 1993
http://www.iain-banks.net/

Tally Ho

An area of grazing farmland until 1536, when it was claimed as a royal park for the palace of Whitehall by Henry VIII, the name Soho is believed to have come from a hunting cry. It was later used as a rallying call by the Duke of Monmouth at the battle of Sedgemoor, half a century after the name was first used for this region of London. The Crown leased the area to a succession of Earls who planned to develop the land to imitate Bloomsbury, Mayfair and Marylebone. But Soho never became as fashionable, mainly due to the French immigrants who flooded the area for work. For a while, Soho was known as '*le petit France*.' By the mid-18th century, the aristocrats of Soho Square and Gerrard Street had moved away. By the mid-19th century, prostitutes, theatres and music halls had moved in, and by the early 20th century, the area was popular among writers, artists and intellectuals. J.K. Rowling's French great-grandfather worked in the area as a waiter in the period before the pubs of Soho became filled with drunken poets and artists.

Soho's reputation as a place of debauchery and hedonism was cemented in their prose, poetry and song.

Today, Soho has retained that slightly grubby image, even though the area has changed a great deal. Due mainly to its fame as a place of entertainment, it's a magnet for the rich and poor, boasting nightclubs, public houses, a few scattered sex shops, late night coffee shops, and chain restaurants side by side with more expensive eateries. There are record shops, London's main gay village, churches and even a Hare Krishna temple. Gerrard Street is now Chinatown. Soho has become home to the media industry. The British Board of Film Classification has its home in Soho Square — the setting in *Dead Air* of Nott's radio station Capital Live! — and the media and post-production community has moved into the area, connecting the heart of London with Pinewood and Shepperton studios. It's this rich and vibrant industry that Iain Banks has brought to life in his novel, the unseen characters and inner workings of a world we take a passive part in, yet know little of, hear but rarely understand. This one square mile has become a world unto itself, so much so that the neighbouring area, on the opposite side of Oxford Street, is 'affectionately' called Noho. There is a deep love for the village and what it represents, past and present, artistic and commercial. Soho epitomises London's diversity, and continues to fascinate both visitors and residents alike.

Courttia Newland

Monica Ali
Brick Lane (2003)

SANCHITA ISLAM

Brick Lane in the East End of London has become something of a tourist hot spot, famous for its curry houses, boutiques and heady vibrant mix. Sunday market in particular is a time when all walks of life congregate to enjoy the array of market stalls and street artists and its infectious energy. Monica Ali's seminal novel, in spite of its title, is not about Brick Lane itself, and has little to say about the commercialised or hip aspects of the locality. Instead she writes about the Bangladeshi community which now predominates — Brick Lane has a rich migrant heritage dating from the French Huguenots and encompassing the Irish, the Jews and more recently the Bangladeshis, who came to London in the fifties and sixties in search of that elusive 'better life' — and hones in on the ghettoised council estates that loom tall like chunky limbs on splinter streets. These often eerily quiet estates are home to thousands of Bangladeshis, primarily from the region of Sylhet — a once poor rural district that has become relatively affluent through remittances from British Bangladeshis. If you visit Sylhet, one of the first things you see driving from the airport into the main town is a massive billboard advertising Taj Stores on Brick Lane — a bizarrely surreal sight and a clear sign that Brick Lane is famous globally as well as locally.

Brick Lane was adapted for the big screen in 2007. Both the book and the film caused controversy. Sections of the Sylheti community were affronted by Ali's depiction of them as insular, backward, conservative and uneducated. Filming in the Brick Lane area had to be clandestine. Monica Ali's book met stern disapproval in Bangladesh, but found a readership there all the same. Stuck in a traffic jam in

247

Dhaka, the capital of Bangladesh and the city of Ali's birth, I was surprised to see street vendors touting pirated copies of the book, shouting 'B-rick L-ane' for everyone to hear as they waved them enthusiastically in the dusty air.

In interviews, Monica Ali has spoken of the fact she has no specific sense of home — something shared by her principal character in *Brick Lane*, Nazneen, who struggles to adapt to London life. It could be argued that Ali's lack of grassroots knowledge of the Sylheti community has an impact on the characters' authenticity. Ali's parentage is half Bangladeshi and half English. She was brought up in Lancashire and is Oxbridge educated and has no personal links to the Brick Lane area. The book was a bestseller and a hit with the critics earning Ali a place on the shortlist for the Man Booker Prize in 2003, which begs the question of whether she created a story and characters that people wanted to hear and believe.

Monica Ali begins the story with the birth of Nazneen in a Bangladeshi village. The untimely death of her mother pushes Nazneen towards an unconventional path. Set between 1985 and 2002, the narrative focuses on three main characters all living on an imaginary East End council estate. Nazneen is introduced as the submissive, village, virgin bride sent to London to begin a new life with Chanu, her rotund, older, opinionated husband. The third character is Karim, a second-generation streetwise Sylheti 'lad' who becomes the 'lover' of Nazneen and is swiftly radicalised after 9/11.

The novel has a three-tier structure that maps the evolving landscape of each principal character. Significantly, Chanu is not from Sylhet. He presents himself as a minority within a minority, suggesting his alienation from a community he perceives to be regressive, parochial and overly religious. An aspirational immigrant, Chanu purports to be highly educated and has framed certificates to prove it. He represents the Bangladeshi immigrant who is brimming with optimism about carving a great, solid future, only to have his dreams consistently thwarted. He idealistically talks about creating a 'mobile' library, which would 'bring the great world of literature to this humble estate' and by doing so would open the eyes of the Sylhetis who seem voluntarily castrated from the rest of the world. He pities those Sylhetis complacent within the parameters of their close knit communities who refuse to learn English and never 'leave home', preferring to keep their hearts 'back there' and 'recreating the village here'.

Nazneen listens submissively to her husband's rants without comment, often whilst cutting his toe nails. Her sphere comprises the dour, brown interior of her small flat, and Chanu is her only connection to the world beyond. Seldom venturing outside, Nazneen endures a claustrophobic, static existence. When Nazneen first entered the world, her parents thought she was stillborn. Nazneen's soul is in effect moribund, stuck in a dusty box that she now calls home, '... the muffled sound of private lives' inhabiting similar boxes is the only sign of a life outside her own. At night, when she has a chance to dream, she reverts 'back' to an idyllic lush Bangladesh where there is light, space, limitless nature and the freedom to roam. She prefers to lose herself in memories and dreams of an earlier life that was so abruptly taken away from her.

Nazneen's grasp of English is poor and Chanu doesn't encourage her to learn the language: 'where's the need, anyway'. On one occasion she does head out, after hearing distressing news about her sister in Bangladesh, and is left walking 'in circles' such is her lack of basic topographical knowledge. It seems that she can only manage 'bird steps' and is forever trapped in the small space she inhabits. Without even a rudimentary knowledge of English she can't ask for help. She's hit inadvertently by a man with a briefcase that swings 'like a mallet', the cold rips through her sari pinching her skin spitefully, and crossing the road is like 'walking out in the monsoon hoping to dodge the raindrops'. The world is hostile, angry and violent and renders her disorientated, small and feeble.

The TV acts like a portal transporting Nazneen into other worlds. A charming metaphor unfolds as she is mesmerised by the fluid movement of the ice-skater, who glides through life unencumbered, in control of her elegant physique and in perfect harmony with her partner. She is derided by her husband for her mispronunciation — 'ice-eskating' — and he comments that failure to grasp the language 'is a common problem for Bengalis'. She clumsily seeks to emulate the ice-skater, trying to renegotiate her body in new forms as if trying to rid herself of the shackle that is her room, home and husband. Her efforts end in failure, but this marks a first real attempt to spin, to move, to find a way to be alive again.

Ali builds up the layers of Nazneen's character, the shock of being in a new country, the trauma of losing her first child, her escapism through dreams of a romanticised childhood homeland, her sister's letters that represent paper fragments of 'home', the meticulous cooking of authentic, tasty Bengali food, her tolerance of Chanu's garrulous wrangling and her gradual adjustment as a wife and mother. Nazneen is slowly redrawing the faint map of her existence with bolder lines.

In the second part of the novel Monica Ali continues to evoke, stroke-by-stroke, Nazneen's growing confidence and subtle transformation from submissive, subordinate wife to someone who has begun to find her voice. She now has two daughters and is more settled into life in London. Conversely, it is Chanu, previously confident and full of grandiose plans, who begins to change and retreat. After failing to be promoted, he finds work as a taxi driver out of sheer necessity. He increasingly uses the internet to gain access to a virtual 'entire world'. Chanu is drifting into an abyss of disillusionment. He is adamant that his daughters only speak Bengali at home and makes them recite the national anthem of Bangladesh. He begins to manifest signs of the 'going home syndrome' to which he has previously been so vehemently opposed. Chanu's displacement is even more evident when he decides to take his family on a day trip to central London, which despite living in England for over thirty years he has never seen. Chanu's parameters are not much wider than his wife's. When a passer-by obligingly takes a photo of the family and then asks where they are from, he states: 'we are from Bangladesh'. His mind is lodged in the space of his much-yearned-for Bangladesh and he feels little sense of being British.

Nazneen, by contrast, is stepping out of the dusty box of her previous existence. Through TV and by conversing with her daughters, she becomes proficient in English and starts working from home. Chanu, perhaps surprisingly, encourages her in this. She begins to sew to earn the much needed money that her husband is failing to provide. He meanwhile is embroiling the family in debt to the local loan shark. Now Nazneen has unwittingly become the head of the family. Her new vocation leads to the introduction of the middleman, British-born Karim, who stammers when he speaks Bengali but 'in English he found his voice'. Karim is shaped through the idealised perspective of Nazneen, who sees this younger man as a means of finding a much yearned for 'place in the world'.

Monica Ali quietly documents the harrowing scenes of 9/11 as seen by millions the world over. Chanu is mesmerised, glued to the TV, and his rants have an ominous foreboding of the Islamic extremism that has become pervasive. His wife, Nazneen, is bewildered, such is her detachment from the outside world. It is events like these that begin to dispel the stillness that she previously inhabited.

The introduction of Karim precipitates Nazneen's sexual awakening. In one pivotal scene she puts on a bright red sari and surreptitiously attends a meeting of the 'Bengali Tigers', the activist Islamist organisation headed by Karim, in order to be close to him. This radical group intends to rise up against the Western powers to defend the Muslim world. Karim's impassioned speeches about the distant war-torn territories of Bosnia, Chechnya and Afghanistan expand her knowledge of the world beyond the flat and the estate.

They stir Nazneen's soul. Ali poignantly describes Nazneen shaving her legs in anticipation of her first major sexual encounter with Karim and an affair ensues in the same stifled interior of the flat. She sees Karim as her ice-skating partner, the antithesis of Chanu who craved her to be still and silent. Karim will, she hopes, help her to 'skate through life' and 'spin, spin, spin'.

In the final section the characters shift further. Chanu surrenders all his dreams and returns to Bangladesh, impecunious, dejected and alone. He prefers the remembered world of 'home' in his head, since the Bangladesh of his youth is no more. Karim ends up pursuing 'jihad in some far away place'. He stammered in English too, we learn, unable ever to articulate clearly in either English or Sylheti. Both men fail to find a place in the world.

Nazneen opts to remain in the flat in London with her children. She has an erstwhile best friend; she learns to stand up for herself by confronting the loan shark; she has found her voice and uses it to protect her family without fear. The story ends with Nazneen on an ice-rink, wearing a sari, but fully prepared to move freely on the ice unaided, finding the courage to 'spin' on her own, finally conquering the space she inhabits and embracing the freedom she discovers within it.

Ever since *Brick Lane* was published I have been asked repeatedly about the book, perhaps because I am Bangladeshi and have worked and lived close to Brick Lane. There is certainly much to discuss about Ali's representation of the Bangladeshi community in east London — the cultural significance of the novel — and about its curious impact on me. Do I relate to the characters Ali portrayed, or are they verging onto generic type? Do I recognise the 'Brick Lane' area that the novel tries to portray? Does she evoke a Bangladesh that resonates with me? Is this novel a credible depiction of a very complex people residing in a mercurial London?

Chanu's character represents a stereotype of the immigrant who is spilling with lofty talk, but fails to make his mark. His fictional antagonism towards the Sylheti community was met by anger among the real residents of the estates in the Brick Lane vicinity. His is a familiar story of discrimination, impoverishment, and shattered dreams. His treatment of Nazneen fits into the patriarchal views that women should be mute, subordinate and stagnant. Nazneen's feisty daughter depicts a new generation of women who will not follow the paths of their docile mothers. Nazneen's daughter speaks in a loud, rebellious tongue that was more interesting to me than her mother's.

Karim's character, it could be argued, is one that we read about in today's papers, the angry radicalised Muslim youth who has turned against the West — the potential terrorist in the making, disaffected and lost. He finds Nazneen attractive because she is somehow untainted, unwesternised and therefore pure. His disappearance at the end of the novel is predictable. We know little more though about the psychological make-up of Karim, apart from the outline of his silhouette.

Nazneen inhabits a cultural image of the enfeebled, reticent, uneducated wife trapped in an arranged marriage with an older man living in a poky council flat. Ali shows how Nazneen's character breaks out of the mould she was initially cast in by not dutifully accompanying her husband to Bangladesh, but rather staying in London to raise her daughters alone, to work, to provide, to step out into the world and explore what it has to offer. Ali's book is not really about Brick Lane, but about a woman who finds herself trapped in a strait-jacketed life in an alien city that is overwhelming. Ali's story reflects the lives of other women that inhabit similar council blocks, women who remain invisible. The narrative charts Nazneen's quest for freedom, but ultimately the transformation Ali painstakingly maps is not as profound as I would have hoped. The experience of the story is too claustrophobic; the area of east London in which it is set, the self-titled Brick Lane it alludes to, is not seen or experienced in a way that is evocative or lasting.

Monica Ali only hints at the complexion of Brick Lane without adding the cacophony of smells, people and colour that it is famed for. Perhaps she intended to show how communities become enclosed and dislocated, stuck in a myopic existence of life on the estates. But the result is that the reader doesn't experience the multi-layered richness of Brick Lane.

The sight of burka-clad women walking down side streets, weighed down with their shopping, wearing socks with sandals to protect their toes from the cold; younger teenagers donning hijabs, zooming about in their cars or chattering with friends, confident and cocky; packs of Asian lads with shaved heads dripping in designer gear as they loiter and heckle; or solitary elders walking slowly in traditional dress — these are all strong visual images that are ubiquitous in the Brick Lane area, and noticeably absent from this novel. The Bangladeshi community may stick to their own, but they slide past other locals and have a visible and audible presence. It is a shame that Ali's story takes place primarily in a flat. We never really get a sense of this 'presence' on the streets or beyond the estate. Nor do we understand the distinct geography of Brick Lane and how communities spill into one another simply because of proximity.

Brick Lane is not the definitive novel about Bangladeshis or about the area. There are richer tales to be woven. The novel comes across as inauthentic in its representation of the residents and the local geography. It is as if the estate is suspended in a different east London that is remote and closed off. Perhaps Mile End would have been a less misleading title. Yet Monica Ali succeeds in giving her key character, Nazneen, a subtle and distinct hue. She seeks to tell a story about a community whose voice is seldom heard, and her novel opens the door a little on a closed and secretive world.

References and Further Reading

Manzu Islam [Syed Manzurul Islam], *The Mapmakers of Spitalfields*, Peepal Tree, 1997

Manzu Islam [Syed Manzurul Islam], *Burrow*, Peepal Tree, 2004

Sanchita Islam (ed.), *From Briarwood to Barishal to Brick Lane*, 2002

Sanchita Islam (ed.), *Avenues*, 2007

Rachel Lichtenstein, *On Brick Lane*, Penguin, 2008

Elisabetta Marino, "From Brick Lane to Alentejo Blue: Cross-Cultural Encounters in Monica Ali's Writings", in *BAS/British and American Studies* (ISSN 1224-3086), (Timisoara, Romania), vol. XIV, 2008, pp. 51–58

Elisabetta Marino, "Intersecting Geographies in Monica Ali's Brick Lane", negli Atti del Convegno AISLI, Cafoscarina, Venezia, 2006

Elizabetta Marino: *Introduzione alla letteratura bangladese Britannica* (An Introduction to British Bangladeshi literature), Roma, Sun Moon Lake, 2005

About Brick Lane

I first came to Brick Lane in 1992 — about the time I became Miss Bengali (my mother entered me in the competition without my knowledge). Brick Lane then seemed a rather non-descript street. I felt intimidated by the place, and unfamiliar with the surroundings which have made the street famous. It's now feted for its vibrant blend of curry houses and trendy boutiques. And it's home to the artistic elite of London with residents like Tracey Emin on Fournier Street where French Protestant refugees once lived, the first of successive waves of immigrants to reside in the East End, each leaving its own distinct footprint.

In 1999, starting out tentatively as an artist, I had my first exhibition on Dray Walk, part of the hip Truman Brewery complex (once the largest brewery in London which stopped making beer in 1988). In the last decade the area has undergone rapid change. Spitalfields has been renovated and blends into the affluent gleaming buildings on Liverpool Street on the edges of the City's 'Square Mile'. The achingly cool (or not so, it's a matter of opinion) Shoreditch is only a hop away.

Brick Lane E1

The Truman Brewery let space to musicians and dot-coms alike, expanding its influence with the establishment of the Vibe Bar in the early 90s to the opening of clubs, an independent record store and more bars and eateries. The complex continues to assert its influence in the realms of art, fashion, design and music. The Brewery neatly slices Brick Lane in two — the section closest to Whitechapel Road is distinctly Bangladeshi in flavour with its restaurants, sari, music and DVD shops and grocery stores selling Bangla food, spices, fish and poultry; the part closest to Bethnal Green Road is lined with boutiques and bars, not forgetting the round-the-clock bagel shops.

The side streets are dominated either by council blocks or brand new flats that have attracted an influx of professionals. There's a strong sense of divide between the impoverished immigrant communities and the pockets of more affluent incomers. In an area already home to top end restaurants and cultural centres, Shoreditch House launched on Bethnal Green Road in 2007. It's not unusual to see paparazzi loitering outside this exclusive private members' club, which boasts a pool on the top floor. I was artist in residence there for two years until 2009, creating graffiti art on the toilet doors and a thirty foot scroll of the panoramic view of east London. As I drew, the landscape changed irrevocably before my eyes. I made it my mission to bring people to the club that otherwise wouldn't have access. But you don't see many Bangladeshis there, apart from the cab drivers waiting for business in the usually cold, dank night. Derek Cox, a dedicated community worker for the last thirty years, says 'Brick Lane is more like Piccadilly Circus on a Saturday night'. It is sometimes not a pleasant place to be at the weekend with drunken revellers stumbling down Brick Lane treading on broken glass and urinating wherever they might fancy. Local residents don't appreciate this new development.

The new Shoreditch train line was finished in time for the Olympics. It severs the East End like a hideous concrete limb and still the restless change in the area does not cease. The East is constantly evolving and will continue to do so. Tesco has found a footing on Whitechapel Road, off Bethnal Green Road and Commercial Road — if a Tesco ever opens on Brick Lane then perhaps it will no longer be deemed 'cool'. Shops open and close with alarming alacrity, a consequence perhaps of the dire economic climate. It's sad that local youth clubs have closed down while clubs and bars flourish. Even an old public toilet — opposite the now defunct Christ Church youth centre — has been converted into a club.

Amid the changing times, there remain some fixtures in the East. The newly renovated Whitechapel Art Gallery stands tall and elegant. It's not uncommon to see the artists Gilbert and George, local residents for decades, popping into the Golden Heart Pub, while a woman with her head covered, laden with shopping, disappears down Hanbury Street. It will be interesting to see how the Somali community, the latest migrant community fleeing from strife in the Horn of Africa, will make its mark on the area. As discussed in my book *Avenues*, there are already tensions developing between Somalis and the more established Bangladeshi enclaves.

All these strains, these contrasts and incongruous juxtapositions, give Brick Lane a strange allure and make life here that little bit more interesting — visually, culturally and socially.

Sanchita Islam

John Lanchester
Capital (2012)

JON DAY

The central character in John Lanchester's novel *Capital* isn't a person but a street. Pepys Road is a fictional road located somewhere to the north east of Clapham Common. The name invokes Samuel Pepys, who retired to a house in Clapham Old Town — then a country retreat, now absorbed by suburban sprawl — near the end of his life. On the 25th July 1663, Pepys was given a tour of the house by Denis Gouden, the merchant who built it, and recorded his impressions in his diary:

> I find it very regular and finely contrived, and the gardens and offices about it as convenient and as full of good variety as ever I saw in my life. It is true he hath been censured for laying out so much money; but he tells me he built it for his brother, who is since dead... Besides, with the good husbandry in making his bricks and other things I do not think it costs him so much money as people think and discourse.

Pepys's interest in house prices anticipates one of the main themes of Lanchester's novel. *Capital* is about speculation, both financial (speculating on the markets), and anecdotal (suspiciously gossiping about others); mutually reinforcing interests encapsulated in the question that echoes through the novel: "did you hear what they got for the house down the road?"

The opening section of *Capital* consists of a biography of Pepys Road; a *buildingsroman* describing the street's changing fortunes as though it were a character in a Victorian novel. The road was laid out in the late nineteenth century, 'during the boom that followed the abolition of the tax on brick', in order to house the expanding lower-middle-classes. Its houses were first inhabited not by 'solicitors or barristers or doctors' but by a new class composed of 'the respectable no-longer-poor.'

Since then the fortunes of Pepys Road have changed dramatically. It was neglected at the start of the twentieth century, suffered damage during the Blitz and finally emerged 'from the dowdy chrysalis of the late 1970s to be transformed 'into a vulgar, loud butterfly of the Thatcher decades.' When the novel opens, in the autumn of 2007, the street is 'like Texas during the oil rush', and ownership of a house on Pepys Road is:

> like being in a casino in which you were guaranteed to be a winner. If you already lived there, you were rich. If you wanted to live there, you had to be rich. It was the first time in history this had ever been true. Britain had become a country of winners and losers, and all the people in the street, just by living there, had won.

Fed by a frenzy of property speculation, contemporary Pepys Road is in a state of perpetual renovation. The houses have become increasingly demanding consumers themselves, 'imperious, with needs of their own', fed by a never-ending stream of supermarket delivery vans and maintained by a caravan of builders who attend to their every whim. The houses, which used to be lived in, are now little more than counters in a game of capital accumulation, and are so valuable that they have 'become central actors in their own right.'

Pepys Road, an invented but familiar place, is a suitably generic setting for Lanchester to explore his themes of boom and bust. South London, what Angela Carter called 'the bastard side of Old Father Thames', has not been mapped in fiction as assiduously as the north or east of the city, perhaps because it lacks the instantly recognisable architectural waypoints that so dominate life north of the river. In 1898 Walter Besant wrote that south London was 'a city without a municipality, without a centre, without a civic history', and Lanchester suggests that it is on these largely anonymous streets that the real dramas of contemporary London are being played out. Though it gestures towards other parts of London — Hoxton, the City, Paddington Green police station — *Capital* suggests that the grand sweep of the city is irrelevant to the more local concerns of the inhabitants of the street. Pepys Road is something of a blank slate; a vaguely identifiable but fundamentally anonymous backdrop against which Lanchester's cast of characters can take their turns.

The novel is divided into four sections encompassing a year of life on the street. It opens in autumn 2007 (before most people had recognised the ominous signs of impending financial disaster), and leads up to the financial crash in 2008. *Capital* is a hugely ambitious novel, and contemporary Pepys Road is populated by a cast which is Dickensian in its range. In attempting to evoke the lives of his representative cross-section of contemporary London, however, Lanchester sets himself a difficult task. Dickens's London was, culturally at any rate, a far more homogenous place than the city is now. For Dickens difference was, above all else, class-based. London has become, more than ever, a city of immigrants, and any novel which hopes to offer a state-of-the-city assessment must attend carefully to its new voices. Whilst Lanchester is confident in his rendering of the lives of indigenous Londoners and those of its wealthy, middle-class migrants, he speaks with less authority in the voices of those of his characters who are drawn from further afield. There is a curious homogeneity in tone: though their interests are very different, everyone in the novel thinks in fairly similar ways.

At 51 Pepys Road live Roger and Arabella Yount with their two children. Roger is a banker who works long hours in the City and is rarely at home. Lanchester presents the modern City of London as a place populated by middle-managers and technocrats aided by mathematical whizzkids whose methods are largely opaque to their superiors and Roger, a clubbable networker from a time 'when the City was more about relationships and less about maths', is a man out of place.

Much of the research Lanchester conducted for *Capital* was annexed to his non-fictional account of the financial crash, *Whoops! Why everyone owes everyone and no one can pay*, and intricate descriptions of the workings of the finance industry are largely absent from *Capital*. This is something of a blessing, and the absence of any laborious narratorial exegesis provides a nice analogy for the impenetrability of modern economics itself. The increasing complexity of the finance industry means that very few people understand how exactly many bankers make their money; fewer still care very much. In *Whoops!* Lanchester traces this increasing complexity to the 'Big Bang', Margaret Thatcher's massive program of market deregulation in 1986 when 'all the historic barriers and separations and rules demarcating different areas of banking and finance and participation in the stock market were simultaneously abolished.' Such massive deregulation led to the creation of increasingly baroque products and markets which were largely incomprehensible to the uninitiated. 'In terms of its basic functioning' Lanchester wrote, the contemporary City became 'a far-off country of which we know little.'

Like us, Roger is both ignorant of and uninterested in the murky details of how he earns his salary. He spends his days in his sound-proofed office fudging his knowledge of the markets and trying to work out if his bonus will come to a million pounds. He doesn't consider himself greedy: with two expensive houses and an expensive family to support he needs his million-pound bonus just to keep afloat. His wife Arabella is addicted to luxury whilst acknowledging the essential wastefulness of anything branded 'luxurious'. She has no time to look after her children but instead spends her days shopping, doing up the house and planning endless holidays. Like Roger, she doesn't consider herself to be truly rich but rather 'typical London struggling well-off.'

Down the street at number 42 lives Petunia Howe, the longest continual inhabitant of Pepys Road. Having lived in her house her entire life, Petunia has witnessed first-hand the massive changes the road has undergone. During that time her house has fossilized around her, becoming a time capsule of 1950s interior design. Petunia is getting old and worries about her health; her daughter lives in Essex and rarely comes to see her. Like most of the inhabitants of the Pepys Road, she rarely engages with other people. Her daughter does her shopping for her on the internet; her doctors are brusque and unfamiliar; her neighbours live lives she can barely comprehend.

Petunia's grandson Smitty, who lives in Hoxton, is a successful street-artist. A composite of Damien Hirst and Banksy, Smitty is interested in the relationship between economic value and cultural capital. Lanchester is sensitive to the arcane and apparently irrational economies of the contemporary art world and Smitty's art, like banking or property speculation, appears to create value out of nothing. He is as canny an economic operator as anyone else in the novel. 'You've got to be a brand, man', he says to his assistant at one point, 'Then you find some shit to flog, yeah? That's the way it works.' Smitty uses his more audacious artistic interventions — erecting giant concrete dildos, digging purposeless holes in the street — to generate interest in his brand:

> "The stuff that can't be sold, that's the stuff which makes everything else seem real. You can't commodify this shit. Which is the whole point. But it adds to your mojo, to your aura. And that allows you to make shit you can sell. See?"

Smitty's practice suggests Walter Benjamin's category of the 'auratic' artwork as outlined in his essay on 'The Work of Art in the Age of Mechanical Reproduction'. For Smitty, the aesthetic 'aura' of the non-reproducible artwork is used merely to add to the economic worth of those works that *can* be commodified and sold.

Other inhabitants of Pepys Road engage in more quotidian means of wealth creation. At number 68 live the Kamals, a hard-working Pakistani family who own and run a corner shop. Ahmed, head of the family, lives above the shop with his wife and two children, and runs the business aided by his brothers: Usman, a rather more devout

Muslim than either of his siblings, and Shahid, their talented and occasionally radical but fundamentally lazy younger brother. Ahmed loves his family and works hard to support them, getting up at 4am every morning to sort out the papers and, pragmatically compromising his Islamic beliefs to sell alcohol and pornography to his customers. He is the archetypal shopkeeper in a nation of shopkeepers, and loves 'the profusion' of his shop and the stability provided by owning goods; 'the sheer amount of stuff in the narrow space and the sense of security it gave him'. His brothers are less responsible and more ideological than he is, however, and as the novel unfurls both are swept up in their own misadventures.

Another of the houses on Pepys Road is owned by Michael Lipton-Miller, a solicitor and factotum for a local football club who is unapologetically 'fluent in money.' At the beginning of the novel he is awaiting the arrival of Freddy Kamo, a talented Senegalese footballer who has been signed to Mickey's club. Kamo, like the Kamals, has come to London with his father to seek his fortune, but he quickly realises that in the modern game players are treated not as people but as bodies; as goods to be bought and sold. The sums involved in the trading of players are vast, and even the bullish capitalist Mickey feels ill when he thinks about 'how much money was knocking around football these days.'

Then there are the walk-on parts, played by people who don't live on the street but are drawn to it for economic reasons. Zbigniew Tomascewski, a Polish builder whom everyone calls 'Bogdan the Builder', appeals to the middle-class inhabitants of the street by making sure he is the opposite of his British counterparts: reliable, hard-working and tidy. Londoners have more money than sense, Bogdan thinks, and he has come to the capital to 'earn it from them'. He dreams of retiring to a cottage in Poland and starting a business with his father. By night he uses his modest earnings to play the stockmarket. But his strictly financial relationship with London is challenged when he falls in love with Matya, the Younts' Hungarian nanny, who is drafted in to help out during a domestic crisis.

Quentina Mkfesi, (BSc, MSc), another occasional visitor to the street, is 'the most unpopular woman on Pepys Road'. A Zimbabwean asylum seeker, Quentina is perhaps the most overqualified traffic warden in south London. She fled Harare after being beaten by police for her political activism and cannot be deported because of the threat of further political persecution. But neither can she work or claim full benefits, and thus dwells 'in a legal state of semi-existence'. Forced to work illegally, she lives in a charitable refuge in Tooting with other asylum-seekers. Quentina's story is typical of modern London, and Lanchester portrays

261

her as having the same concerns as any of his other characters. Her harrowing experiences are kept in the background, hovering over her day-to-day life but rarely intruding on her thoughts.

The strongest theme that emerges from Lanchester's novel is that of isolation. Everyone in the novel is, in one way or another, connected to London primarily as a self-interested speculator, and their relationship with the city and with each other is based almost exclusively on selfishness. Roger Yount trades financial products in the world's economic capital; Smitty bestows value on overlooked walls and canvases with a squirt of paint. Even the most modest characters are invested in this game of capital accumulation: Bogdan the builder and Matya service the needs of the wealthier residents of Pepys Road and Quentina the traffic warden, on the bottom rung of the economic ladder, exists only in the cracks of the system. The circulation of wealth has always been a potent metaphor for novelists, and in this case it is echoed in the movement of people and the suspicion such movement can engender, something reflected in the fact that most of the characters in *Capital* are from elsewhere: brought to London for political or economic reasons. Some, like Freddie Kamo, come as celebrities. Others, like Quentina, arrive as pariahs.

Lanchester suggests that money insulates people not only from the shocks of poverty but also from one another, and the isolation of these lives is mirrored in the structure of the book. The 107 chapters of *Capital* are all told from the perspectives of individual characters, formally enacting something of their alienation. People are presented as closed and unreadable, brought together only briefly through financial transactions or in order to participate in the co-creation of wealth. The cumulative effect is somewhat bleak: *Capital* presents a London made up of atomised lives which overlap and inhabit the same geographic space, but never truly connect.

The inhabitants of Pepys Road are united, briefly and only superficially, when their suburban idyll is threatened by a murky campaign of harassment. Postcards depicting the houses on the road accompanied by the motto 'We Want What You Have' are sent to its inhabitants. The message is an enigmatic truism: 'who in the world', thinks Freddie Kamo's father, 'wouldn't want what he had?'

At first many of the residents are troubled by the campaign, fearing that house prices will be affected; others are intrigued but dismissive. After a while the harassment becomes more serious. Graffiti is daubed on some of the houses and dead birds are posted through letterboxes. The lack of any clear meaning behind the campaign is unsettling, but its anonymous ambiguity allows the cards to be incorporated by the residents of Pepys Road into the stories of their own

262

lives. Arabella Yount interprets the campaign as a marketing gimmick from an estate agent, and is vaguely flattered, relishing the 'compliment they paid to the desirability of her house'; whereas Smitty assumes they're an artwork. Like money itself, the cards are symbols; ciphers to be invested with meaning by those they are addressed to. They are not things in and of themselves, but the source of myriad potential meanings. In their differing interpretations of the campaign, the residents of Pepys Road are further isolated.

Capital is an ambitious novel which tries to picture the ways in which economic change influences the geography and social structures of London. Lanchester tells a familiar story of gentrification, suggesting that the movement of capital tends to create barren islands of wealth by pricing poorer people out of the areas that had originally been designed to house them. London remains one of the most economically unequal cities in the world, and there is undoubtedly an increasingly huge divide between those who work in the finance industry and the City (parasitic on the advance-guard of artists seeking cheap rents whose diasporas generally provide the first waves of gentrification), and the rest: people whose lives are dictated by their relative poverty. In an article for the *London Review of Books* Lanchester wrote:

> City money is strangling London life. The presence of so many people who don't have to care what things cost raises the price of everything, and in the area of housing, in particular, is causing London's demographics to look like the radiation map of a thermonuclear blast.

In this analogy only the City types can survive close to the heart of the explosion.

In *Capital* he suggests that money, which has no value in and of itself, functions mainly to divide people from one another. It can be conjured at the flick of a switch and some nifty moves on a balance sheet; or it can be created by the daubing of paint on a wall. Those who manipulate it successfully can generate wealth seemingly without effort, but it can also lose its value overnight. Late in the novel, Bogdan uncovers a cache of bank notes hidden by Petunia's dead husband in the walls of her house. They turn out to be worthless — out of date tenners that it would be impossible to exchange without questions being asked by the tax man. Money, the message seems to be, retains its value only when it's circulated: only when it remains part of the community. As soon as it's hoarded and cut off from the economy, it begins to lose its value.

The economic and social isolationism which is the dominant theme of *Capital* is reflected in prose which staunchly resists representing

263

character through the idiosyncrasies of differentiation. With such a varied cast of characters, it's little wonder that Lanchester's portraits occasionally lack depth. His tone remains similar no matter who he's describing, which tends to homogenise the voices of his cast. His ear for dialogue extends to the odd spattering of slang, but, unlike the polyphonic ventriloquism of Will Self or Martin Amis, or the patient attention to the details of idiomatic diction displayed by Zadie Smith, Lanchester's characters can tend to feel inauthentic; cut off from themselves.

This is partly a problem of scale. London is such a hugely varied place that *Capital* — despite its ambition — can't hope to capture all its facets. Other contemporary London novels, especially those focussed on such a specific geographical area, tend to confine themselves to particular groups of people: the Bangladeshi community in Monica Ali's *Brick Lane*; disenfranchised white working-class in Martin Amis's *Lionel Asbo: State of England*. Nevertheless *Capital* is an unsettling and thought-provoking (if occasionally flawed) novel because it pictures a world in which individuals are all islands, living in a time when the values that once united communities have been given over in favour of those of monetary worth. As Petunia Howe speculates at one point: 'We're all in this together: Petunia was the right age for that once to have been a very important idea, a defining idea, about what it meant to be British. Was it still true? Were they in it together? Could she look around the surgery and truthfully say that.' At the end of the novel, we are led to ask similar questions of contemporary London.

References and Further Reading

Patrick Brantlinger *Fictions of State: Culture and Credit in Britain, 1694-1994,* Cornell University Press, 1996

John Lanchester, 'Cityphilia', http://www.lrb.co.uk/v30/n01/john-lanchester/cityphilia

John Lanchester, *Whoops! Why Everyone Owes Everyone and Nobody Can Pay,* Penguin, 2010

Nicky Marsh *Money, Speculation and Finance in Contemporary British Fiction,* Continuum, 2007

Samuel Pepys, *The Diary of Samuel Pepys, a new and complete transcription,* HarperCollins, 1995

http://www.pepysrd.com

'Pepys Road' Today

As a fictional street it is hard to say precisely where Pepys Road is located, though Lanchester provides enough information to narrow its location down to the north east tip of Clapham Common. Denis Gouden's house at the junction of Clapham North Side and Long Road, to which Pepys retired at the end of his life, was demolished in the mid-eighteenth century. An elegant house was built on the site, where the architect Charles Barry once lived. It now houses Trinity Hospice, the oldest hospice in the UK, founded by the Hoare family in 1891. At number 14 North Side is a plaque commemorating Graham Greene, who lived there during the war. In 1940 a bomb destroyed the house, an event he later described in *The End of the Affair*.

The wide streets surrounding the hospice are very much as Lanchester describes *Pepys Road*: imposing Victorian mansions punctuated every so often by a few more recent developments. This used to be a rather more bohemian location — Angela Carter lived on The Chase, the street next to Trinity Hospice, in the 1980s — but it's now extremely well kept and obviously affluent. A blue plaque on the wall near Carter's old house commemorates a street party held for the wedding of Prince William and Katherine Middleton.

To the south spreads Clapham Common, referred to throughout *Capital* familiarly as 'the Common'. Though Pepys Road is the focus of the novel, the Common forms the dividing line between many of the lives described within it: Quentina lives to the south, in Tooting; the Kamals worship in Brixton Mosque, to the east. In the middle of the northeastern spur of the Common next to Cock Pond stands Holy Trinity Church, where William Wilberforce and the anti-slavery 'Clapham Sect' once worshipped.

Jon Day

Kilburn High Road NW6

Zadie Smith
NW (2012)

Philippa Thomas

Zadie Smith's London exhausts me. It's relentless and remorse-less. The London of *NW* traps you, grinds you down, never lets you go. It's weighed down by the tensions of class, race and casual violence. The in-your-face realities of curses and coarseness.

It's strange to write this in the afterglow of London's Olympic summer. On 25th July 2012, the *Brent and Kilburn Times* reported that thousands of residents had gone out onto the streets to welcome the Olympic torch relay. Those privileged to run with the torch included local figures 'nominated for their tireless community work'.

On 27th August 2012, *NW* was published... "Crack. Filthy habit! See them down our end every day, by the station"... "Ain't seen him in two years. Abusive. Violent. Had issues... Broke my arm, broke my collarbone, broke my knee, broke my fuckin face."

Zadie Smith's vision is a visceral contrast — perhaps a corrective — to those weeks of communal euphoria.

Her novel revolves around the fictional Caldwell estate, but its setting is real. She gives us both Kilburn's skyline, 'brutal, high-rise towers', 'ungentrified, ungentrifiable', and the pretensions of the posher bits of Willesden, 'little terraces, faux-Tudor piles'. There's some space for maneouvre but not much. Like her characters, we rarely get out of this two-mile square of the city for long.

Of the three key figures, we begin and end with the girls: Leah of Irish descent; Keisha, Jamaican. They 'went Brayton' together, to the 'thousand-kid madhouse' of the local school. The story of Felix flares up and flames out in between them. In different ways, all three try to move on. They're all brought back or brought down. Smith's *NW* isn't a land of opportunity.

Leah

From the beginning, the writing makes me claustrophobic. Leah is in the garden, superficially free and easy, swinging in her hammock. But she's in the garden of a basement flat. 'Fenced in, on all sides', and already oppressed by the sound of a string of curses from a neighbour's balcony.

'A grim girl on the third floor screams Anglo-Saxon at nobody. Juliet balcony, projecting for miles. It ain't like that. Nah it ain't like that. Don't you start.'

Leah does start. She goes to college, 'a state-school wild card', 'the graduate', but as an adult, comes home. She meets French-Algerian hairdresser Michel, whose personal ambition would delight Margaret Thatcher. He wants to move on from the council flat into 'a proper flat, a mortgage'. He has a dream. "If we ever have a little boy I want him to live somewhere — to live proud — somewhere we have the freehold."

But Leah can't. At the community charity where she works, the only white girl in the office, she's teased every day for taking one of "their" men. She can't move on. She can't face getting pregnant, and she ends it — again. We last see her back in the hammock, dazed, defeated, getting blistered by the sun.

She can't sustain the motivation, can't find a way out. She stays with what she knows. 'Leah, born and bred, never goes anywhere'.

Felix

Our second protagonist, Caribbean Londoner Felix Cooper, is still pushing to get on.

We join him on a journey to the West End — travelling by tube, Kilburn to Baker Street, Baker Street to Oxford Circus. We look through his outsider's eyes at the discreet gleam of wealth on the side streets, 'slick black doors, brass knobs, brass letterboxes'. We meet the callow posh boy Tom, selling off a car for his father, quite unable to treat his potential buyer on equal terms. Shocked that Felix is black. Asking clumsily if he has any dope.

We also learn, incidentally, about Felix's roller coaster ride through London life — adventure, drugs, descent, and now a renewed sense of mission. He believes he's going to escape the world of 'sitting on concrete steps in a stairwell somewhere on Caldwell estate'. 'Start all over again, fresh'. But for the alert reader, Felix's end has already been foreshadowed in a briefly mentioned news event before we even meet him.

The incident that for Felix is the beginning of the end made me shudder, and put down the book. He's on the Tube, heading home, daydreaming. And in one fell swoop, he's stereotyped — by the pregnant white woman who assumes he's with the black guys opposite. He acts — "your man's got his feet on her seat, blud" — and he's targeted, all because of the colour of his skin. Zadie Smith absolutely captures the body language of the London Underground. Nobody else speaks but the group's disapproval is clear, conveyed in fleeting glances full of meaning.

In *NW*, there is one explicit allusion to the death of Stephen Lawrence — 'that poor defenceless boy', the black teenager infamously stabbed to death at a bus stop in South London. I sat in court as a journalist throughout the case that put two of his killers away. No Londoner could fail to be aware of the crime or the official complacency that initially greeted it. The awareness of gang life, of knife crime, of a city that's home to fits of swift and bloody violence, adds to the sense of low level threat that seeps through these pages.

But then Smith drives home another point. Felix meets danger not at the hands of a gang of racist white youths — but one of his own.

Keisha

The real character with destiny, the book's success story, seems to be Keisha Blake — Leah's best friend from school — a girl who's on the move and on the make. At university she's 'crazy busy with self-invention'. She becomes Natalie de Angelis. She becomes a barrister, practicing commercial law.

She lives in the London world of those who've made it. One perfect husband, two perfect children, one fabulous house ('twice the size of a Caldwell double'.) 'Private wards. Christmas abroad. Security systems. Fences. The carriage of a 4x4 that lets you sit alone above traffic.' When she sets out to define herself, she writes: 'I am a highly educated black woman. I am a successful lawyer.'

But she's hollowed out by the effort of playing a part, and we follow her spiralling down, losing it. I didn't quite believe the speed of her slump. It felt to me as if the structure of the novel demanded she pay the price. But it does lead us to another stretch of London entirely.

For most of Zadie Smith's novel, I felt pulled down as a reader, forced to idle in the basement flat, to hang out on street corners and at bus stops and in the 'boxy cramped Victorian damp' of Leah's office space. One Caldwell character, the old man Tom, talks about Londoners needing their bit of green, but there's precious little of it here.

269

There are two memorable scenes where the horizon lifts. But they're both about false promise. At the top of a flight of stairs in Soho, Felix visits an old flame Annie. She's stuck in her own life, stupid with booze and coke. They head up through the trap door to the roof where he worked with a film crew in more glamorous days. There's a view. He tries to match it, talks about getting on with his life. But it's a squalid meeting — they grapple through sex, a clumsy shag — and as they look out at a man and a woman and a toddler trying to picnic on a nearby terrace, Annie loudly mocks the aspiring happy family. In a way, it's very funny. But cruel. So much for that.

Back then to Natalie's journey — or Keisha's, as she walks out of her life and drops back in, via the Caldwell estate, with her old class mate Nathan Bogle. The boy who was so fine at ten is now an addict and a wreck: a man whom it emerges is running girls and ruining lives.

'They stood in the centre of Caldwell's basin. Five blocks connected by walkways and bridges and staircases, and lifts that were to be avoided almost as soon as they were built.'

They head out and up, climbing the 'great hill' that begins in Willesden and ends in Highgate. 'They crossed over and kept climbing, past the narrow red mansion flats, up into money. The world of council flats lay far behind them, at the bottom of the hill'.

They stumble up to a beautiful corner of London. Up to the top of Hampstead Heath. But even this scene is written as if they're the outsiders. They're depicted like animals, scurrying, creeping, crouching to piss in the woods.

They reach Hornsey Lane, and the grand iron bridge that stretches over the Archway Road. It's a part of London where you gain a sweeping view of the city. It's also known by locals as 'Suicide Bridge'. As Smith writes: 'Here nothing less than a break — a sudden and total rupture — would do'.

All of London is out there. But it's not there for them. The narrative climax is empty. The author demands that her characters retreat.

Zadie Smith's *NW*

The world of *NW* isn't simplistic. It's more confusing than that. There are all sorts of racial currents, reflecting the ebb and flow of different communities. A young Sikh runs the corner shop. The quiet old Anglican church now gathers a congregation of 'Polish, Indian, African, Caribbean'. Women 'from St. Kitts, Trinidad, Barbados, Grenada, Jamaica, India, Pakistan', doll themselves up for a warm night out on the Edgware Road.

There are comparisons and tensions. Leah's mum thinks about the 'wily Nigerians... owning things in Kilburn that once were Irish'. She 'looks pointedly towards their old estate, full of people from the colonies and the Russiany lot'. But Leah's Michel says: "I'm not like these Jamaicans [who] still have no curtains".

Zadie Smith writes from experience. She was brought up in this corner of north-west London and went to a local comprehensive school. In a personal essay published in the *New Yorker* in 2008, she tells us more about her father Harvey, who grew up in 'a poky housing estate' in Willesden Green, and committed a 'late, failed marriage to a Jamaican girl less than half his age'.

She writes an *NW* that we can almost inhale — sight, sound, smell. At one point, she literally invites us in. 'A local tip: the bus stop outside Kilburn's Poundland is the site of many of the more engaging conversations to be heard in the city of London. You're welcome.' It's all there in the details. 'Sweet stink of the hookah, couscous, kebab, exhaust fumes of a bus deadlock.'

And it's there in the bigger picture. As a writer, Smith is adept at sketching out just what 'social mobility' means to those moving up in the world by moving a mile down the street.

In her first novel *White Teeth* (2000) she wrote of the Bangladeshi couple Samad and Alsana Iqbal that 'it had taken a year... of mercilessly hard graft to make the momentous move from the wrong side of Whitechapel to the wrong side of Willesden'. There's also a pitch-perfect description of the relief felt by Clara to be improving her lot as she arrives at the house in Willesden Green that her new husband has picked out: 'She'd seen the high road and it had been ugly and poor and familiar, but then at the turn of a corner suddenly roads had exploded in greenery, beautiful oaks, the houses got taller, wider and more detached, she could see parks, she could see libraries. And then abruptly the trees would be gone, reverting back into bus stops as if by the strike of some midnight bell'.

But what really strikes me in *NW*, in this latest version of Zadie Smith's London, is the relentless pull of the meaner spaces. Every protagonist in her class-conscious, boundary-conscious London wants the door to be open — wants to be able to leave.

NW gives more emphasis to the getaway postcodes: the places her characters mention fleetingly, with envy or with longing. We hear that 'Wimbledon' is the countryside, 'Pimlico' pure fiction. The Khan kid tells Felix: "I'm in Hendon now, innit", speaking 'a little bashfully, as if it was too much good luck to confess to'.

In her contribution on *White Teeth* in this book, Lisa Gee celebrates that novel's optimism, while noting that Smith has referred back to

271

the earlier incarnation of a London 'melting pot' as somewhat naïve. As a reader, I also feel there's a stark difference in tone between the jaunty narrative of *White Teeth*, published the year before 9/11, and the sense of paralysis that permeates *NW*. In the earlier book, Zadie Smith muses about the twentieth century as a great immigrant experiment, at the end of which 'we have finally slipped into each other's lives with reasonable comfort.' In the year 2000, the harder bitten vision of London life is an undercurrent. Twelve years later, it takes centre stage.

Taken together, *White Teeth* and *NW* make me think about a changing city. They also made me wonder about a changing author. *White Teeth* is alive with the exuberance of a twenty-four year old writer gleefully creating teenage characters who are making their first big choices. The thirty-six year old author of *NW* feels the need to spell out the fact that few of her cohort have significant choices.

Her own life story is one of opportunity gained. Sadie Smith changed her name to Zadie at fourteen. She went to Cambridge University. She kept on moving. She wrote in her *New Yorker* essay in 2008 that 'class-wise each year placed us [Smith and her father] further apart. As in many British families, it was university Wot Dunnit.' She pulled free in a way that Keisha never did.

She concludes that piece bluntly, describing modern Britain as 'a nation divided by postcodes and accents, schools and last names.'

Could it get worse? She's written more recently about opportunity lost, the slow slide of the enabling state. In the *New York Review of Books* in June 2012, Smith talks about Willesden public libraries threatened by government spending cuts. She reminisces about a state which gave her everything from her NHS specs aged nine to her NHS baby aged thirty-three, and concludes that 'the state is not what it once was'.

Is she too pessimistic? Your answer might depend on your experience — and your politics. There are other success stories out there, such as Smith's old school Hampstead Comprehensive. Like Brayton in *NW*, it was founded as a secondary modern, basically an education factory for the masses. In 2008, it was described in glowing terms in the *Times Educational Supplement* as a successful comprehensive 'remade' under visionary leadership.

Zadie Smith hasn't left the world of Willesden behind and she cares passionately about how it fares. But perhaps she sees it through a different lens after moving up and away. In the *New Yorker*, she remarked of a rising young comedian: 'Can't go home, can't leave home — a subject close to my heart'. Today, in 2012, she lives with the smarter set in Queen's Park, NW — and New York.

NW denies her characters any such luxury. They act out a morality tale — which has at its heart the sinking belief, that in twenty-first century London, it's still class not character that is destiny. She may be right. In the end, I don't want to believe her. I find *NW* to be a counsel of despair.

Zadie Smith's Essays

'Dead Man Laughing', a revealing personal essay about social class and situation comedy, published in the *New Yorker* in December 2008: http://www.newyorker.com/reporting/2008/12/22/081222fa_fact_smith

'The North West London Blues', an essay published in the *New York Review of Books* in June 2012, and republished in the neighbourhood blog 'Keep Willesden Green'. Smith writes about the campaign to keep open a local library, and its worth as an essential public space in an increasingly privatized world. http://www.nybooks.com/blogs/nyrblog/2012/jun/02/north-west-london-blues/ http://keep-willesdengreen.blogspot.co.uk/2012/06/zadie-smith-north-west-london-blues.html

Climbing the Great Hill

'Walking was what she did now, walking was what she was. She was nothing more or less than the phenomenon of walking. She had no name, no biography, no characteristics.'

Towards the end of *NW*, Keisha/Natalie stalks out of her home, her family, her old life. 'She turned left. Walked to the end of her road and the end of the next. Walked quickly away from Queen's Park. She passed into where Willesden meets Kilburn. ... Without looking where she was going, she began climbing the hill that begins in Willesden and ends in Highgate.'

Whatever truth you're looking for in a novel, it's not cartographical precision. Yet simply the chapter heads of this night time tramp, an arc across north London, are sufficient to delineate the route: Willesden Lane — Kilburn High Road — Shoot Up Hill — Fortune Green — Hampstead Heath — Archway — Hornsey Lane. The walk is twenty pages, or two-and-a-half hours at a decent pace if you are minded to follow in Keisha's footsteps.

Tracing the journey suggests just how much *NW* touches on the author's own life. Keisha's point of departure, close to Queen's Park, is near where Zadie Smith was brought up, where she went to primary school, where she still lives in a house a lot like Keisha's. Within minutes, she's walked past the other key locations, her friend Leah's house and the composite and imprecisely located Caldwell estate, with its five blocks named after those north London street heroes, Smith, Hobbes, Bentham, Locke and Russell.

A moment later, Keisha is making her way along Albert Road, hemmed in by a police cordon as she tries to reach the tube station. This is Caldwell territory. A bleak landscape of harsh council blocks, the other side of the tracks from fashionable Queen's Park. In spite of the high-density flats all around, if you walk down Albert Road, even on a sunny Sunday afternoon, it's empty — because there's nothing there. No shops, no pubs, nothing to suggest community.

At the heart of this early part of the walk is Willesden Lane — with its estate boundary walls, basketball court, and 98 bus route. Near here, Keisha stumbles across her old schoolmate Nathan, 'flying' on some substance or other and incessantly rolling joints. They lounge by the 'high iron gates' of Paddington cemetery, among the most tranquil of London's Victorian valhallas, opened in the 1850s and now hidden behind late nineteenth-century terraced streets. Keisha recalls childhood figure-of-eight walks round the grounds with her mother, looking in vain for the grave of Arthur Orton, the Tichborne claimant. No wonder — he had a pauper's burial.

Keisha and Nathan strike out north, pausing near Kilburn tube station as he talks to two women in the doorway of a Chinese takeaway. He seems to be their ponce. Then along Shoot Up Hill, and at its crest — close to Zadie Smith's secondary school — striking out east (as best one can tell) towards Golder's Hill. 'Victorian houses began to appear, only a few at first, then multiplying. Fresh gravel in the drives, white wooden blinds in the windows. Estate agent's hoarding strapped to the front gate.' Across an outlying part of the Heath, through rain and darkness, to Jack Straw's Castle, once a coaching inn and now top-end flats. The walk is relentlessly up hill, to about the highest spot in the city.

"Suicide Bridge", on Hornsey Lane high above the dual carriageway of Archway Road, is journey's end. 'The lamp posts at either end were cast iron, and their bases moulded into fish with their mouths open wide. They had the tails of dragons, winding round the stem, and each lamp was topped by an orange glass orb.' Keisha had 'forgotten that the bridge was not purely functional. She tried her best but could not completely ignore its beauty.'

The bridge was built in 1897, replacing an earlier structure from which Archway got its name, an arch over an unsuccessful attempt to tunnel through Highgate hill. Between the dog teeth railings you get a marvelous view south over the heart of the city, but you are no nearer to it than at the walk's starting point.

Andrew Whitehead

Contributors

Andy Croft's most recent books of poetry are *Ghost Writer, Sticky, Three Men on the Metro* (with Bill Herbert and Paul Summers) and *1948* (with Martin Rowson). He writes a monthly poetry column in the *Morning Star* and runs Smokestack Books. He is currently writer-in-residence at HMP Moorland.

Valentine Cunningham is Professor of English Language and Literature at Oxford University and Senior Fellow and Tutor in English at Corpus Christi College, Oxford. He writes on the Victorian Novel, Victorian Poetry, Shakespeare, the 1930s, the Spanish Civil War, Religion and literature, the Bible and literature, and Literary theory. He's spent more years than is healthy, he says, reviewing new novels and judging literary prizes, including the Booker (twice!).

Jon Day was born in north London, and now lives in Hackney. He is writing a PhD about modernist fiction at St. John's College, Oxford, and a book about bicycle couriers for Notting Hill Editions. He is a regular contributor to the *London Review of Books* and *n+1*.

Zoë Fairbairns, novelist, journalist, short story writer and playwright, has lived in London and its south-of-the-river suburbs for most of her life. Her books include *Benefits* and *How Do You Pronounce Nulliparous?* Her website is at www.zoefairbairns.co.uk.

Susan Alice Fischer is Professor of English at Medgar Evers College of The City University of New York. She is editor of the online journal *Literary London Journal* www.literarylondon.org and co-editor of *Changing English: Studies in Culture and Education*, published by Routledge/Taylor & Francis. She writes mostly about contemporary British literature.

Bogdan Frymorgen studied English at the Jagiellonian University in Krakow. He worked for the BBC World Service for over 24 years. He is a journalist, a photographer and an art curator. He collaborates with many cultural institutions in his native Poland and is a member of the Association of Polish Art Photographers (ZPAF).

Lisa Gee has lived in Harlesden since 2000. She is the author of *Friends: Why men and women are from the same planet* (Bloomsbury) and *Stage Mum* (Hutchinson, Arrow) and the editor of *Bricks Without Mortar: the selected poems of Hartley Coleridge* (Picador). She writes about books for the *Independent on Sunday* and the *Independent* and makes stuff out of words, sound and video. www.lisagee.net.

Sanchita Islam is an artist, writer and film maker. She runs Pigment Explosion www.pigmentexplosion.com, an organisation specialising in international and London-based art projects. She has been artist-in-residence at Shoreditch House and at the Whitechapel Art Gallery. Her diverse range of books include a novel *Gungi Blues*, poetry and a volume connecting the Bangladeshi diaspora, *From Briarwood to Barishal to Brick Lane*. She has been preparing for a mid-career retrospective at Rich Mix. She lives and works in Brussels and London.

Angela V. John is Honorary Professor of History at Aberystwyth University and a vice-president of Llafur, the Welsh People's History Society. She lived and worked in south-east London for thirty years. Her books include *War, Journalism and the Shaping of the Twentieth Century; The Life and Times of Henry W. Nevinson* (I.B. Tauris, 2006); a biography of his second wife, Evelyn Sharp, *Rebel Woman, 1869-1955* (Manchester University Press, 2009) and *Turning the Tide: The Life of Lady Rhondda 1883-1958* (Parthian, 2013). See http://www.angelavjohn.com/ for details of her publications.

John King is the author of seven novels including *The Football Factory* (1996) and his most recent, *Skinheads* (2008). With Martin Knight, he founded and runs London Books www.london-books.co.uk. He lives in London.

Andrew Lane is the author of some fourteen original novels and eight books of non-fiction looking at the world of films and TV programmes. Most recently he has been writing a series of novels about the early years of Sherlock Holmes — the fifth of these books, *Snake Bite*, came out in October 2012 and the first book in a new Young Adult series, *Lost Worlds*, is published in May 2013. Andrew is proud of having been born in central London and bought up in east London.

Rachel Lichtenstein is an artist and writer. She is the co-author, with Iain Sinclair, of *Rodinsky's Room* (Granta, 1999) and the author of *On Brick Lane* (Hamish Hamilton, 2007), the first of a trilogy of books on London streets. The second in the series, *Diamond Street: The Hidden World of Hatton Garden* was published in June 2012; a volume on Portobello Road will follow. Her website is www.rachel-lichtenstein.com.

John Lucas is a poet, novelist, biographer, literary historian and critic. Recent books include *92 Acharnon Street* (2007, paperback 2011), Eland Publishing, winner of the 2008 Dolman Award for Travel Writing, *Things to Say: Poems* (2010), *Next Year Will be Better: A Memoir of England in the 1950s*, (2010, paperback 2011), both Five Leaves Publications, and a novel *Waterdrops*, (2011), Greenwich Exchange. He runs Shoestring Press.

Jane Miller first worked in publishing, then as an English teacher in a large London comprehensive school and finally at the London University Institute of Education, where she retired as Professor Emeritus in 1998. Since then she has continued to edit the academic journal, *Changing English*. Her most recent publication is *Crazy Age: thoughts on being old* (2010). She is a contributing editor of the American magazine, *In These Times,* for which she writes a monthly column.

Courttia Newland is the author of four novels and two collections of short stories — the latest, *A Book of Blues*, was nominated for the Frank O'Conner Award and the Edge Hill Prize. His forthcoming novel is entitled *The Gospel According to Cane*. For more, see www.courttianewland.com.

Heather Reyes is co-founder, with Malcolm Burgess, of Oxygen Books and edits their anthologies of writing on major world cities, including *London* (2009). She is author of a novel, *Zade* (Saqi Books, 2004), many short stories, and a number of articles on the novels of Christine Brooke-Rose. Her most recent offering is *city-pick ISTANBUL* (April 2013).

Bill Schwarz teaches in the School of English and Drama, Queen Mary, University of London. He is an editor of *History Workshop Journal* and the first volume of his *Memories of Empire* appeared in 2011.

Philippa Thomas is a BBC news journalist who's lived in different corners of London for much of the last twenty years. She's currently to be found in N7, off the Holloway Road. She blogs at www.philippathomas.com and tweets @Philippanews.

Susie Thomas has written about British authors from Aphra Behn to Martin Amis. She is the editor of *A Reader's Guide to Hanif Kureishi* (Palgrave Macmillan, 2005), and has interviewed Hanif Kureishi and written about his work for the journal *Changing English*.

Cathi Unsworth is the author of three London-based pop-cultural crime novels, *The Not Knowing* (2005), *The Singer* (2007) and *Bad Penny Blues* (2009), the last of which is set in a similar milieu to *The L-Shaped Room*. Her latest novel is *Weirdo* (2012). She is also the editor of *London Noir* (2006), a compilation of stories set within the city. All these books are published by Serpent's Tail. For more information please see www.cathiunsworth.co.uk.

Nadia Valman is Senior Lecturer in Victorian Literature at Queen Mary, University of London. She is the author of *The Jewess in Nineteenth-Century British Literary Culture* (2007) published by Cambridge University Press, and co-editor of several books on British-Jewish cultural history. She is currently researching the literature of the East End of London.

Jerry White has been writing about London since the early 1970s. His first two books were oral histories of contrasting London communities and he is the author of a large-scale study of modern London. *London in the Twentieth Century: A City and Its People*, won the Wolfson History Prize in 2002; this was followed by *London in the Nineteenth Century: 'A Human Awful Wonder of God'* in 2007; the final volume of the trilogy, *London in the Eighteenth Century: A Great and Monstrous Thing*, was published by the Bodley Head in 2012. Since 2009 he has been teaching London history at Birkbeck. He is a former Chief Executive of the London Borough of Hackney.

Andrew Whitehead has spent his career as a news journalist and is currently the editor of BBC World Service News. He is an editor of *History Workshop Journal* and runs a website devoted to London novels www.londonfictions.com as well as his personal site www.andrew whitehead.net. He is the author of a history of the origins of the Kashmir conflict in the 1940s, *A Mission in Kashmir* (2007).

Sarah Wise's *The Blackest Streets: the Life and Death of a Victorian Slum* (2008) was shortlisted for the Ondaatje Prize. Her debut, *The Italian Boy: Murder and Grave Robbery in 1830s London*, was shortlisted for the 2005 Samuel Johnson Prize and won the CWA Gold

Dagger for Non-Fiction. Her latest book, *Inconvenient People: Lunacy, Liberty and the Mad-Doctors in Victorian England* was published in 2012 by the Bodley Head.

Anne Witchard lectures in English Literature and Culture at the University of Westminster. She is the author of *Lao She in London* (Hong Kong University Press 2012) and *Thomas Burke's Dark Chinoiserie: Limehouse Nights and the Queer Spell of Chinatown* (Ashgate 2009) and co-editor with Lawrence Phillips of *London Gothic: Place, Space and the Gothic Imagination* (Continuum 2010). Her forthcoming edited collection, *Modernism and Chinoiserie* will be published by Edinburgh University Press in 2014. Her *China in Britain* project website is www.translatingchina.info.

Gregory Woods is Professor of Gay and Lesbian Studies at Nottingham Trent University. He is the author of *Articulate Flesh: Male Homo-eroticism and Modern Poetry* (1987) and *A History of Gay Literature: The Male Tradition* (1998), both from Yale University Press. His poetry is published by Carcanet Press and Shoestring Press. His website is www.gregorywoods.co.uk.

Ken Worpole is a former English teacher and oral historian who has lived in Hackney for more than forty years. His 1983 book, *Dockers & Detectives* (updated edition, Five Leaves, 2008), brought to light many forgotten writers of the 1930s and 1940s, and he has written biographical introductions to Alexander Baron's *King Dido* (Five Leaves, 2009) and Simon Blumenfeld's *Jew Boy* (London Books, 2011). He has also written books on public architecture, landscape and social history, and is Emeritus Professor at The Cities Institute, London Metropolitan University. His latest publication is *Contemporary Library Architecture* (Routledge, 2013). Website: www.worpole.net.

Afterword and Acknowledgements

This book has not been designed as a 'top twenty' of London fiction — though it would be difficult to imagine most of the novels here failing to make the charts. The selection has an element of the arbitrary, reflecting the interests and enthusiasms of editors and contributors. There is no claim to comprehensiveness. And lest anyone doubt, we are all too well aware of what we have left out. Of commanding London novels, we can offer no convincing excuse for the absence of Conrad's *The Secret Agent*, Bennett's *Riceyman Steps*, or Priestley's *Angel Pavement*. There's no Margaret Harkness or John Galsworthy, chroniclers of Victorian-into-Edwardian outcast and propertied London respectively; Mr Pooter would (we trust!) be mortified by the omission of the Grossmiths' *Diary of a Nobody*; Gerald Kersh, whose *Night and the City* is the epitome of London Noir, has escaped the net; that quartet of modern sages and visionaries of the city, J.G. Ballard, Michael Moorcock, Peter Ackroyd and Iain Sinclair, are all distressingly absent. We weren't intending that any author would feature twice, but made an exception for Zadie Smith simply because *NW*, published just as this book was being put to bed, has such a powerful sense of place.

All this is offered up not as ritual self-flagellation, but as a simple admission of the limitations of this project. And to whisper the idea that there is plenty of material for an encore, if there's an appetite.

There are other places to turn to celebrate London's representation in fiction. The London Fictions website (www. londonfictions.com) was the first home of a handful of the articles in this book – though by far the greater number are entirely new, and indeed most of the contributions on the site have a digital only existence. We have also appended a list of websites, articles, anthologies, guides and studies which deserve the attention of those who have enjoyed this book.

For the evocative photographs which grace this book, we have Bogdan Frymorgen to thank — a visual chronicler of another aspect of London, the BBC's departure from Bush House where he (and one of us) worked for many years, and now capturing the contemporary aspect of our chosen London fictions.

Ross Bradshaw of Five Leaves has been a model publisher – embracing this book, sticking with it through the sort of turbulence which is alas the lot of small publishers, and cajoling several of his writers to contribute. He also enlisted Andy Croft as project manager, himself both writer and historian, who was inveigled to write for the book as well as seeing it to press. The ever excellent Bishopsgate Institute, and its events organisers Kira Milmo and Lucy Kerr, have hosted evenings which have had the happy consequence of helping *London Fictions* on its way. Our contributors have displayed an enthusiasm for the idea behind this book, providing not simply sparkling content but the intellectual drive and energy which saw this initiative to fruition. We're grateful. Not least for their patience. Several have written a book or two while waiting for these articles to appear in print.

Still more deserving of our gratitude are our respective partners, Anuradha Awasthi and Rosie Cooper, who must at times have thought their husbands' preoccupation with London to be — to borrow Defoe's comment on the city — 'a great and monstrous thing', given the drain imposed on our time and resources. Without their forbearance and support, it would never have happened.

Andrew Whitehead and Jerry White

Books, Articles and Guides:

Tom Bullough, *The Rough Guide to London by the Book*, Rough Guides, 2006

Merlin Coverley, *London Writing*, Pocket Essentials, 2005

Ian Cunningham, *A Reader's Guide to Writers' London*, Prion Books, 2001

David Daiches and John Flower, *Literary Landscapes of the British Isles: a narrative atlas*, Penguin, 1981

Andrew Davies, *Literary London*, Macmillan, 1988

Ed Glinert, *A Literary Guide to London*, Penguin, 2000

Christina Hardyment, *Writing Britain: Wastelands to Wonderlands*, British Library, 2012

P.J. Keating, *The Working Classes in Victorian Fiction*, Routledge & Kegan Paul, 1971

Lawrence Manley (ed.), *The Cambridge Companion to the Literature of London*, Cambridge U.P., 2011

Tony Murray, *London Irish Fiction: Narrative, Diaspora and Identity*, Liverpool University Press, 2012

Nick Rennison (ed.), *Waterstone's Guide to London Writing*, Waterstone's, 1999

Sukhdev Sandhu, *London Calling: How Black and Asian Writers Imagined a City*, HarperCollins, 2003

Iain Sinclair, *Hackney, that Rose-Red Empire: a confidential report*, Hamish Hamilton, 2009

Roger Tagholm, *Walking Literary London*, New Holland Publishers, 2004

Jerry White, 'Unreal City: reflections on London and the novel in the twentieth century', *History Workshop Journal*, autumn 2003

Ken Worpole, *Dockers and Detectives*, Verso, 1983, republished by Five Leaves, 2008

Ken and Larraine Worpole, *20,000 Streets under the Sky: the London novel, 1896-1985*, Royal Festival Hall exhibition catalogue, 1986

Anthologies:

Julian Evans (ed.), *London Tales*, Hamish Hamilton, 1983

Peter Haining (ed.), *London After Midnight*, Little, Brown, 1996

P.J. Keating (ed.), *Working-class Stories of the 1890s*, Routledge & Kegan Paul, 1971

Heather Reyes (ed.), *City-Lit: London*, Oxygen Books, 2009

Iain Sinclair (ed.), *London: City of Disappearances*, Hamish Hamilton, 2006

Cathi Unsworth (ed.), *London Noir: capital crime fiction*, Serpent's Tail, 2006

Websites:

www.londonfictions.com/

www.lostlondonlit.blogspot.co.uk/

www.literarylondon.org/london-journal/

New London Editions
from Five Leaves

King Dido by Alexander Baron*
Introduced by Ken Worpole

Rosie Hogarth by Alexander Baron*
Introduced by Andrew Whitehead

Scamp by Roland Camberton
Introduced by Iain Sinclair

Rain on the Pavements by Roland Camberton

October Day by Frank Griffin
Introduced by Andy Croft

Adrift in Soho by Colin Wilson*

The Furnished Room by Laura Del-Rivo*

Baron's Court, All Change by Terry Taylor*
Introduced by Stewart Home

This Bed Thy Centre by Pamela Hansford Johnson
Introduced by Zoë Fairbairns

London E1 by Robert Poole
Introduced by Rachel Lichtenstein

---

*also available as eBooks

Available from bookshops or, post free,
from www.fiveleaves.co.uk